Revisioning
Social Work Education:
A Social Constructionist
Approach

Revisioning
Social Work Education:
A Social Constructionist
Approach

Joan Laird
Editor

The Haworth Press, Inc.
New York · London · Norwood (Australia)

Revisioning Social Work Education: A Social Constructionist Approach has also been published as *Journal of Teaching in Social Work,* Volume 8, Numbers 1/2 1993.

The development, preparation, and publication of this work has been undertaken with great care. However, the publisher, employees, editors, and agents of The Haworth Press and all imprints of The Haworth Press, Inc., including The Haworth Medical Press and Pharmaceutical Products Press, are not responsible for any errors contained herein or for consequences that may ensue from use of materials or information contained in this work. Opinions expressed by the author(s) are not necessarily those of The Haworth Press, Inc.

The Haworth Press, Inc., 10 Alice Street, Binghamton, NY 13904-1580 USA

Library of Congress Cataloging-in-Publication Data

Revisioning social work education : a social constructionist approach / Joan Laird, editor.
      p. cm.
      "Has also been published as Journal of teaching in social work, volume 8, numbers 1/2 1993"–T.p. verso
      Includes bibliographical references and index.
      ISBN 1-56024-615-4 (acid-free paper)
      1. Social work education. I. Laird, Joan.
HV11.R399 1994   94-2853
361'.0071–dc20   CIP

INDEXING & ABSTRACTING

Contributions to this publication are selectively indexed or abstracted in print, electronic, online, or CD-ROM version(s) of the reference tools and information services listed below. This list is current as of the copyright date of this publication. See the end of this section for additional notes.

- *Applied Social Sciences Index & Abstracts (ASSIA)*, Bowker-Saur Limited, Maypole House, Maypole Road, East Grinstead, East Sussex, RH19 19 1HH, England

- *Contents Pages in Education*, Carfax Information Systems, P.O. Box 25, Abingdon, Oxfordshire OX14 3UE, United Kingdom

- *Human Resources Abstracts*, Sage Publications, Inc., 2455 Teller Road, Newbury Park, CA 91320

- *Index to Periodical Articles Related to Law*, University of Texas, 727 East 26th Street, Austin, TX 78705

- *International Bulletin of Bibliography on Education*, Proyecto B.I.B.E./Apartado 52, San Lorenzo del Escorial, Madrid, Spain

- *Inventory of Marriage and Family Literature (online and hard copy)*, National Council on Family Relations, 3989 Central Avenue NE, Suite 550, Minneapolis, MN 55421

- *Referativnyi Zhurnal (Abstracts Journal of the Institute of Scientific Information of the Republic of Russia)*, The Institute of Scientific Information, Baltijskaja ul., 14, Moscow A-219, Republic of Russia

- *Social Care Update*, National Institute for Social Work, 5 Tavistock Place, London WC1H 9SS, England

- *Social Planning/Policy & Development Abstracts (SOPODA)*, Sociological Abstracts, Inc., P.O. Box 22206, San Diego, CA 92192-0206

- *Social Service Abstracts*, Department of Health, Room G12, Wellington House, 133-135 Waterloo Road, London SE1 8UG, England

(continued)

- *Social Work Research & Abstracts*, National Association of Social Workers, 750 First Street, NW, 8th Floor, Washington, DC 20002

- *Sociological Abstracts (SA)*, Sociological Abstracts, Inc., P.O. Box 22206, San Diego, CA 92192-0206

- *Studies on Women Abstracts*, Carfax Publishing Company, P.O. Box 25, Abingdon, Oxfordshire OX14 3UE, United Kingdom

SPECIAL BIBLIOGRAPHIC NOTES

related to special journal issues (separates) and indexing/abstracting

❑ indexing/abstracting services in this list will also cover material in the "separate" that is co-published simultaneously with Haworth's special thematic journal issue or DocuSerial. Indexing/abstracting usually covers material at the article/chapter level.

❑ monographic co-editions are intended for either non-subscribers or libraries which intend to purchase a second copy for their circulating collections.

❑ monographic co-editions are reported to all jobbers/wholesalers/approval plans. The source journal is listed as the "series" to assist the prevention of duplicate purchasing in the same manner utilized for books-in-series.

❑ to facilitate user/access services all indexing/abstracting services are encouraged to utilize the co-indexing entry note indicated at the bottom of the first page of each article/chapter/contribution.

❑ this is intended to assist a library user of any reference tool (whether print, electronic, online, or CD-ROM) to locate the monographic version if the library has purchased this version but not a subscription to the source journal.

❑ individual articles/chapters in any Haworth publication are also available through the Haworth Document Delivery Services (HDDS).

Revisioning Social Work Education: A Social Constructionist Approach

CONTENTS

ABOUT THE EDITOR

Joan Laird, MS, ACSW, is Professor at the Smith College School for Social Work in Northampton, Massachusetts, where she teaches family theory, family therapy, and social theory. Previously, she taught for many years at Eastern Michigan University and was a co-founder of the Ann Arbor Center for the Family, a clinical, research, and training center for family therapy. Professor Laird is the author of many articles and book chapters in the social work and family therapy fields and is co-author of *Family-Centered Social Work Practice,* a text used in social work programs throughout the country and overseas. Recently, her interests have centered around social constructionist and narrative ideas, the use of myth, ritual, and story in family therapy, and on issues of gender and sexual orientation. A member of the National Association of Social Workers and the American Anthropological Association, and a charter member of the American Family Therapy Association, Professor Laird has nearly completed a joint PhD program in social work and anthropology.

Preface

We are pleased to introduce Joan Laird as editor of this book. She is Professor of Social Work, Smith College School for Social Work, and is the co-author with Ann Hartman of *Family-Centered Social Work Practice* as well as author of many articles. Her contributions from an anthropological perspective have enriched social work practice and education. We believe the chapters in this book represent important, highly meaningful approaches for contemporary teaching and practice.

Florence Vigilante, DSW
Harold Lewis, DSW

[Haworth co-indexing entry note]: "Preface," Vigilante, Florence, and Harold Lewis. Co-published simultaneously in *Journal of Teaching in Social Work* (The Haworth Press, Inc.) Vol. 8, No. 1/2, 1993, p. xv; and: *Revisioning Social Work Education: A Social Constructionist Approach* (ed: Joan Laird) The Haworth Press, Inc., 1993, p. xi. Multiple copies of this article/chapter may be purchased from The Haworth Document Delivery Center [1-800-3-HAWORTH; 9:00 a.m. - 5:00 p.m. (EST)].

Introduction

Joan Laird

Our theories are not descriptions of nature, but only of some little feathers which we picked out of nature's garb, more or less accidentally.

Popper (1950, p. 193)

In 1932, Bertha Reynolds exclaimed, some time after the publication of Virginia Robinson's 1930 book, *A Changing Psychology for Social Work*, "Miss Robinson has published her book and we will never be the same again" (p. 109). She might have said the same thing, had she been here to read Martha Heineman's 1981 article, "The Obsolete Scientific Imperative in Social Work Research." Robinson's work sparked the diagnostic-functional debate and launched a long and deeply divisive battle in the profession; her work threatened the very "truth" that had been gaining such a hold on social work theory and practice development. Similarly, Heineman's challenge to the stranglehold of logical positivist thought on social work research catalyzed a long, often acrimonious, but also healthy and fascinating dialogue in the social work field and in the literature. Actually, the issue of social work and "scientism" had been raised earlier by Carel Germain in her 1970 historical analysis titled "Casework: An Historical Encounter," but apparently the field was not yet ready to engage the debate. It is a dialogue that continues today.

A second marker in social work of what was beginning to take shape as a major epistemological revolution in the arts, humanities,

[Haworth co-indexing entry note]: "Introduction," Laird, Joan. Co-published simultaneously in *Journal of Teaching in Social Work* (The Haworth Press, Inc.) Vol. 8, No. 1/2, 1993, pp. 1-10; and: *Revisioning Social Work Education: A Social Constructionist Approach* (ed: Joan Laird) The Haworth Press, Inc., 1993, pp. 1-10. Multiple copies of this article/chapter may be purchased from The Haworth Document Delivery Center [1-800-3-HAWORTH; 9:00 a.m. - 5:00 p.m. (EST)].

and social sciences was the gathering of (at first) a small group of social workers at Council on Social Work Education to talk about "philosophical issues." This group, organized by Roberta Imre, consisted of a number of dissidents, social work educators who were discontented with the hegemonic positivist emphasis and its "truth-telling" status, and wished to explore together "alternative" ways of knowing, ways that had indeed been subjugated in social work. The group soon acquired a name, "The Study Group for Philosophical Issues," attracted more interest, launched a newsletter, and gained "symposium" status; our existence as a group enhanced the likelihood that at least a few papers at CSWE would challenge and offer alternatives to the predominant epistemology of logical empiricism. The "Philosophical Issues" group has given birth to at least one offshoot, this one in the Northeast, which has been a valued gathering place over the last several years for a number of social workers, including me, interested in "other" ways of knowing. A number of the "constructionist" papers published in the social work literature in the last few years have had their first reading in this group.

The debate of the 1980s was not simply about research, however, but also about practice. Social work practitioners were repeatedly criticized for being non-rigorous, haphazard, and muddle-headed, exhorted to make their practices more empirically-based, more "scientific." Only behavior modifiers seemed to come close to fitting the prescription. The extreme position on the "scientific" side was taken by researcher Walter Hudson (1982), who wrote: "If you cannot measure a client's problem, it does not exist" (p. 252). These early volleys were followed by a charged exchange between Joel Fischer (1981, 1984) and William Gordon (1983, 1984) on the pages of *Social Work* concerning the relationship between research and practice.

It is not my purpose here to review the debate; many readers probably know it intimately. My own sense is that it was a most healthy conversation, a time of intellectual ferment which, like the diagnostic-functional split, paved the way for social work thinkers to re-examine their epistemological allegiances, something that rarely happens in a profession where the critique often stays at the level of theory, model, or technique. The challenges to "science" and the accusations of "scientism" in social work were timely;

originally provoked by thinking from philosophy of science and followed up by, among other directions, challenges from feminist thought, they perhaps allowed us to glimpse the beginnings of the revolution against modernist thought, the coming of the postmodern era, earlier than we might otherwise have done.

It wasn't until the late 1980s, however, that the field began moving in any major way beyond a critical stance, beyond a deconstruction of prevailing doctrines toward what are becoming major reformulations of approaches to research, theory, and practice in the profession. And it was the early 1990s before a revisioning of social work education entered the realm of possibility. This volume, then, is most timely, for it brings together a number of social work scholar-educators who have been bringing a postmodern and social constructionist epistemological lens to social work theory-building, to their own practices, to their research, and especially to their teaching.

So far I have been flinging about such terms as postmodernism, constructivism, deconstruction, and social constructionism, as if we all might agree about what they mean. Nowhere in this collection will the reader find a thorough exposition of these terms or a full analysis of the postmodern revolution in social thought, which bridges multiple disciplines from the hard sciences through the social sciences to art and literary criticism. Each of the authors herein was asked to briefly introduce the ideas from postmodern thought that have informed his or her thinking and to go on to demonstrate how those ideas are re-shaping their approach to social work education and their teaching. Thus we assume a certain level of familiarity with the shape and direction of the postmodern movement, with constructivist and social constructionist thought.

The postmodern movement has taken place in an era of uncertainty, ambiguity, and paradox, and has brought with it both a sense of liberation from epistemological positions that, for all their alleged rigor, were not bringing us a better world, and a new set of uncertainties, ambiguities, and paradoxes. Modernism seemed to represent order and clarity, a nailing down, while postmodernism welcomes an unbridled eclecticism, an endless pluralism, multiple reflections, extreme relativism, a bungee-jumping, free-flying time with no certainty about where we will land. Our grandparents and parents seemed to be more sure about what was true and who they were, what comprised a "self" or a family, and communicated to us, with some authority, the meanings of life, of marriage, of politics.

Postmodern thinkers, anti-truth tellers, enamored of language, of story, of the narrative, of the words we use to construct our worlds, abhor absolutist positions. Gone is the search for underlying deep structures in language, in society, in the family. Postmodernists teach us that history itself is a changing narrative, open to endless recasting, that experiences are not "real" until they are interpreted, given meaning in language; meanings themselves are contextual and intersubjective, co-created in dialogue with others. Knowledge does not develop from "proven" or empirically-tested theory or hypothesis, it does not reflect any objective truth but is rather a product of social discourse; particular "knowledges" are seen as social constructions, stories that have been shaped in contexts of relationships of power. Certain knowledges achieve dominance, become accepted as truth, re-creating, then, the contexts of power relationships in which they were crafted.

Modernism brought us a sense of hope, in social work a belief that if we could be "scientific" enough we could locate the causes of our clients' miseries and, with a high level of certainty, intervene appropriately to eliminate the problems. Postmodernism, on the other hand, perhaps reflecting a world in which constant change rather than stability is the norm, a world in which individualism has run rampant and the self has become "saturated" (Gergen, 1991), in which many have given up hope for any future, brings with it a profound skepticism, a sense of irony, and even a troubling level of cynicism. It is not surprising that the turn is toward a search for meaning in a world in which "truths" have led to repeated genocides and to other appalling abuses of power/knowledge.

Where will the postmodern path take us? Is is just "a pastiche of discordant styles, a mindless jumble of theories and fancy vocabulary" (Doherty, 1991, p. 42)? Will it become just another ephemeral "truth"? In my own admittedly biased view, social constructionist thought, deconstructionism, whatever terms we use to describe this epistemological revolution, is bringing a new level of freedom and intellectual creativity to social work thought, practice, research, and teaching. It is a "meta-level" movement, a refashioning of thinking at the paradigmatic level; in that sense, like some of the promises of the systemic and ecological stance that preceded it, it is thinking about thinking, it is not so much about specific truths as about the nature of meaning-making itself. No particular sets of meanings are privileged; there is room here for Joel Fischer, for Walter Hudson, for the kinds of questions their particular ways of knowing may help answer, and for Martha Heineman-Peiper and her intellectual pursuits. But does it mean chaos?

What implications does postmodern thought have for social work teaching? How does the classroom change? What is the relationship between the taught and the learned, between teacher and student? What happens to the "truths" we as educators have leaned upon, the values and ethics of the profession, our central theories of human behavior and social environment, our approaches to assessment and intervention, our models of practice, our tried and true assumptions about how research should be taught and practice evaluated? Contributors to this volume tackle these kinds of questions as they bring to life the ways postmodern thought is shaping their educational philosophies and classroom experiences.

The book is organized as the social work curriculum is organized, that is, along the lines of practice, Human Behavior in the Social Environment, and so on. (There is one major gap—we do not have represented a teacher of social policy, although certainly the work of many of these chapters carry implications for policy.) *Ann Weick*, a pioneer in thinking about positivist epistemology and its relationship to social work values and issues of power, leads off this collection of essays with a vision of how social work education might be reconstructed in the postmodern era. She believes that social work has been pulled away from its value moorings and has increasingly depended on other disciplines, dividing education and practice. Taking a constructivist perspective, Weick advocates a de-centering of knowledge as fact, moving to knowing as a process in which "lived experience" becomes the focus for professional attention.

In a second framing of some of the larger issues surrounding education, *Jo Ann Allen* uses a constructivist lens to re-examine social work values and ethics. In her view, a constructivist paradigm is highly consistent with existing social work values, but it also challenges us to take another look at how we have interpreted their meanings as, for example, in the case of self-determination. Focusing on clinical social work, she believes that postmodern thought offers a new vision for a non-hierarchical, collaborative, more empowering relationship between worker and client as well as a renewed commitment to goals of social justice.

These frame-setting essays are followed by a series of articles authored by teachers of direct practice. *Ruth Dean,* whose work has been seminal in this field, offers a gold mine of teaching suggestions in an educational approach which offers a process parallel to what one envisions happening in the very content and process of clinical practice itself. In her classes, as in the classes of other contributors to this volume, students have firsthand experiences of examining how their own "knowledges" derive from individually and socially constructed experiences. Students learn in a context in which multiple ideas are generated; the class co-constructs meaning in a teacher-student learning environment in which hierarchy is minimized and students participate in shaping their own learning, at the same time learning how this approach might be empowering in work with clients. Dean also raises some of the risks and challenges in this approach.

Her article is followed by a description of the directions my own work has taken in teaching family theory and family-centered practice. The family field has been a lively stage for trying out constructionist ideas, as a number of new models inspired by an international cast of characters have generated much interest. Many of those ideas are gathered here and their integration into an approach to teaching described, but what is emphasized is the stance of always taking a critical stance toward one's own work, one's use of theory and practice technique. I truly believe that our words create our worlds, at least in the sense of our understandings of whatever world lies out there beyond perception and language. Students are encouraged to think about the worlds their categories conjure up and to discover new language that will be more empowering.

In the work of my colleague at Smith, *Phebe Sessions,* the psychological and the social come together in a postmodern context; the world of individual meanings is located in the world of social discourse. In a third-summer course she developed (inspired by C. Wright Mills' famous metaphor) to examine anew the relationship between private troubles and public issues, Sessions challenges students to critically examine, in the context of major social trends of the 20th-century, the popular diagnostic categories of our time, categories which have shaped student thinking about human beings and the models of clinical practice they have learned. Here again are suggestions for how a critical thinking stance can be fostered in the classroom.

Ruth Middleman and *Gale Goldberg Wood* blend three perspectives, constructionism, their own structural approach to practice, and issues of power and conflict in the United States. Consciousness-raising is used to illustrate how these three perspectives translate into direct practice. They, too, like all of the authors here, are concerned with raising a critical consciousness in the classroom. Their chapter is followed by the work of *Liane Davis* on the tensions between constructivism and feminism, mirroring some of the tensions I find in the family therapy field. She describes the thinking behind her development of a course on social work practice with women and raises several of the dilemmas she faces in trying to juggle several seemingly disparate or contradictory educational goals at the same time.

Two more articles round out the material on practice. *Howard Goldstein*, using a social discourse perspective in a paper that will surely stimulate debate, revisits the history of the field experience in social work education. He argues that the heart of education for practice should be located in the field rather than in the classroom, a more facilitating context for the development of the "reflective" practitioner. And *Joan Hardcastle*, a recent M.S.W. graduate from the University of Georgia, describes her experience as a student in a practice course shaped by social constructionist theory. She kept a journal during this "shared learning" experience. Of particular interest is her discussion of the parallels between student experiences of the class and client experiences of the worker.

The direction then turns to Human Behavior and the Social Environment. The similarities and differences between the approaches of *Dennis Saleebey* and *Ann Fleck-Henderson* in conceptualizing and teaching required courses in HBSE are intriguing, particularly in their treatment of developmental theory. Although both take a constructivist perspective, Saleebey is perhaps more critical of developmental and other theories as explanatory "truths" for human behavior, envisioning a radical transformation of the curriculum and detailing how the central metaphors of constructivism can be used to shape HBSE. Fleck-Henderson, not uncritical of our familiar and dominant theories, neverthe-less argues that it is important to continue to teach the central and most useful "abstract" theories we can locate. She argues that students also need more specific testable and operational theories as well. Interest-ingly, as the reader will see, Saleebey and Fleck-Henderson, although they teach in quite different contexts in schools with very different histories, end in a similar place.

Three research articles, each unique, conclude this volume. Here is evidence of how researchers have moved beyond critique of the scientific model to clear demonstrations of how postmodern ideas can be translated into the doing and teaching of research. *Stanley Witkin's* paper illustrates how human rights and social work re-search and evaluation can be integrated in social work education. In his teaching of research, the moral and value implications of inqui-ry, as well as issues of language and theory, critical thinking, and historical and cultural sensitivity, become more central than a focus on research method. *Kathleen Hannigan Millstein*, who teaches in a clinically-focused program historically dominated by psychoanalyt-ic theory, offers carefully thought-out guidelines for how the re-search teacher can use a social constructionist perspective for inten-sive case study and practitioner self-evaluation, an alternative approach to empirically-based single subject designs, which typi-cally best fit behavioral models of practice.

In the final chapter, *Catherine Kohler Riessman*, who has long been interested in narrative analysis, tackles the question of how, in the research pursuit, the subject's responses to questions will be "represented" and "re-presented." She very colorfully illustrates, on one level, how a narrative changes as it is retold in shifting contexts by shifting narrators and interpreters and, on another, how she helps both masters' and doctoral students come to interpret their own narrative stances in the research process, how to place the researcher into the researched.

This book holds between its covers a provocative and innovative collection of ideas for re-visioning social work education. But it is not "right," or "true," or even complete; it is a collection of narratives and descriptions of experience to which the reader will bring her or his own history of ideas. It cannot be easily transformed into a new "Curriculum Policy Statement." But the "reflective" reader will find here a rich treasury of thought and experience that can stimulate dialogue about how to bring social work fully into the postmodern era.

The idea for this collection of original, invited papers belongs to Florence Vigilante, co-editor of the *Journal of Teaching in Social Work*. After she and Harold Lewis published several key articles on a social constructionist stance in social work education, Professor Vigilante recognized the need for a more wide-ranging and thorough exploration of how constructivist and social constructionist ideas are filtering into the curriculum. I was very pleased to have been asked by her to plan such a volume and to work with the group of creative social work educators whose ideas are reflected on these pages. Social constructionists may not overly value "reliability," but this was certainly a reliable group of author-philosophers, for each came through in timely fashion and those who needed to responded good-naturedly and diligently to reviewer suggestions for revision.

Special thanks must be given to Barbara Fenby, a critic in the best sense of that term (who is a practitioner rather than an educator and so was not herself represented in these pages) for her incisive readings of several of the contributions. She is a member of the Northeastern branch of the "Philosophical Issues" study group that I find such a nurturing context for the exchange of ideas. Howard Goldstein, who has become a neighbor in Maine (on the next lake over), also deserves special thanks. He finished his contribution so early that I was able to persuade him to comment on the work of many of his colleagues, which he did with his familiar sense of the ironic. And, finally, I would like to thank Ann Hartman, who stole rare and precious time from her roles as dean of my school and as editor of *Social Work* to read yet a few more papers. Her constructions are always meaningful and helpful.

REFERENCES

Fischer, J. (1981). The social work revolution. *Social Work, 26*, 199-207.

Fischer, J. (1984). Revolution, schmevolution: Is social work changing or not? *Social Work, 29*, 71-74.

Germain, C.B. (1970). Casework: An historical encounter. In R. Roberts & R. Nee (Eds.), *Theories of social casework* (pp. 3-32). Chicago: University of Chicago Press.

Gordon, W.E. (1983). Social work revolution or evolution? *Social Work, 28,* 181-185.

Gordon, W.E. (1984). Gordon replies: Making social work a science-based profession. *Social Work, 29,* 74-75.

Heineman, M. (1981). The obsolete scientific imperative in social work research. *Social Service Review, 55*(3), 371-396.

Hudson, W.H. (1982). Scientific imperatives in social work research and practice. *Social Service Review, 56*(2), 246-258.

Popper, K. (1950). Indeterminism in quantum physics and in classical physics. Part 1. *British Journal for the Philosophy of Science, 1,* 117-133.

Reynolds, B. (1932). A changing psychology one year later. *The Family, 13,* 107-111.

Robinson, V. (1930). *A changing psychology in social case work.* Chapel Hill, NC: University of North Carolina Press.

Reconstructing Social Work Education

Ann Weick

SUMMARY. Understanding social work education requires a long view of history as well as a sense of where social work fits in a larger process of social change and how it can contribute to a radical revisioning of professional education. In this paper a dynamic educational model is proposed, in which the de-centering of knowledge as a fact to knowing as a process is proposed and "lived experience" becomes the central focus of professional attention. At the center of this construction is a new relationship among theory, values, and practice.

INTRODUCTION

The field of social work education rarely takes the opportunity to examine itself through a wider lens. If it were to do so, it would see that there is a crisis in professional education which extends far beyond important but transient issues such as mandated curriculum reviews, concern about student enrollment, and the problems produced by dwindling state budgets. In forging its early alliance with a scientific model of knowledge-building, social work was gradually pulled away from its value moorings. The consequence for the profession has been an erosion of its unique perspective, an increasing dependence on other disciplines to validate its worth, and a

---

Ann Weick, PhD, is Dean of the School of Social Welfare, Twente Hall, The University of Kansas, Lawrence, KS 66045.

[Haworth co-indexing entry note]: "Reconstructing Social Work Education," Weick, Ann. Co-published simultaneously in *Journal of Teaching in Social Work* (The Haworth Press, Inc.) Vol. 8, No. 1/2, 1993, pp. 11-30; and: *Revisioning Social Work Education: A Social Constructionist Approach* (ed: Joan Laird) The Haworth Press, Inc., 1993, pp. 11-30. Multiple copies of this article/chapter may be purchased from The Haworth Document Delivery Center [1-800-3-HAWORTH; 9:00 a.m. - 5:00 p.m. (EST)].

11

dangerous bifurcation between education and practice. While the pressure of immediate challenges conspires against a broadly-based critique, it is precisely at this historical juncture that such an analysis is so urgently needed. From this critique can come a stronger base on which to construct professional education. At the center of this construction is a new relationship among theory, values, and practice.

The road to this revaluation consists of a close examination of some of the major influences which shaped social work education. As will become obvious, social work is part of a much larger cultural-historical process and thus is not unique among professions for its particular development. However, the impact of these forces on social work education and practice deserves an analysis which untangles some of the threads and makes clearer the new directions which are possible. This analysis becomes the base for reconstructing social work education.

It is tempting to imagine that professional practice and professional education developed in the only, and therefore best, way possible. However, that assumption anesthetizes our judgment. In keeping with a constructivist perspective, we assume instead that our perception of the world, including the world of professions, is profoundly influenced by the sociopolitical-historical context within which we live our lives (Gergen, 1985). In spite of the fluid, interpretative way in which reality is constructed, human beings are pattern-makers. They create standard interpretations which become deeply embedded in the interpretive frameworks which govern everyday life. The roles and rules which circumscribe virtually all human exchange are rarely recognized as constructions which could be changed. Rather, they are seen as reflecting the "real world," whether it is family life, government, religious expression, or education. Thus, an essential paradox of human life is that we live in a world of our own construction but we treat it as though it was constructed by powers outside ourselves. The meanings we attach to everything in this world could be other than they are but we do not claim the power to revise them.

The power to revise flows from the assumption that what has been constructed can be reconstructed. In order to revise, we must know that we can re-view, that is view from another perspective, our usual patterns of thinking and acting. Re-viewing can then become the base for revisioning, a process which challenges us to create new constructions which better fit our experience and our needs.

PROFESSIONS AND THE ACADEMY

Understanding social work education requires a long view of history. To say that social work asserted itself as a profession by establishing its first professional association in the mid-1870s does little to explain why social work took the particular course it did. Nor does it explain the intellectual and political forces which gave it, along with other professions, a particular configuration. The classic work by Greenwood (1981) describes attributes of professions, but these attributes primarily serve to justify his argument that social work is indeed a profession, although not as completely one as law or medicine. In order to move beyond the descriptive, we need to create a different frame for analysis. That frame will focus on the phenomenon of professional knowledge, particularly as it has developed within the university, and the crucial relationship between professional knowledge and professional power. Only by understanding this relationship can we critically assess the nature of social work education and construct an alternative view.

Throughout human civilization, universities have been viewed as seats of learning. They have served as both repositories and generators of human knowledge. Because knowledge is treated as a valuable commodity, the enterprise of knowledge-building and transmission is accorded a special status within our culture. Certain people are seen as "learned" or educated because they have experienced a college or university education, while others are considered unschooled and, sometimes, ignorant because they have not. The process of education is often mystified so that those who do not partake are unsure about what actually occurs. From ages old, the university has served to divide people in a society along the lines of formal knowledge training. That this division, even today, is so rarely questioned shows how deeply we believe that there is a significant difference between people who are formally educated and those who are not.

It is instructive to see how professions such as social work, emerging in the late 19th century, connected with the university and how this gave the professions their inevitable shape. The first notable step in this process was essentially political in nature. The turf over which the battle was played was the world of human experience. In order to achieve status within society, the emerging professions cordoned off the world of common experience. During the course of the 19th century, such pervasive human troubles as disease, poverty, and criminality came under the purview of the budding professions (Bledstein, 1976, p. 80). What was customarily viewed as a person's own experience about which he or she had intimate knowledge was given to the new professional class. People who were poor or sick became objects whose knowledge of their own experience was no longer valid.

The second step in the process of professionalization is connected to the professional schools' drive for status within the university. The writing of Donald Schön (1983) is helpful in showing what the stakes were. As envisioned by Thorsten Veblen (Schön, 1983), there would be a division between universities and professions. The "lower schools," namely professions, would be consigned to "instilling such knowledge and habits as will make their pupils fit citizens of the world . . ." (pp. 35-36), while universities would have the more elevated mission to "fit men for a life of science and scholarship" (p. 30). As Schön points out, the professions paid a price for gaining access to the university by having "to accept the Positivist epistemology of practice" (p. 36). In doing so, they accepted that "university-based scientists and scholars [would] create the fundamental theory which professionals and technicians would apply to practice" (p. 36).

As a strategy to diminish this division, professions adopted a model of knowledge which was firmly lodged in 16th century science. The Newtonian revolution, which freed the world from medieval strictures on inquiry, was resoundingly empirical. A scientist investigated the world of nature by putting her to the test through carefully executed experiments (Pagels, 1982, p. 172). These experiments came to define human experience by creating boundaries around what could be investigated and thus was considered a legitimate source of knowledge (Weick, 1990). The scientific model of knowing treats knowledge as an objective reality. Facts float "out there," unsullied by the passions and preoccupations of the observers. These facts can collectively form a "corpus," a body of knowledge which becomes an entity in itself. Thus, the act of knowing and the content of what is known are radically separated from the one who knows. It was this model of knowledge which set the parameters for professional practice.

The history of the social work profession has been consistently marked by both its adherence to and its attempt to maximize its linkage to a scientific model of knowledge. As with other professions, the scientific model which has held the longest sway and greatest prestige is an experimental model derived from the natural sciences. Experimentation allows scientists to act upon matter to see what secrets it might reveal, but it is ultimately a disembodied empiricism, because the observer's influence is purposely removed through the imposition of objective measurement. Although this position of objective observation has been resoundingly challenged by contemporary scientific theory, social sciences and the professions such as social work, which borrowed these assumptions, are still deeply influenced by them (Weick, 1990).

It is important at the outset to recognize the consequences to professions of this strategic linkage with science. While it cleared the path to social recognition for emerging professions by removing what were seen as vestiges of moralism, charlatanism, and amateurism, it created a new class–"the professionals"–and a counterpart class–"the clients." By developing jurisdiction over large areas of human experience, professionals created a new power relationship, based largely on their claim of having expert knowledge about the human condition. As Bledstein (1976) notes, "Common sense, ordinary understanding, and personal negotiations no longer were the effective means of human communication in society [and] . . . clients found themselves compelled to believe, on simple faith, that a higher rationality called scientific knowledge decided one's fate" (p. 94).

POWER AND KNOWLEDGE

The inextricable relationship between professional knowledge and professional power is of utmost importance in understanding the crisis of professions in general and social work in particular. When social work aligned itself with an empiricist or positivist model of science, it adopted, however inadvertently, a valuing system about human knowledge. In keeping with the model of knowledge implicit in empiricist science, social work developed an elite knowledge system, in which clients did not know and could not know precisely what was wrong with them or what they could do to "get better." (The language of the disease model crept early into social work vocabulary.) Instead, it was the social worker who determined what the problem was, giving rise to sophisticated and widely-varied diagnostic catalogs. It was the social worker who orchestrated the course of treatment, presumably based on the diagnosis. The social worker took the role of actor and organizer; the client took the role of obedient recipient.

What should be remarkable about this state of affairs, however starkly drawn, is its poignant inconsistency with social work values. From the origins of the profession in the 1870s, there has been a persistent, if sometimes faint, consensus that asserts belief in people's innate capacity for growth and their ability to direct the course of their lives. And yet the model of social work knowledge adopted by the profession allows no fundamental valuing of clients' own knowledge and experience. Instead, it places expert knowledge and its consequent power directly and almost solely in the hands of the practitioner. It is at the discretion of the practitioner to determine whether and how much to share either one. Thus the model of knowledge, which Schön (1983) calls "technical rationality" (p. 30) became the model for practice.

Foucault (Gordon, 1980) has written eloquently about the dynamics of this exclusion. The voices of such apparently disparate groups as psychiatric patients (Foucault, 1973), prisoners (Foucault, 1977), and penitents (Foucault, 1978) have been systematically silenced through the development of expert knowledge systems which disqualify and disregard their experiences. I have referred to this in another context (Weick, 1983b) as a "giving over" process, because the person is expected to relinquish the power of interpreting his or her own experience in favor of the judgment of the professional.

It is not surprising, then, that professions are in crisis. They have sought to enhance their status by ever more closely allying themselves with a scientific-technical world view. This is evidenced in the increasing demand for research which meets narrow scientific standards; the bias toward rational, problem-solving models; and the conception of human problems in esoteric and power-denying language. The upshot has been a deepening rift between research and practice, a public clamor for an expertise in solving human problems which professionals do not have, and an increasing cynicism and despair about dealing constructively with the world we have created. Doing more of the same is clearly not the answer. Instead, the crisis prompts us to find another angle of analysis which can reconstruct the problem and lead us to a new level of understanding of professional practice and education for practice.

RETHINKING THE NATURE OF PRACTICE

Three essential and related elements combine to form the basis for this reconstruction: knowledge, power, and the professional relationship. The nature of professional practice is intimately connected with the way in which these aspects are conceived. It is only by being clear at the practice level that social work education can find its moorings. This approach is significantly different from the current model, where practice is seen as an outcome of, not as an influence on, education. Turning things upside down can be a helpful way to shift our perception and it allows us to see something we had not seen before.

The bridge to the development of an alternative view is based on a constructivist approach, which assumes that processes of human knowing are deeply rooted in and shaped by our culture, conditions, and psyches. Because perception itself is mediated by constellations of factors, the possibility of seeing something "as it really is" is no longer tenable. In contrast to traditional science, where it has been thought that nature can be observed independently of the observer, the social sciences and humanities have begun focusing on the interpretive nature of human knowledge. Rather than establishing a subject-object relationship, human discourse is seen as intensely subjective.

The knower always intimately influences what is known and how it is known. Human beings are pattern-makers because they inter-pret or attach meaning to what they observe. The phenomenon of human experience suggests that people are active shapers of their reality, not passive observers of events played out on a screen. If, through interpretation, human beings create what they see, then we can no longer claim that truth rests on an absolute standard existing outside ourselves. Instead, the world of social discourse and social judgments must be seen as a process, not a product to be judged by standards external to ourselves.

The shift from viewing knowledge as a product to knowing as a process is profoundly important for the way in which we conceive of professional knowledge. When emphasis is placed on process, attention slips away from the accumulation of facts or the construc-tion of truth statements. Instead, concern is squarely centered on knowing and, more specifically, on the process by which our expe-rience comes into knowing. Bernstein (1985), borrowing from Ga-damer, emphasizes the importance of dialogue in the process of human knowing. We need to see ourselves as "truly dialogical beings–always in conversation, always in process of understand-ing" (p. 165). The attempt to understand is a quest for meaning. As we think, reflect, and converse, we are engaged in an interpretive process which is fluid, influenced by context, tentative, and collab-orative. Because it is so provisional, what we say may be less important than our experience of communicating it. Focusing on process rather than content brings about a radical shift in our way of viewing knowledge. Instead of the source of knowledge being lo-cated outside ourselves, we can begin to see ourselves as knowl-edge-creators. Human experience, a universal commodity, belongs to all of us. No one person or group can be said to exclusively possess this source of knowledge. In fact, the varieties of human knowing make it impossible to create a monopoly on knowledge. All human beings are meaning-seekers and can make the same provisional attempts to communicate meaning.

It is important to understand how radically this view changes the authority of the dominant knowledge systems. If power resides in people because of what they know, that is, the content of their knowledge, then there will always be classes of people who have more of this content than others. People are called scientists because they have a store of knowledge which sets them apart from non-scientists. People are called professionals because they are thought to possess specialized knowledge about the human condition which non-professionals do not have. The boundaries of knowledge and power are thus constricted. If knowledge of a particular type is socially valued, and if only certain people possess it, then power will reside with those who have it. A permanent inequality (Miller, 1976) will exist between the possessors and the dispossessed.

Consider the difference when the process of knowing is valued over the content of knowledge. Everyone suddenly emerges as a knower. Everyone, by virtue of their common humanity, is actively engaged in making sense of their world, of constructing meaning in their lives. Everyone is an interpreter, a creator, a seer. The method of human knowing is dialogue, where individuals negotiate the meaning of human events. When we lodge human knowing within the world of human interpretation, it is much more difficult to assert that any group has a monopoly on knowledge. If every interpretation, including empiricist science, is treated as provisional, then the knowledge-constructing enterprise of humankind is greatly expanded. Knowledge of human experience which has not met the standards of science suddenly becomes accessible. Actors who have been long excluded can enter the stage.

This egalitarian view of human knowing serves to reconstruct the idea of the professional relationship. In contrast to the traditional conception of the professional as one who possesses privileged and esoteric knowledge, a practitioner is one who seeks to activate, support, and honor people's ability to know their own knowing. Rather than re-interpreting a person's own experience of their life, a social worker helps to uncover and make more vivid the meanings attached to life events and issues.

This process of hearing the person's story is the fertile ground in which the relationship is formed. Active, non-judgmental listening is the medium through which important practice orientations are conveyed: respect for the person's own experience as a source of knowledge, validation of the person's capacity to make sense of their situation, acknowledgement of the resiliency shown in surviving and trying to grow, and appreciation for the talents and resources they can use in directing the course of their lives. The skill of professional practice rests on the ability to activate and nurture people's own abilities to grow according to their best lights.

PROFESSIONAL EDUCATION REVISITED

If professional practice is construed as a process whereby people can use and enhance their own deep knowledge about themselves, then some broad outlines for professional education begin to emerge. As may be apparent, these outlines diverge significantly from education as it is traditionally conceived. The focus on content–information, facts, data, and theory–is not sustainable as a primary emphasis because the idea of facts as sources of knowledge are suspect. The goal of mastering certain content flies in the face of a constructivist view which maintains that knowledge is always mediated and thus shaped by language. There is no canon, whether in literature or science, which can be taken to represent ultimate knowledge or objective truth.

Nor can the sharp division between instructor and student be sustained. The stark inequality which exists when the instructor is the preeminent possessor of knowledge is challenged when knowledge is no longer viewed as a scarce and privileged commodity. If knowledge itself rests on shifting sands, then it must always be considered provisional and subject to new interpretations. Because learners also bring their own interpretative powers to life experiences, they must be considered co-sharers in the creation of what is known.

A social constructivist view of education points to a dramatic shift in the source of social power. What is believed to be known at any one point in time loses its central place. Thus, the class divisions based on the possession of certain knowledges is blurred. Neither the professor, the professional, nor the priest can be seen as having a monopoly on knowledge or on the power which flows from it. They, along with all others, are viewed as having equal capacity to interpret, revise, and negotiate the meaning of human events. At the heart of a constructivist view, then, is a radical egalitarianism. All human beings are meaning-makers and no person or group can claim to have exclusive rights as interpreters.

These assertions about education in general have particular poignancy for professional education. For deep in the heart of professional practice lies the intuitive recognition that knowledge about human behavior and social institutions is breathtakingly imprecise. The traditional model of knowledge, based on facts, theory, and research, is frail and superficial in the face of people's quirks, passions, resilience, and nerve. Good practitioners know that the quality and course of each encounter is unpredictable and infinitely fluid. However, unknowingly, good practitioners have already accepted the premise of a constructivist view. They already know that theory and technique are a backdrop against which the negotiation of meaning occurs.

If one accepts the essentially constructivist nature of professional practice, it is interesting to consider what sort of educational orientation might best support it. Not surprisingly, the guidelines for this orientation do not center on content. There is a place for curriculum content but it is not at the starting point. Instead, the focus is on elements which support students' capacity to understand and act within an interpretive world.

Elizabeth Minnich and her colleagues (Minnich, O'Barr, & Rosenfeld, 1988) have identified elements which form a preliminary shape for discussion. Drawing from their collected essays on women's place in and contributions to the academy, they point to "critique, reflexivity, conversation, action, and cross-cultural understanding . . . [as] a web that is complex enough to hold us while restraining us from spinning off on our own single thread . . ." (p. 7). The image of a web of such elements is a congenial way to approach the challenge of rethinking professional education.

CRITICAL PERSPECTIVE

The importance of critique is inherent in a constructivist view of education. When no particular interpretation deserves to have a privileged status, then the intellectual skill of critique is essential. Students must learn how to approach whatever content is presented with a means for critically assessing its virtues and shortcomings. In stark contrast to traditional education, which emphasizes the skill of mimicry, that is, sounding like the professor, the art of critique begins with the assumption that what is presented must always be seen and evaluated within a larger socio-political context.

An instructor facilitates this process by always placing content within this larger context. At one level, this occurs through a process of critical thinking: Students are supported in asking questions about why certain interpretations of human behavior emerged or why certain policies gained or lost favor. Critical thinking engages curiosity and healthy skepticism. At another level, it becomes part of a larger critique. Students begin to see that there are patterns of interpretation, where global assumptions are apparent. This is the level of ideology, where certain patterns of belief can be seen as pervasive ways of viewing the world.

Being able to identify broad patterns of belief provides a base for assessing their origins and consequences. For example, there is a general belief in the authority and preeminence of traditional curricula in American universities. Students are expected to learn the canon, those texts deemed to best exemplify the thinking of the culture. However, as Minnich (1990) points out, this belief rests on a false universalization that has taken a very few privileged men from a particular tradition to be the inclusive term, the norm, and the ideal for all (p. 2). If one only learns the text, one does not have an opportunity to place it in critical perspective. Obviously, such critique goes beyond an assessment of the quality of a particular author's work. Instead, it places all authored works into a larger frame, so that one can observe that the writings of women and people of color are excluded, and that such exclusion reveals the implicit devaluing of voices other than those in the dominant tradition.

A multicultural perspective further fortifies the need for including and valuing the history and experiences of all cultures. This perspective challenges the arrogance of any group who would propose that their interpretation of history or their understanding of human relations deserves preeminence. Instead, multiculturalism invites the richness of all human experience to display itself, with its wisdom and foibles, its conflicts and striving. By attending to the multiplicity of meanings humans have attached to their lives and their societies, we cannot help but achieve a more modest and respectful view of the limits and contributions of all.

The larger critique therefore deals with broad themes: the persistence of certain knowledges and the exclusion of others, the use of power to squelch other voices, and the dynamics of oppression which cause the majority of people in our society to disqualify their own experience. It is through this critical perspective that subjugated knowledges can begin to emerge.

REFLEXIVITY

The human ability to construct patterns of meaning has a strong counterpart in our ability to reflect on our own thinking. We don't simply create meaning; we can also judge, evaluate, and change it. This reflexive quality is an essential component of good practice. As Schön (1983) has so aptly pointed out, "Practitioners do reflect on their knowing-in-practice" (p. 62). Sometimes this occurs after the fact, when one ruminates on a past interaction and distills certain aspects which are significant for future encounters. But it is equally true that practitioners "reflect-in-action" (p. 62), by actively and spontaneously knowing and acting in the moment. This action tends to flow from tacit knowledge–past knowledge, intuitions, artistic flashes–which instantaneously evolve from the meaning of the moment. Trusting and using tacit knowledge gives practitioners a virtuosity which allows them to engage fully in the process of making meaning with their clients.

To prepare students as reflective practitioners, there need to be expanded ways for them to appreciate their own wisdom and creativity. While it is generally thought that field practicum offers the needed opportunity to practice, it is not clear that either field or classroom settings adequately provide the atmosphere where creative reflexivity takes place. By creative reflexivity I mean the opportunity to reflect on one's practice, not just in terms of its consonance with facts, information, or theory but with the entire array of experiential knowledge available to each of us.

Finding ways to heighten self-awareness has received sporadic attention in social work. In the earlier days of professional education, students were expected to undergo their own therapy in order to be prepared to practice. In the 1960s, "T groups" and sensitivity training offered another venue for achieving a similar goal. The 1990s have brought us self-help groups and the recovery movement, in which many students participate. The critical issue is how to incorporate opportunities for increasing reflexivity so that practice is enhanced, not subverted.

We can draw some preliminary guidelines from our discussion of knowledge and power. If good practice seeks to honor and draw from people's own experience, their opportunities for self-awareness need to focus on student's own wisdom about how they have lived their lives. The context for this will be discussed shortly. But suffice it to say that providing experiences in which students can recognize and appreciate what they bring to the educational process is crucial for reconstructing traditional professional education.

A STRENGTHS PERSPECTIVE

A constructivist view in social work education acknowledges the frailty of "truth" as a standard against which to measure human activities. The notion that there is some truth safely preserved "out there" for us to discover fails to account for the ways in which humans constantly construct and reconstruct interpretations of their social and physical worlds. Critics of a constructivist view suggest that it will lead to chaos and nihilism, where nothing matters and nothing can be judged in moral terms.

The irony is that constructivism, rather than traditional models of truth and authority, can lead to a more genuine moral perspective (Imre, 1991). When truth is defined by institutions radically separated from the everyday world of people's lives, the only role for citizen, student, or worshiper is that of believer. They do not participate in shaping "the truth." Instead, they are recipients or consumers of it. In contrast, a constructivist view assumes that people not only have the ability but also the responsibility to negotiate human meaning. It is in this process of negotiation that individuals are called upon to become intensely aware of their own assumptions and, more specifically, their own values. Ultimately, it is the negotiation of values which characterizes the importance of a contructivist view in social work.

Being able to explicitly and unashamedly focus on the value base of the profession provides a refreshing corrective to a 50-year trend which has buried values under the mantle of objective, value-free science. Now we must once again engage in the profoundly challenging task of discussing the values which shape professional practice. We enter this discussion to stimulate debate, not to authoritatively set out a new value agenda for the profession.

Perhaps this direction can best be understood through an example. The strengths perspective, as it is being called by its developers (Saleebey, 1992), is an orientation to practice based on the conscious valuing of people's own innate talents, abilities, and resources. Social workers' belief in and explicit attention to these strengths is seen as a key element in supporting people to direct the course of their lives according to their own lights. As a value orientation, it stands in contrast to the dominant pathology model, where deficit, illness, and problems are given central place. The strengths perspective makes the assumption that people are more likely to be able to grow and develop when their strengths, rather than their problems, are recognized and supported (Weick et al., 1989).

Those familiar with early social work writings know that the strengths perspective draws from a long-held practice maxim of building on people's strengths. In that sense the orientation is not new. However, the development of an approach which is explicitly value-based, rather than method-based, is new to the field. The assumptions upon which the orientation is based are not hidden from view. Instead, they are laid out with as much initial clarity as possible. This strategy invites dialogue and debate, an opportunity to consider whether the assumptions about human resilience and aspirations provide a good match with our constructions about how people can best grow and change. It provides, perhaps for the first time, an opportunity to match theory with values with practice.

THEORY, VALUES, AND PRACTICE

With the opening of debate on the relationship of theory, values and practice, it should be clear how important conversation becomes. The act of dialogue is the vehicle through which meaning gets made. In a constructivist arena, no one comes to the conversation with preeminent authority. It is true that some may have had more opportunity than others to think through issues. But the tone of conversation is provisional and exploratory. Things can be

learned in the making of a meaning which revise previous interpretations. When one listens intently to another's story, understandings emerge which make and test theory in the moment. Theory is
not an external knowledge-packet but a fluid, creative process of
constructing new guesses. The urge to make sense of something
continues but it is, at best, a provisional sense. There is always room
for learning, reflecting and creating new responses.

Good practices (and good education) has been likened to good
conversations (Saleebey, 1989). It is characterized not by logical
steps or an action plan but by the components of good conversation,
"simile, memory, metaphor, recounting, irony, analogy and declara-
tion (which) take shape in forms that could hardly have been predicted" (p. 558). Through the medium of conversation, people explore, evaluate and engage with each other. The qualities with
which they imbue this dialogue affect the process. Compassion,
respect, affirmation, and interest heighten the chances that the dialogue will realize its creative potential.

Because neither party to the conversation can claim to know all
that is relevant to the situation, other grounds for negotiating meaning must be found. In place of authority, other elements emerge.
There is the criterion of pragmatics: that some interpretations seem
to provide a better fit with human experience than others. For example, human development theory is typically lodged in linear, age-re-
lated assumptions about how people change. Most people probably
experience a much more convoluted process. Devising an interpretation which seems to fit this experience is a pragmatic approach
(Weick, 1983a).

Another criterion is simplicity. Interpretations which stay close to
everyday life in both language and experience seem to have more
power and appeal. So do those which elicit people's wisdom. The
evidence of wisdom can come to light when knowledge is not
defined as information and facts. It is the deeper part of one's
knowledge, which draws from broad understandings about the human condition and involves the heart. To understand (to stand under) and to be compassionate (to feel with) are at the core of wisdom. Ultimately, all of these qualities join with values as the new
context for education and practice. Instead of seeking to be value
free, a constructivist view is value-based (Murphy, 1989). It explic-

itly recognizes the importance of values and allows a discussion of values to take center stage.

The opportunity for a dialogue on values is, in itself, a liberating move. Rather than artificially cleaving knowledge and values, as required in a traditional scientific perspective, a constructivist view recognizes that there is little else but values. Every interpretation is profoundly influenced by beliefs and their underlying values. Whether one is assessing a family situation, organizing a community, spotting an issue for research or promoting a policy change, values set the orientation for action. Thus, values deserve a prominent place in discussions of both education and practice.

Because professional values have had to exist in subterranean regions throughout most of this century, a focus on social work values would be bracing. For example, trying to understand the meaning of self-determination is no small challenge. The values of respect, dignity, equality, and social justice fall from our lips and textbooks as leaves from a tree. But we have yet to seriously take up the challenge of inquiring about how they would reshape both education and practice if they were given a central place.

Because a constructivist view necessarily emphasizes process rather than product, it is interesting to consider another area of values, namely, those which support social work process. If education were conceived as a process which engaged students' intellectual, emotional, and spiritual resources, then it would matter how this engagement occurred. The model of instructor as the "talking head" would be seen as pitifully inadequate.

SOCIAL WORK AS ART

When we acknowledge the value-process context of social work, the metaphor of art, rather than science, comes into sharper focus. One virtue of the artistic metaphor is that it applies equally to education and to practice, or perhaps more accurately, it applies to education because it is true in practice. If social work practice is a value-oriented art form, then preparation for practice must be art-sensitive. In order to accomplish this, students must be helped to develop their natural talent as artists by creating a milieu where their virtuosity can come to light and be supported.

Just as with other art forms, students study about and with other artists. They study painting or music or dance as it has evolved over time. They learn to critically assess works of art. They learn techniques of the art and they practice those techniques until they are no longer conscious of applying them. What they produce is subject to other's comments and views. But through all of this, it is recognized that the performance or product is a creative act which happens in a never-to-be duplicated moment. It is guided by an amalgamation of intentions, knowledge, and experience whose boundaries are lost in the act of doing. Social work, as with other art, is holistic by nature.

Emphasizing the artistic essence of social work may seem a dangerous strategy when doing so threatens the scientific basis upon which the profession has so carefully anchored itself. It is true that the scientific paradigm still has preeminence in many quarters. However, it is also true that the limits of the scientific world view are becoming increasingly evident. The fervid application of a scientific approach to the physical and social worlds is outrunning its problem-solving potential. From the environment to medical science, sounds of crisis are becoming more urgent. In every sphere, the assumptions of a scientifically-constructed world view are receiving critical review.

A constructivist perspective has the potential to free us from a self-imposed attachment to an outmoded view. If a scientific world view is no longer sufficiently helpful in providing meaningful future directions, then it is possible to create other constructions which might do so. In the more modest realm of social work education, if we find that the bifurcation of knowledge and values estranges us from a richer and fuller view of both education and practice, then we can re-vision our practice and the learning environment which prepares students to do it well. In doing so, we may discover a new creative spirit within faculty and students which justifies the profession's enduring commitment to social work values.

The social work profession, by virtue of its long commitment to values and to process, is in an ideal position to "open (a) space for the dreaming of humanity" (Minnich et al., 1988, p. 7). Rather than continuing to copy an approach which may never have served us well, the profession could reach into its own considerable reservoir of wisdom and begin dreaming a new vision of practice and education. The vision would draw from our remarkable strengths as a profession, particularly our stubborn loyalty to radical, egalitarian values and our deep understanding of human process. If we can rise to the challenge of honoring these strengths, we may find that social work can, indeed, help lead the way into a new and more hopeful century.

REFERENCES

Bernstein, R.J. (1985). *Beyond objectivism and relativism: Science, hermeneutics and praxis*. Philadelphia: University of Pennsylvania Press.

Bledstein, B. (1976). *The culture of professionalism*. New York: Norton.

Foucault, M. (1980). *Power/knowledge*. Gordon, C. ed. New York: Pantheon Books, New York: Vintage.

Foucault, M. (1978). *The history of sexuality* vol. 1, New York: Pantheon.

Foucault, M. (1977). *Discipline and punish: The birth of the prison*. New York: Pantheon.

Foucault, M. (1973). *Madness and civilization: A history of insanity in the age of reason*. New York: Vintage.

Gergen, K.T. (1985). The social constructionist movement in modern psychology. *American Psychologist, 40*(3), 255-275.

Gordon, C. (1980). *Power/knowledge* by Michel Foucoult. New York: Pantheon Books.

Greenwood, E. (1981). Attributes of a profession. In N. Gilbert & H. Specht (Eds.). *The emergence of social work and social welfare* (pp. 302-318). Itasca, IL: F.E. Peacock.

Gergen, K.T. (1985). The social constructionist movement in modern psychology. *American Psychologist, 40*(3), 255-275.

Imre, R. (1991). What do we need to know for good practice? *Social Work, 36*, 198-200.

Miller, J.B. (1976). *Toward a new psychology of women*. Boston: Beacon.

Minnich, E. (1990). *Transforming knowledge*. Philadelphia: Temple University Press.

Minnich, E., O'Barr, J., & Rosenfeld, R. (1988). *Reconstructing the academy*. Chicago: University of Chicago Press.

Murphy, J.W. (1989). Clinical intervention in the postmodern world. *International Journal of Adolescence and Youth, 2*, 61-69.

Pagels, H. (1982). *The cosmic code*. New York: Simon and Schuster.

Saleebey, D. (1992). *The strengths perspective in social work practice*. New York: Longman.

Saleebey, D. (1989). The estrangement of knowing and doing: Professions in crisis. *Social Casework, 70*, 556-563.

Schön, D. (1983). *The reflective practitioner* New York: Basic Books.

Weick, A. (1983a). A growth task model of human development *Social Casework,* *64*(3), 131-137.

Weick, A. (1983b). Issues in overturning a medical model of social work practice. *Social Work, 28*(6), 467-471.

Weick, A. (1990). Knowledge as experience: Exploring new dimensions of social work inquiry. *Social Thought, 16*(3), 36-46.

Weick, A. (1991). The place of science in social work. *Journal of Sociology and Social Welfare, 18*(4), 13-34.

Weick, A., Rapp, C., Sullivan, W.P., & Kisthardt, W. (1989). A Strengths Perspective for Social Work Practice. *Social Work, 34*(4), 350-354.

The Constructivist Paradigm: Values and Ethics

Jo Ann Allen

SUMMARY. Values and ethics are central, everyday concerns in clinical social work based on a constructivist perspective. Key assumptions of the constructivist paradigm preclude the ethic of objectivity and neutrality associated with the positivist and empiricist traditions. In constructivism, the active role of social context and practitioner values in shaping the descriptions and problems of clients is acknowledged and an ethic of responsibility and collaboration is called for. The constructivist paradigm is highly congruent with existing social work values. However, at the same time, it challenges clinical social work to re-examine the meanings of its values and to give social justice a practice priority.

INTRODUCTION

The values and ethics of a profession reflect the assumptions and theories in which it is grounded. In this chapter, I examine the ways in which key assumptions of the constructivist paradigm move values and ethics to center stage as practice issues in clinical social work. I also contrast the values and ethical positions of the

---

Jo Ann Allen, MSW, is Professor Emerita, University of Michigan School of Social Work, Ann Arbor, MI 48109 and is a staff member of Ann Arbor Center for the Family, where she does supervision, training, and direct clinical practice in family therapy.

[Haworth co-indexing entry note]: "The Constructivist Paradigm: Values and Ethics," Allen, Jo Ann. Co-published simultaneously in *Journal of Teaching in Social Work* (The Haworth Press, Inc.) Vol. 8, No. 1/2, 1993, pp. 31-54; and: *Revisioning Social Work Education: A Social Constructionist Approach* (ed: Joan Laird) The Haworth Press, Inc., 1993, pp. 31-54. Multiple copies of this article/chapter may be purchased from The Haworth Document Delivery Center [1-800-3-HAWORTH; 9:00 a.m. - 5:00 p.m. (EST)].

constructivist paradigm with those of the modern/positivist paradigm which has long guided much of clinical social work practice. Constructivism challenges some of our cherished beliefs but it also offers an opportunity for new and beneficial directions in ethics and values.

Many clinical social workers base their practices upon the logical positivism of Freudian psychoanalysis or the empiricist tradition of classical behaviorism. Although very different, both share the modern, scientific view that "an objective and reductionistic stance is best suited for explaining the true nature of the expansive human state" (Goldstein, 1986, p. 353). Reality is out there and can be discovered by an objective observer. Many family systems practitioners also subscribe to the idea of a discoverable reality which can be viewed through lenses of normative interaction, structure, and communication. From the modern perspective, the only ethical stance for the clinician is that of a value-free, objective expert.

A fundamental assumption of the constructivist paradigm leads to the rejection of objectivity and suggests a stance of responsible participation instead. Constructivists believe that reality is invented, constructed largely out of meanings and values of the observer. They hold that an observer cannot help but change that which is observed. In this paper, I explore the ethical mandate for clinical social workers to acknowledge their active participation in creating images of their clients, their problems, and their possibilities for change.

By challenging the "postivist presumption that it is possible to distinguish facts from values" (Hare-Mustin & Maracek, 1988, p. 6), constructivists bring values into focus as a central issue in therapy. The meanings, values, and attitudes of both clients and clinicians determine what are to be taken as facts. It is the responsibility of practitioners to bring values openly into conversations with their clients.

Another assumption of constructivism with important implications for values and ethics is that of language as a mediating influence in all constructions, from our ideas, concepts, memories, to our very sense of self. We bring forth our realities, our worlds, through conversations with others. According to Maturana and Varela (1987), "We work out our lives in a mutual linguistic coupling, not because language permits us to reveal ourselves, but because we are constituted in language in a continuous becoming that we bring forth with others" (pp. 234-235). In a sense, conversation creates reality. As we talk, we are not revealing truths about a problem, a family, or an individual; we are creating them with others. In this paper, I explore the ethical dimensions of the power of meaning-making through language and propose that the newly developing language-based therapies which take dialogue, conversation, and narrative as metaphors are an ethical fit for clinical practice.

The constructivist paradigm, as it is interpreted here, stresses the inevitable link between knowledge and power, particularly in the political sense that some knowledge is privileged and some is subjugated. One person's or a profession's knowledge may become more valued, more "true" than another's, depending upon sociopolitical context. The ethical and value implications are profound. Therapy, then, is always a political act and discussions of client problems and solutions should take into account sociopolitical context. One ethical question to be raised is whether the "knowledge," the story of the clinical social worker, is to take precedence over that of the client. This also suggests the ethical necessity for a collaborative, rather than a hierarchical, relationship between clinicians and clients as truly supportive of such values as self-determination.

In a constructivist perspective, it is proposed that truth and reality are inevitably intertwined with social context and meaning and that values should be examined in that light. In this paper, I suggest that current social work values reflect an ethnocentric preference for a Western point of view, particularly with respect to self-determination and respect for the individual. Because of the importance of social context in shaping lives, a values framework in which connectedness and social justice are more prominent is considered.

Perhaps the most demanding challenge of the constructivist paradigm to social work education is to devote adequate space and energy to the teaching of values and ethics. These are central concerns in constructivist practice and need the same centrality in education. Students should be encouraged to examine all theory, research, social policy, and practice methods courses for value biases and ethical implications. The sociopolitical contexts for clinical social work in particular agency settings should be part of the dialogue between practicum supervisors and their students. Students should be asked to reflect upon how their personal values are affecting their work with every client. They should be encouraged to bring their own ethical dilemmas openly into the supervisory process and helped to find ways to examine these dilemmas with clients when necessary. Goldstein (1986), describing a humanistic approach, suggests that "educational programs would include a strong foundation of moral philosophy and ethical reasoning to enable students to grapple with both social and personal ethical dilemmas" (p. 356).

A CONSTRUCTIVIST ETHIC

Rhodes (1986), in her excellent book on ethical dilemmas in social work, speaks of an "odd ethical stand" (p. 14) in the Code of Ethics of the National Association of Social Work. On the one hand, the Code acknowledges that ethical choices must be seen in the context of a broader political framework. On the other hand, it remains silent about any political/social/ethical basis of practice. She calls upon each social worker to develop an informed ethical and political position that is relevant to daily practice. In addition, she believes that it is the responsibility of every practitioner to enter into an open dialogue about his or her ethical stands. I enter the dialogue on behalf of constructivist practice in a way which is quite consistent with Rhodes' insistence on acknowledging the sociopolitical aspects of professional ethics.

"Ethics" has been defined as "a set of moral principles" and "the rules of conduct recognized in respect to a particular class of human actions or a particular group" (Webster's, 1989). As Rhodes (1986) points out, "Almost every decision that a social worker makes, even a technical one, is a decision about ethics" (p. 10). The everyday conduct and decisions of clinical social workers require an underlying ethical framework. Every practice paradigm has an implicit ethical and political basis although these often are not made explicit. Every theory about therapy, explicitly or implicitly, prescribes ways of being with and acting towards clients.

Rules of conduct or ethics flow from the underlying belief system of the clinician. The ethical mandate for the modern, "scientific" clinician/expert is to be objective, neutral, and value-free. Such "objectivist therapists" believe that "objective truth is discoverable and, when, properly revealed, leads to improved psychological health" (Efran, Lukens, & Lukens, 1988, p. 28). Therapy then becomes a hierarchical affair in which the clinician is accorded ultimate power, based upon superior knowledge, to diagnose and treat problems. In essence, the therapist is to behave in accord with an ethic of objectivity.

Ethic of Responsibility

The constructivist paradigm represents a dramatic shift in the ethical framework of clinical practice. Keeney (1983) discusses the shift as moving from an ethic of objectivity to an ethic of responsibility. In fact, he proposes that the alternative to objectivity is ethics itself. Constructivists recognize the connection of the observer with the observed and "acknowledge the active role they play in creating a view of the world and interpreting observations in terms of it" (Efran, Lukens, & Lukens, 1988, p. 28). An examination of our ethics, that is, how we participate, the effect of observing, our lenses of observation, our values, and how we behave towards clients, *is* the ethic. The ethic is played out in practice through a co-evolutionary process in which clients and clinicians are equal participants in defining problems and creating change. The hallmarks of such a process are *mindfulness, respect,* and *empowerment.*

The ethic of responsibility repositions the therapist from expert to participant-observer. As Weingarten (1991) points out, constructivists are not the first to consider the participatory role of therapists. Psychiatrists such as Sullivan and Fromm, identified with the interpersonal school of psychiatry, introduced this concept some years ago. Nevertheless, postmodern therapy has incorporated the idea of the co-participant therapist as essential to sound, ethical practice. In order to participate responsibly, the practitioner must develop an active mindfulness focused on "the intentions that underlie our punctuative habits" (Keeney, 1983). This self-referential attitude is as much concerned with what questions, hypotheses, and conclusions reveal about the practitioner as what they reveal about the client. In addition, the ethic of responsibility suggests that the practitioner must be as open to change as the client, and even invite it.

Social work educators, too, must incorporate an ethic of responsibility. Instructors need to be alert to what their teaching methods convey to students about their views of educational responsibility and self-determination. Teachers can study their styles and methods for what they reveal about their own beliefs. They may even ask their students to comment on what they surmise about the teacher's beliefs, values, and ethics. Instructors may reflect openly about what their preferences for certain theories reveal about them, inviting students to do the same and, thus, modelling the co-evolutionary process in the classroom; here both students and teachers are learners.

Helping students move from an objective stance requires exercises that promote a self-evaluative attitude, as well as an appreciation that others legitimately make sense of the world in ways that may be very different from their own. To do this, it may help to think of teaching in more personal ways. Tice (1990), writing of feminist models of teaching, suggests that teaching "become not only intellectual but emotional engagement" (p. 139). She encourages students to enter into the experiences of others by listening to oral histories from a wide diversity of people who vary in terms of race, class, ethnicity, gender, and so on. Her students may "try on" the experiences of others through simulated activities. For example, they may try to understand a gay client by writing a "coming out" letter to their own parents. Gay and straight students alike can process their own feeling responses to the material in peer discussion groups. Such exercises sensitize students to the importance of an ethic of listening and can open them to the idea of multiple truths.

Dialogue as Ethics

Language-based or dialogic therapy (e.g., Anderson & Goolishian, 1988; White & Epston, 1990) is one way an ethic of responsibility is realized. Such an approach employs narrative, conversation, and dialogue as practice metaphors, and is evolving in part as a response to the ethical charge to practitioners to become participant-observers. This is the natural outgrowth of constructivism's recognition of language as a mediating influence in the social construction of systems and their problems as well as their meanings and values. Therapy, from this perspective, is a collaborative, change-oriented conversation.

The idea of therapy as dialogue fits the ethical framework of the constructivist paradigm in a comfortable fashion for several reasons. One is that dialogue is focused on meaning-making. David Bohm (1990), a theoretical physicist, describes dialogue as "a stream of meaning flowing among us and through us and between us–a flow of meaning in the whole group, out of which will emerge some new understanding, something creative" (p. 1). Dialogue, in other words, brings people together for the express purpose of learning what is on each other's minds and not necessarily to reach conclusions or make judgments.

An ethic of responsibility constantly reminds the therapist of her or his role as a co-constructer of "truth," rather than a discoverer and conveyer of "truth." In the therapeutic dialogue, the therapist is invested with the responsibility to be passionate about understanding the meanings of others, in this case the clients' meanings and those of anyone else within the therapeutic system. As Bohm (1990) points out, "This sharing of mind, of consciousness, is more important than the content of the opinions. You may find that the answer is not in the opinions at all, but somewhere else" (p. 22). So long as the dialogue moves forward, there is hope for the co-construction of new and more satisfactory meanings.

An ethic of responsibility makes special and difficult demands upon therapists who engage in dialogue as the main instrument of change. For one thing, it requires a constant mindfulness, an ability to be as totally present as possible. A constructivist therapist is fully aware that everyone, including the therapist, enters the dialogue with opinions and "knowings" in the form of values, theories, hypotheses, and perhaps conclusions. But the ethical stance I am describing counsels the therapist to enter the situation from what Anderson and Goolishian (1990) have called a "not-knowing" position (1990). This means that therapists must be aware of their opinions but able to bracket them, to adopt a learning stance. They are required constantly to question what hypotheses and "stories" are influencing their own thinking, behavior, and decisions. Very importantly, they must be willing to change. As Anderson and Goolishian (1988) have said, "For us, the willingness to risk and undergo change is the essence of therapeutic ethics. We would hold that the only person the therapist changes in the therapy consultation is himself or herself" (p. 385). This is quite different from describing clients as resistant to change if they fail to move towards an acceptance of the practitioner's ideas.

Another property of dialogue which fits well with the ethics of constructivist practice is its requirement to open space for multiple realities and perspectives. Multiple realities offer the seeds for change, for constructing new stories in which the problem ceases to be a problem or new alternatives are generated. Epstein and Loos (1987) note, "A dialogical constructivist position implies that every person's reality has validity within their own domain of existence" (p. 19). In the language-based approaches, it is the ethical responsibility of the clinician to behave in ways that maintain the dialogue and foster an atmosphere of respect for a multiplicity of views. The practitioner is always guided by an understanding of the connection between the observer and the observed. This recognition extends to all who participate in that all are observers and all are observed. Everyone in the dialogue is a participant-observer.

The dialogical constructivist position described above requires the clinician to shed power but not responsibility. Therapists occupy the position of what Anderson and Goolishian (1988) call the "participant manager of the conversation" (p. 384). From this position, they take on the responsibility to open space for all stories in an atmosphere that respects and values diversity as a creative force for change. One of the most important ethical and therapeutic roles for the practitioner is to bring forth "subjugated knowledge" (Foucault, 1980) in the personal, family, and social lives of clients. These are the untold stories and ways of thinking and being that have never been admitted to the mainstream conversation.

One of the most effective ways to teach dialogue as ethical practice is for the teacher to take the role of participant manager of the classroom conversation. It is her responsibility to keep the dialogue flowing, whatever the topic, by drawing upon the diversity of class members for multiple perspectives. She may ask students deliberately to take alternative views and defend them, particularly marginal or fringe viewpoints. Role plays can be devised in which students are asked to take opposing positions but are required to converse until they can fully understand and present the other's beliefs and rationale. Students can also identify what they learned from each other that may modify their original views.

Power and Ethics

The constructivist paradigm and the dialogical models of therapy have sharpened the focus of ethical issues concerning power, especially that of the therapist in relation to clients. In recognizing the power of the practitioners's voice to shape problems and outcomes, every attempt is made to empower clients by creating a respectful, egalitarian climate. Ethical codes have always encouraged clinical social workers to be self-aware and to examine their personal and family of origin issues with respect to their actions and reactions towards clients. But an analysis of the effect of power on the relationship between practitioner and client has seldom been a serious consideration. Postmodern writers and therapists such as White and Epston (1990) speak of the inseparability of power and knowledge. Given that condition, practitioners cannot simply take a benign view of their own practices in the belief that "we can avoid all participation in the field of power/knowledge through an examination of such personal motives" (White & Epston, 1990, p. 29). We are ethically required to examine how our own belief systems contribute to meaning-making around clients and their problems.

Postmodern therapists realize that whoever has the power to construct meaning has the power to construct reality. In other words, as many (e.g., Foucault, 1980; White & Epston, 1990) have argued, power is constitutive of meaning and experience. From this point of view, the sociopolitical context of a client's problem is inevitably a consideration. The meaning-making process by which problems and desired solutions are determined is a critical ethical and clinical concern. Whoever joins the conversation about clients and their problems is not just making conversation but is making meaning. As a result, it is an ethical responsibility for the clinical social worker to push the boundaries of therapy outward beyond individuals and families.

Sociopolitical concerns require the inclusion in the therapeutic system of those powerful voices who may be part of the problem they are so active in defining. As Hoffman (1985) points out, "The problem is the meaning system created by the distress and the treatment unit is everyone who is contributing to that meaning system. This includes the treating professional as soon as the client walks in the door" (p. 387). The ethical dimension of this view for the clinical social worker lies not just in the recognition and bringing forth of multiple opinions. It lies in the responsibility to advocate and to open space for client voices in the developing conversation so that they can define themselves, their problems, and their preferred solutions. Sometimes this means actively trying to change rigid definitions about the client and the problem which actually impede needed change.

One of the most controversial and difficult areas, and one having also to do with power, is that of expert knowledge. Postmodern ethics require that diagnosis be a joint endeavor of client and clinician. Otherwise, as Anderson and Goolishian (1988) hold, "It is easy to slide into certainties, into monologues" (p. 389) in which the voice of the client is lost. There is no escaping the idea that, ethically, in postmodernism, the diagnostic categories of the "expert" therapist are called into question as value-laden and self-referential. What has often been overlooked, until recently acknowledged in the work of language-based therapists, is the fact that diagnoses are meanings and represent the values and cultural and gender biases of the dominant voices of the therapy world. The socio-political context of diagnostic systems will be explored more fully in a later section on values.

Questioning the position of the therapist as expert does not mean that the therapist abandons all knowledge and expertise. The ethical challenge is not so much to the knowledge of the practitioner but to the notion of the practitioner as the possessor of the only "truth" that matters. Coming from the "not-knowing" position does not mean that the practitioner lacks a knowledge base or hypotheses. It means that there is no "pre-knowing," no drawing of irrevocable conclusions which are substantiated by selectively gathering and attending to data which support the theory. Weingarten (1991) speaks of the responsibility to share expertise as needed, for example, about drug or sexual abuse. Constructivism's ethical charge does not dampen the clinician's interest in change but only the passion to be the one who changes the other. The passion may be transferred to helping to free clients from rigid descriptions which they had little part in making.

The ethical questions raised by the constructivist paradigm are clearly centered in the issue of power. A resolution to these issues lies, in part, in the therapist's willingness to "shed power" (Hoffman, 1985, p. 393). The dialogical models of therapy are constructed to empower clients in their relationships with therapists and anyone else in the problem-determined system. These are collaborative, change-oriented conversations rather than hierarchical, instrumental therapies. As clinical social workers relinquish their faith in objectivity and invite clients into a partnership, all voices are respected. As Maturana (Simon, 1985) remarks, "with objectivity in parentheses, it is easy to do things together, because one is not denying the other in the process of doing them" (p. 43).

The shift to an ethical stance of collaboration and dialogue has far-reaching implications for education as well as clinical practice. First of all, the moral dimension of language (Rhodes, 1986) is to be emphasized. That is, the question of what political and value judgments are being made when a client is diagnosed as having a "borderline personality," for example, is to be kept in the forefront of the classroom conversation. Teachers need to find ways to sensitize students to the fact that when they talk of who needs treatment, for what and to what purpose, they are "making (and accepting) judgments about how people should function and what their lives should be like" (Rhodes, 1986, p. 85).

To help students appreciate the power of words to influence our feelings and judgments about clients, students can be asked to describe the same client situation using different language. For example, one student might discuss the client in terms of basic needs while another speaks of the same situation as basic rights. Or a client might be described as dependent on extended family or as someone who has a strong family network as a resource. The class members can then discuss different perceptions of the client generated by these descriptions.

Every case presentation should be evaluated in terms of how the client participates in decision-making and problem determination. Students can be asked to elaborate on what they did to invite the client into the definition of the problem and into defining goals.

They can be asked to consider such questions as: "What happened when the client and the worker disagreed?" "How was it resolved?" and "Who changed?"

A CONGRUENT STANCE:
THE FIT BETWEEN VALUES AND CONSTRUCTIVISM

The constructivist paradigm promotes congruency between clinical practice and values by accommodating social justice concerns and by a collaborative stance supportive of all social work values. Social justice as a guiding value is embraced by most clinical social workers, but we often have difficulty figuring out how to express it in clinical practice. Social work values, as they are currently defined, seem largely grounded in individualism and rationalism and are often treated as universal truths without respect to culture. Values that honor the individual, such as self-determination and dignity of the individual, are, therefore, a central priority in clinical practice. But there is a discrepancy between honoring the individual while neglecting the social contexts which may define the lives, needs, and problems of individuals. The result can be a feeling of incongruency and discomfort for both clients and clinicians.

The constructivist paradigm, with its both/and approach, comfortably embodies self-determination, dignity of the individual, empowerment, and social justice as basic social work values. The sociopolitical aspect of individual and family life is emphasized along with the psychological. Values themselves become part of the conversational domain of therapy. Later discussion will explore specifically how constructivism provides congruence by elevating social justice as a value that actively finds its way into the clinical arena. By so doing, it also bridges the gap between clinical and community-oriented practitioners.

As clinicians move the therapeutic conversation beyond the psychological into the sociopolitical realm of meaning, a working alliance can emerge between clinical and community workers. Would it not be possible, for example, for the clinician to ask for consultation from a community organizer and/or an agency administrator about the impact of a particular community problem, such as unemployment, on an individual client or family? Would it not make sense for the community worker to consult with clinical workers about the experiences and needs of their clients as they plan community responses?

The issue of congruence is critical because some of the ethical/clinical tensions and dilemmas experienced by clinical social workers can be attributed to the lack of fit between the values of the profession and some traditional clinical practices. Many practitioners experience the tension between values and practice dramatically. Hoffman (1988) speaks of it in this way: "Therapy became like a military operation–either a straightforward campaign we had to win, or an underground guerilla war. I don't know which made me feel more uncomfortable" (p. 58). In modernist practice, the client's view of reality and interpretation of her or his world is subjugated to that of the practitioner, who is presumed to know what is good for the client. From this perspective, the social work dictum of "always start where the client is" often unwittingly masks a therapeutic agenda to get the client to end up where the practitioner is.

Another source of tension between values and practice is woven into ideas of objectivity and neutrality. When the clinician operates from the objective, value-free position of the expert, he or she may feel restrained in bringing up the ethical and value dimensions of a client's behavior. Yet, the clinician may indeed experience ethical and moral dilemmas around such things as abusive and illegal activities on the part of the client. The constructivist, collaborative approach invites conversation about meaning so that values, ethics, and context clearly are relevant topics. It is more likely that a client's experience of abuse, injustice, and inequity will be heard. In addition, the egalitarian quality of dialogical therapy opens up space for the clinician to be self-revealing about significant values and ethical concerns.

A major teaching point to emerge from the constructivist paradigm is that there is no choice about bringing values into clinical work. Teachers can influence a student's vision of the ideal practitioner. For some teachers, it will represent a change to teach, as Rhodes (1986) insists, the idea that "the ideal of value-free counseling is impossible and dangerous" (p. 87). Probably one of the best ways to teach this is through case studies in which the focus is on the value assumptions of the student clinician. Questions to be asked are: "What value assumptions am I making?" "What values need to be shared with the client in our dialogue?" "How do we resolve differences and learn from each other?" "What value tensions does my client's behavior generate in me?" "How do values relate to other clinical issues in this case?"

Students can practice including a values focus in work with clients through role play and case example. For example, in my own practice, I have learned to ask clients questions about what values will help them make a certain decision. One client decided, through such a dialogue, how to respond to a legal situation which could cost him thousands of dollars. He felt that the decision could be made on an economic basis, on the basis of his feeling that the situation was unfair to him, or on a value basis rooted in his own standards for honesty. In our discussion, he emotionally identified a deep sense of shame about his family of origin which was linked to his view that "my family had no honor." He perceived his parents as always "lying to protect themselves." In the interest of his own growth and the opportunity to alter a disturbing intergenerational pattern which he felt might affect his own children, he made his decision according to his own ethical standards.

Self-Determination

Self-determination does not fare well in the hierarchical structure of many objectivist-based therapies. Hierarchy is built upon the idea that the therapist possesses superior knowledge about what constitutes problems and desired solutions. Such a stance does not honor the client's agency and experience in determining the problem or the outcomes so vital to her or his life. A client can end up feeling grateful for the expert effort and help but feel disempowered at the same time. The collaborative stance of constructivism is naturally supportive of self-determination because it enhances the voice of the client. It is a stance that feels "right" to many practitioners.

It is very difficult to operate from the normative perspective of most modern therapy without interfering with the self-direction of clients. Collaborative therapy does not erase all differences between client and clinician, but it does invite therapists to abandon diagnoses and interventions. Normative theories, based upon the assumption that Western values apply to all, are usually silent on cultural differences and political issues in the lives of individuals and families. Karl Tomm (1990), in critiquing DSM-III-R, reminds us "that human behaviour, the mind, and its disorders, may be more fundamentally grounded in social phenomena rather than individual phenomena" (p. 6). It is all too easy inadvertently to impose the "normal" view of the dominant society even though the practitioner is well-intentioned.

Perhaps one of the most difficult problems to be faced by educators in clinical social work has to do with the ethical charge to disavow reliance on diagnostic categories such as DSM-III-R. The economic and political climate of clinical practice is not altogether favorable to this point of view. At the very least, however, students can be sensitized to the impact of such labeling not only on their clients but also on their own thinking and their abilities to assist clients. Students can be taught that it is an ethical responsibility to be aware of the sociopolitical and economic contexts of such diagnostic systems and to learn to question why they have preferred status over other ways of knowing. Social work teachers would do well to assign readings such as Tomm's (1990) critique of the DSM-III and Cutler's (1991) deconstruction of the DSM-III.

One does not need to look far to find examples of what has been called "therapeutic imperialism" (Watts-Jones, 1992) and violation of self-determination. In structural family therapy, for example, the normative family is traditionally described as a hierarchical nuclear family, a view not adequately reflective of the extended family and network models upon which many cultures thrive. Also, it is not uncommon in family therapy literature to be instructed to give the male more power. The self-determination of many women does not seem to be a consideration. Presenting the two-parent family as the functional ideal has resulted in many single parents being made to feel that their models of family life are deficit based and dysfunctional. The dilemma between practicing from such a theoretical orientation and honoring self-determination is quite pronounced, especially for female practitioners.

A collaborative partnership between client and clinician may prove comfortable but there is potentially a discomfort to be resolved. The practitioner is asked to give up or at least bracket her or his favorite theories, lenses, or ways of knowing. Cherished theories that clinicians practiced with confidence and even time-honored ideas of developmental stages of individuals and families are being questioned. Lacking an external "truth" in the form of a theory, therapists may feel bewildered about what to do. Goolishian and Anderson (1991) refer to this as the "Cartesian anxiety." They explain, "It seems as if it is either a case of there being meaning and knowledge to which we have the capacity for objective determination, or no meaning or knowledge is possible" (p. 9). Ethical behavior requires each clinician to face this anxiety. In the end, the struggle is between therapy that welcomes self-determination of the client and therapy that too easily becomes a normative form of social control in which the ideas of the therapist are privileged above those of the client. The idea that there are "always dialogic opportunities for change and movement" (Goolishian & Anderson, 1991, p. 9) guides the postmodern clinician and ultimately can resolve anxiety about the "not-knowing" stance.

One of the most serious implications for self-determination to arise from constructivist thinking has to do with the nature of self. Many postmodern thinkers have questioned the traditional view of self as reflecting a Western ethnocentric preference for individualism and rationalism. This thought underscores the growing number of writers who, in recent years, have acknowledged the cultural and gender bias of traditional therapies and have urged the development of ethnic and gender-sensitive approaches. Hermans, Kempem, and van Loon (1992) argue that, from a constructionist perspective, "the self can be conceived of as basically dialogical, and in this respect can transcend the cultural limits of individualism and rationalism" (p. 23). For them, the self is a multiplicity of dialogically interacting selves. Gergen (1991) speaks of laying to rest the self as a serious reality and thinking of self as constructed and reconstructed in multiple contexts. He conceives of the relational self in which "individual autonomy gives way to a reality of immersed interdependence, in which it is relationship that constructs the self" (p. 147). From his postmodern perspective, moral decisions are made through active dialogue. Individuals act as "local representatives of the larger relationships in which they are enmeshed" (p. 169). As I will maintain, shortly, this view is much more in tune with ideas of self that exist in cultures not dominated by Western white, middle-class meaning systems. It is also consistent with writers such as Gilligan (1982) and Surrey (1985) who find interdependence and connectedness as values which are central to women's development.

If the self is socially constructed, then what does this mean for our ideas of self-determination? If the Western emphasis on the individual self is recognized as an ethnocentric view, then we cannot comfortably assume that clients from diverse cultural backgrounds value autonomy and self-determination as white middle-class therapists may. Charles Waldegrave (1990), a New Zealand family therapist, writes that people from communal and extended family cultures are confused and alienated by questions relating directly to self-assertion and self-exposure. For such groups, identity is expressed in extended family rather than in individual terms. Questions and practices that are essentially focused on issues of individual self-worth and self-determination rupture "the co-operative sensitivity among people in such cultures, sensitivity which provides the framework of essential meaning required for solution of their problems" (p. 16). To be responsive, the therapist must be interested in learning how self-determination is perceived and how it is played out as a family matter.

With a new understanding of self, clinicians will accept the ethical responsibility to extend their curiosity to the web of connectedness manifested in how clients perceive themselves, their lives, their problems, and their possibilities. As our value base is broadened to include connectedness and relatedness, practitioners will become sensitive to the multiple voices that influence the decisions of their clients and those voices will be attended to in the total therapeutic process. Respect for the individual will be taken to include respect for family, community, and culture.

Probably one of the best ways to help students examine their notions about the meaning of self and self-determination is to study their own families of origin. One assignment I often use is that of having students interview someone from a different culture, comparing the meanings and beliefs of that person with their own family belief system. They explore attitudes about helping and asking for help. They ask questions about who relies upon whom, what it means to be dependent, who is included within the family boundaries, and how outsiders are treated. This kind of exercise surfaces some deeply held beliefs about what families ought to be like and about the place of the individual in relation to the family. I am reminded of one student from a small African country who simply could not conceive of living safely in a nuclear or even an extended family as described by most of the other students. For him, family is an entire interdependent community with individual well-being intertwined with the well-being of the group.

Respect for the Individual

One value dilemma clinicians often experience around respect has to do with the modern-based idea that therapists must take the neutral position of the objective observer. The "neutral" therapist, however, can also be seen as non-involved, lacking in strong values and reinforcing the status quo, particularly with reference to power inequities. In postmodern dialogical therapies, a kind of respectful curiosity replaces neutrality.

Cecchin (1987) describes neutrality as "the creation of a state of curiosity in the mind of the therapist" (p. 406). This is not a curiosity concerned with locating the cause of a problem. It is derived from an aesthetic base (Keeney, 1983) in which the focus is on "the multiplicity of possible patterns" (Cecchin, 1987, p. 407). From this frame, the clinician is enthusiastically interested in bringing forth multiple descriptions of a problem rather than in finding the best or most logical description. We are curious about how different descriptions fit with each other, why they are different, how they may have changed over time, and how they may fit with our descriptions.

Curiosity generates respect and respect generates curiosity. It is the responsibility of therapists to stay curious and to generate curiosity within the client system. Otherwise, the dialogue will cease. When we already "know" what is happening, we lose curiosity and respect suffers. This kind of curiosity depends upon a collaborative approach and at the same time invites collaboration. Family therapists have developed tools which support the ethical mandates for collaboration, conversation, and respectful curiosity. It is not within the scope of this paper to detail these techniques but all are designed to stir alternative ways of thinking about problems and to co-create pathways to change. Circular questioning (Penn, 1982) is a way of encouraging a participatory conversation that helps maintain dialogue. The reflecting team approach developed by Tom Andersen (1987) and his colleagues in Norway is an innovative example of how to "shed power" and establish a collaborative context. An intriguing spin-off of the reflecting team technique is Stephen Madigan's (1991) "listening therapist" approach which lays out the thoughts and often the values of the therapist for the clients to consider. All of these techniques convey respect while promoting collaboration and dialogue.

The reflecting team and the listening therapist techniques provide exciting tools for teaching the values and ethics dimensions of clinical practice. Students can be encouraged to present their work for consultation from other class members. Small groups can form reflecting teams or there may be role plays utilizing the listening therapist approach. In both instances, the classroom consultation can be focused on bringing forth ethical dilemmas the student clinician may be facing and values which may be influencing the student's relationship to clients. Students can practice how and when to share these thoughts with clients.

SOCIAL JUSTICE AND A "JUST" THERAPY

There is controversy about whether clinical social work seriously addresses issues of social justice or tends to reinforce the status quo. O'Connor (1990), for example, speaks to schisms that have developed between clinical and community-oriented social work practice as a result of the dispute over values. He calls for social work to adopt a justice framework based upon the assumption of satisfying human needs rather than wants. Otherwise, he believes that social work is in danger of supporting a status quo in which many are disadvantaged.

Critics who espouse social justice and the need for social change fault clinical workers for their seeming preference for pathological explanations. Such explanations ignore the powerful influence of external conditions such as unemployment and lack of opportunity and resources and can feel blaming to clients. Too often a focus on psychological symptomatology can result in "unwittingly adjusting people to poverty and other forms of injustice" (Waldegrave, 1990, p. 6).

Constructivist therapy and the collaborative stance bring values and the social context of problems into the conversational domain of therapy. A group of postmodern family therapists from New Zealand has been particularly zealous in articulating a "just" therapy (Waldegrave, 1990). They believe that "therapy can be the vehicle for addressing some of the injustices that occur in society" (p. 5). A "just" therapy is one that takes into account the gender, cultural, social, and economic contexts of any person or family seeking help. Central to this approach, as with all constructivist therapy, is an understanding of the manner in which people give meaning to their experience. Crucial to such therapy is the elevation of social factors to a position that is as important as psychological factors.

From the point of view of a just therapy, therapeutic ethics and values require that political work be conducted in association with the psychological. Postmodern therapy brings social, gender, cultural, and political data squarely into the therapeutic conversation. A father's violent abuse can be looked at from the perspective of the harmful impact of patriarchy. A woman's depression may be treated as a disorder of power rather than as a biological or psychological matter. As Waldegrave (1990) states, "Clinical work that addresses suicidal feelings, periods of depression, or unhappy sexual experience, but does not address the underlying political agendas, will merely be incorporated into the old meaning filter" (p. 11). A therapy that potentiates social and political explanations for problems may bring about social change through a change in personal meanings and values.

Therapy that deals directly with social justice issues is ultimately supportive of the social work value of empowerment. As it opens a dialogue about values and meanings and links these to the problems experienced by clients, there is a new possibility for clients to examine their values in the light of choice. Which do they cherish and which do they choose to change and with what consequences? Such therapy does not need to stop at the talk level. It is quite feasible, under these circumstances, for values associated with problems such as gender inequities and racial intolerance to become an appropriate goal for change. For example, as Rhodes (1986) suggests, racism is severely harmful to individuals and to society. There is no reason, other than a political one, to exclude it from therapy.

Perhaps the most difficult context and yet one greatly in need of a "just" approach is the situation where the practitioner is invested with a social control role. Cecchin (1987) notes that when practitioners accept the role of social controller they are guided by a sense of moral linearity rather than the respectful curiosity of postmodern therapy. Even though clinicians are often required to act legally, for example in cases of abuse, it is still possible to focus on meaning, values, and justice. Postmodern therapist Alan Jenkins (1990) is a case in point as he works with men who are violent and abusive. His is an empowering approach, fully sensitive to the sociocultural context, in which he invites men to take responsibility for and to alter the meaning and value systems which contribute to their abusive styles.

A just therapy is not an either/or approach in which psychological and internal family system dynamics are lost. It is a both/and approach in which all factors are considered relevant. Ritterman (1985) speaks of a therapy in which the dignity of the individual is elevated "above the context which has transgressed his [sic] humanity" (p. 54). The constructivist paradigm with its emphasis upon social context moves beyond pathology and blaming. Clients are much better able to marshal their internal resources when relieved of the idea that problems are entirely the result of their own deficiencies. With the focus on both the inner and the outer worlds, wrongful environments can be changed along with internal difficulties. In Ritterman's (1985) words, "In this way, further encroachment into the person's private reality is prevented by a new social process, a therapy for restoring human dignity . . ." (p. 54).

In the classroom, through the use of case studies and role plays, students can be encouraged to conceptualize private troubles in terms of public issues, and to consider how such a conceptualization might cause them to think and behave differently with clients and others involved with their clients. For example, in a marital or family problem they may consider power inequities rooted in patriarchal notions of gender, or the despair and frustration generated when an unemployed father cannot adequately fulfill his socially prescribed male tasks. In another situation, the rage and helplessness stimulated by racism may be enacted in an adult partnership. Role plays can be used to help the student clinician practice collaborative, change-oriented, "just" conversations with clients around these issues.

CONCLUSIONS

A constructivist stance has profound implications for revisioning social work values and ethics in clinical social work and represents changes from a practice based on the modern, scientific paradigm. Its basic call is for an ethic grounded in what Rhodes (1986) describes as "informed relativism" or understanding that objectivity involves a particular point of view and is always partial. Theories and hypotheses are to be valued for their utility rather than reified as truth. Constructivist assumptions lead to an ethic of responsibility in which the clinician and the client are equal participants in creating a context in which both may change. This collaborative therapy takes full account of the power of language, position, and social context to shape problems and lives. As a result, constructivists highlight social justice as a value to guide clinical practice.

Postmodern teaching parallels practice and is characterized by collaboration, dialogue, and respectful curiosity. Students are invited, in various ways, to take responsibility for creating new stories about and pathways to their own learning. As Anderson and Goolishian (1990) envision in their discussion about supervision, the teacher becomes "more of a mentor than an expert" and "acts as a resource person or a catalyst for learning" (p. 3).

From a postmodern perspective, teaching can be thought of as an unfolding conversation in which the participants co-create a learning system. As part of the dialogue, students are provided the space to identify their own learning needs and styles, their goals, and what they bring into the classroom experience. They can be asked such questions as: "How do you want to be different at the end of this course?" "How do you want to be the same?" Together, teacher and students can construct a context in which roles may be differentiated but in which respect for different voices is clear.

One challenge for the postmodern teacher is to "shed" the power of the teaching role and be willing to be a learner as well. To do so, however, is an effective way to underscore the value and ethical stance of the constructivist-based social work practitioner. Such a collaborative stance no more precludes a strong and active role for the teacher than it does for the clinician. A dialogue contains ample room for the voices of all participants; the postmodern teacher finds a space for his or her voice without restraining the voices of the students. Teaching based upon postmodern ideas instills the values and ethics of the constructivist paradigm through "lived experience" (White & Epston, 1990). The vital significance of values and ethics in practice becomes difficult for students to ignore after such an experience.

REFERENCES

Andersen, T. (1987). The reflecting team: Dialogue and meta-dialogue in clinical work. *Family Process, 26,* 415-428.

Anderson, H., & Goolishian, H. (1988). Human systems as linguistic systems. *Family Process, 27,* 371-395.

Anderson, H., & Goolishian, H. (1990). Supervision as collaborative conversation: questions and reflections. In H. Brandau (Ed.), *Von der supervision zur systemischen vision.* Salzburg: Otto Muller Verlag.

Bohm, D. (1990). *On dialogue.* Ojai, CA.: David Bohm Seminars.

Cecchin, G. (1987). Hypothesizing, circularity, and neutrality revisited: An invitation to curiosity. *Family Process, 26,* 405-413.

Cutler, C. (1991). Deconstructing the DSM-III. *Social Work, 36,* 154-158.

Efran, J., Lukens, R., & Lukens, M. (1988). Constructivism: What's in it for you? *The Family Therapy Networker,* Sept./Oct., 27-35.

Epstein, E., & Loos, V. (1987). Some irreverant thoughts on the limits of family therapy. Paper presented at the 45th annual conference of the American Association for Marital and Family Therapy. Chicago, IL.

Foucault, M. (1980). *Power/knowledge: Selected Interviews and other writings.* New York: Pantheon Press.

Gergen, K. (1991). *The saturated self.* New York: Basic Books.

Gilligan, C. (1982). *In a different voice: Psychological theory and women's development.* Cambridge, MA: Harvard University Press.

Goldstein, H. (1986). Toward the integration of theory and practice: A humanistic approach. *Social Work, 31,* 352-357.

Goolishian, H., & Anderson, H. (1991). An essay on changing theory and changing ethics: Some historical and poststructural views. *American Family Therapy Association Newsletter,* No. 46, 6-10.

Hare-Mustin, R., & Marecek, J. (1988). The meaning of difference: Gender theory, postmodernism, and psychology. *American Psychologist, 43*, 2-41.

Hermans, H., Kempen, H., & van Loon, R. (1992). The dialogical self: Beyond individualism and rationalism. *American Psychologist, 47*, 23-33.

Hoffman, L. (1985). Beyond power and control: Toward a "second order" family systems therapy. *Family Systems Medicine, 3*, 381-395.

Hoffman, L. (1988). Like a friendly editor: An interview with Lynn Hoffman. *The Family Therapy Networker, 12*(12), 55-58 and 74-75.

Keeney, B. (1985). *Aesthetics of change.* New York: Guilford Press.

Jenkins, A. (1990). *Invitations to responsibility.* Adelaide, So. Australia: Dulwich Centre Publications.

Madigan, S. (1991). Discursive restraints in therapist practice: Situating therapist questions in the presence of the family. *Dulwich Centre Newsletter: Postmodernism, deconstruction, and therapy.* No. 3, 13-40.

Maturana, H., & Varela, F. (1987). *The tree of knowledge: The biological roots of understanding.* Boston: New Science Library.

O'Connor, G. (1990). Assessing social work values. *Philosophical Issues in Social Work, 1*(3), 4-5.

Penn, P. (1982). Circular questioning. *Family Process, 21*, 267-280.

Rhodes, M. (1986). *Ethical dilemmas in social work practice.* Boston: Routledge and Kegan Paul.

Ritterman, M. (1985). Symptoms, social justice and personal freedom. *Journal of Strategic and Systemic Therapies, 4*(2), 48-63.

Simon, R. (1985). An interview with Humberto Maturana. *Family Therapy Networker, 9*(3), 36-43.

Surrey, J.L. (1985). Self-in-relation: A theory of womens' development. Stone Center for Developmental Services and Studies at Wellesley College. Working paper.

Tice, K. (1990). Gender and social work education: Direction for the 1990s. *Journal of Social Work Education, 26*, 134-144.

Tomm, K. (1990). A critique of the DSM. *Dulwich Centre Newsletter, Reflections on our practices. Part one,* No. 3, 5-8.

Waldegrave, C. (1990). Just therapy. *Dulwich Centre Newsletter, Justice/therapy,* No. 1, 5-47.

Watts-Jones, D. (1992). Cultural and integrative therapy issues in the treatment of a Jamaican woman with panic disorder. *Family Process, 31*, 105-118.

Webster's encyclopedic unabridged dictionary of the English Language. (1989). New York: Portland House.

Weingarten, K. (1991). The discourses of intimacy: Adding a social constructionist and feminist view. *Family Process, 30*, 285-306.

White, M., & Epston, D. (1990). *Narrative means to therapeutic ends.* New York: Norton.

Teaching a Constructivist Approach to Clinical Practice

Ruth Grossman Dean

SUMMARY. Constructivism and social constructionism provide the philosophical underpinnings of an approach to practice teaching that emphasizes the ways knowledge derives from individually and socially constructed experience. Constructivist practices such as generating multiple ideas through questioning or collaborating with clients in the co-construction of meaning and the creation of alternative narratives are taught through an experiential format. The exercises presented provide students with firsthand experiences of seeing how they shape their own learning. While the conceptual challenges inherent in teaching from this position are many, a constructivist approach is ideally suited to practice in a multicultural society.

INTRODUCTION

Constructivism and social constructionism have become the basis of a reconceptualization of practice, creating an atmosphere of

Ruth Grossman Dean, DSW, is Associate Professor, Simmons College School of Social Work, 51 Commonwealth Avenue, Boston, MA 02116. The author wishes to acknowledge the contributions to the evolution of these ideas of colleagues Sallyann Roth, Kathy Weingarten, and Corky Becker through their teaching in The Program in Systemic Therapies at The Family Institute of Cambridge 1989-1990. She is also most appreciative of the generous editorial advice of friend and colleague Margaret Rhodes.

[Haworth co-indexing entry note]: "Teaching a Constructivist Approach to Clinical Practice," Dean, Ruth Grossman. Co-published simultaneously in *Journal of Teaching in Social Work* (The Haworth Press, Inc.) Vol. 8, No. 1/2, 1993, pp. 55-75; and: *Revisioning Social Work Education: A Social Constructionist Approach* (ed: Joan Laird) The Haworth Press, Inc., 1993, pp. 55-75. Multiple copies of this article/chapter may be purchased from The Haworth Document Delivery Center [1-800-3-HAWORTH; 9:00 a.m. - 5:00 p.m. (EST)].

55

excitement in the classroom as new approaches are introduced and former ways of thinking about practice are challenged. In a constructivist approach, experience is at the center of learning and this belief permeates the classroom. The Kantian tradition, on which constructivism is based, posits that learning occurs through sensory experiences and interaction with the environment. Thus, the experiential emphasis in teaching constructivism reinforces the philosophical position being taught. The teacher creates a process and environment in which students have a firsthand experience of seeing how they shape their own learning experiences and, then, how these experiences shape what they know. The following example may help to clarify this relationship.

In the classroom, a student interviews two classmates role playing a couple who complain that intense fighting over disciplining their children is destroying their relationship. The interviewer carefully elicits each person's story of the fighting. They examine the differences in the stories each tells and the implications these differences have for their relationship. Then, the interviewer asks–"Has there ever been a time when you didn't fight about disciplining your children?" As the couple recall an exception to their usual behavior they are asked for the details of this experience. The "worker," by asking questions, encourages the "clients" to become curious about understanding this exception. Gradually an alternative narrative emerges that highlights more cooperative behavior. Then the teacher stops the action and invites each member of the class to say an idea they have in response to the interview. Next, the student who has conducted the interview expresses her ideas about the situation. This might be followed by asking the "clients" for their thoughts now that they have heard the reflections. In a second go round, each member of the class is asked to state another idea about the interview and to notice how his or her thinking has changed.[1] Finally, all participants may be encouraged to ask about the interviewer's way of conducting the interview. In both the interview and the classroom discussion there is an emphasis on generating multiple ideas, comparing and contrasting these, and seeing which are more useful. No attempt is made to reach consensus or develop the "right" hypothesis about the material. Students discover how meaning is co-constructed as they integrate ideas expressed by others into their own explanations and questions. They are learning the practices of questioning, generating multiple ideas, and making the context for the interviewer's ideas more transparent (Epston & White, 1992.) They are *experiencing* an idea associated with constructivist practice–that change occurs through the discovery of new meaning and new ideas in dialogue and conversation (Anderson & Goolishian, 1988, p. 382).

The values in this approach to practice and teaching will become apparent as this discussion continues. Perhaps most important is the inherent respect for diversity contained in the constructivist model, as students see that many approaches are valid and expertise is not the exclusive property of the teacher or the clinician. Therapy and learning are revealed as collaborative processes.

The paper begins with definitions of constructivism and social constructionism. Then the meaning of grounding practice teaching in underlying philosophical assumptions is discussed. The next sections combine an explication of constructivist ideas for practice with a discussion of constructivist teaching methods. Many examples of teaching exercises are offered.[2] Since it is not possible to cover all aspects of practice within the confines of this paper, the focus is on the treatment process, with a limited discussion of assessment. The paper concludes with an examination of the challenges of teaching a constructivist approach.

It is important to note that incorporating new ideas and approaches into the teaching of practice does not mean throwing out all other theories and practices. Instead, teachers and students must evaluate which concepts from other paradigms are useful and important to retain, as they explore the new framework. The material that follows shows constructivist views being taught along with other models. This is particularly important when students' field (and later work) experiences occur in practice contexts where psychodynamic and systemic models prevail, and constructivism is barely understood or even rejected. (The problem of dissonance between field and class will be discussed more fully in the section entitled "Challenges.")

DEFINITIONS

Two intellectual discourses form the basis of the new paradigm (Hoffman, 1990). *Constructivism* is the belief that we cannot know an objective reality apart from our views of it. This philosophical position is derived from a tradition that includes Wittgenstein and Piaget, in which knowledge is seen as resulting from interactions with the environment. The values and interests of the observer are always operative. Knowledge is not so much discovered as created. This Kantian notion is in opposition to the Lockean belief that objective observations about the world can be made from a neutral position. Constructivists point to neurological and biological writings and experiments to support the idea that we cannot get "outside" our own observing systems (Maturana & Varela, 1987). The emphasis is on the individual structural determinants of knowledge.

Social constructionism, in contrast, stresses the social aspects of knowing and the influence of cultural, historical, political, and economic conditions. While agreeing with constructivists that we cannot know an objective reality, social constructionists stress the interpersonal rather than the neurological imprints on our ways of knowing the world. According to social constructionists, our categories and assumptions are fluid, continually influenced by the communities to which we belong. As Kenneth Gergen (1985) states: "The terms in which the world is understood are social artifacts, products of historically situated interchanges among people" (p. 266). Those in power are able to determine the definitions and categories that are used.

Social constructionism offers an extremely relevant focus for clinicians working in a pluralistic, multicultural society with clients who suffer from social and economic inequities, because it highlights the extent to which beliefs and ideas are determined by one's position in the world. Constructivism also carries important messages with its emphasis on the limits on our abilities to know another and the need to construct meaning together. Although the differences between the discourses of constructivism and social constructionism are important, for purposes of simplification the term constructivism will be used in this paper to represent both constructivism and social constructionism.

THE ROLE OF UNDERLYING ASSUMPTIONS

Social workers need to be aware of the philosophical assumptions that underlie their clinical theories and practices (Dean & Fenby,

1989). This learning can quite naturally become a part of clinical courses and forms an important introduction to the profession. In a constructivist approach, the teacher can help students become more aware of the many influences on their ways of knowing and the tacit assumptions that guide their thinking (Dean, 1989).

Students can be encouraged to think as social constructionists beginning with the first practice class. When they introduce themselves to one another, they are asked to mention the communities of which they are members that they think will be most influential in shaping their clinical work. This immediately leads to an awareness that it is easier to talk to classmates about some memberships than others–a situation parallel to the one that clients are in at the beginning of a clinical encounter. So, some aspects of identity are shared and some remain private from classmates, but self-awareness and identification with clients is heightened as students begin to consider personal influences on their ways of knowing and being in the world.

Constructivism fosters a questioning of theoretical and personal assumptions about the world in which we live and our ability to know it. In a constructivist approach students are taught to consider theories as metaphors, with different theories providing more or less helpful ways of conceptualizing practice. Several theoretical perspectives (such as ego psychology, object relations and family systems theory), introduced in human behavior courses are reviewed and utilized in the practice course as ways of conceptualizing assessment and treatment. There is an emphasis on preserving those aspects of theories that are useful as well as a focus on the viability of multiple perspectives.

Once distanced from a tendency to cling to a single theory, as if it could provide all the answers, students are helped to consider their own assumptions about the world and human nature, how people come to grief and how they change. In an exercise that aids this process, students are asked to write down one of their assumptions about change. Some questions that might stimulate awareness include: How long does change take? How much do people change in treatment? Can old people change? Are patterns formed in childhood with adult influences having little impact or does growth and development occur throughout the life span? Is it more important to change ideas or feelings? Having identified at least one basic assumption, students are asked to list the sources of this belief. Then, they list the ways the assumption might affect their work. The process of making tacit beliefs explicit and questioning them is further enhanced when students read their lists aloud in class and discuss each others assumptions. This exercise can be extended by asking students to compare their assumptions (on subjects such as child rearing) to those held by clients and to think about the origins of their own and their clients' assumptions.

Differences in assumptive frameworks observed in the classroom are echoed across the curriculum. A healthy tension can be fostered in social work schools when some courses are taught from objectivist and others from constructivist perspectives, if faculty are accepting of these differences. Until recently, little attention has been given to the philosophical underpinnings of courses and teaching strategies (Berman-Rossi, 1988; Dean & Fenby, 1989). Students whose teachers hold different stances have the opportunity to compare epistemologies, an experience conducive to an appreciation of the viability of multiple views.

ABOUT WORDS

Since constructivists believe that words shape our views of the world,[3] it is impossible to proceed with a discussion of practice without considering some of the words used to describe this process. The expressions "diagnosis," "assessment," "therapy," and "treatment" derive from medical and research models and suggest that the client is sick and needs to recover. In addition, these terms turn the client or problem into a finite entity to be studied and diagnosed. Similarly problematic, the term "intervention" defines a process in which the clinician does something to the client (or situation).

Recently Scott (1989) has recommended the term "inquiry" to describe the assessment process. She draws attention to the work of Rodwell (1987) with "naturalistic inquiry as an alternative model of social work assessment to that derived from linear positivist assumptions" (Scott, p. 40). While hardly ideal, and reminiscent of a legal investigation, "inquiry" is intended to suggest a mutual, circular interaction in which both client and therapist expand their awareness and self-knowledge. According to Scott, social workers have always practiced naturalistic forms of inquiry but have turned these into linear forms in writing assessments. Anderson and Goolishian (1988) use the term "therapeutic conversation" to describe the "linguistic activity" through which "fixed meanings and behaviors (the sense people make of things and their actions) are given room, broadened, shifted and changed" (p. 381). While all of these expressions can be used in the classroom, students need to be alerted to implicit meanings carried by particular expressions.

TEACHING ASSESSMENT AND INQUIRY

Social work is taught in the context of a practice community where students are often expected to evaluate clients, write diagnoses and diagnostic formulations, and use these to guide decisions about treatment. While diagnostic categories are usually taught in psychopathology courses, the practice teacher is called upon to help students make sense of these designations and consider how to use them. Thus, the practice teacher attempting to teach from a constructivist position has the challenge of teaching students to use diagnoses derived from more objectivist ways of thinking while proposing an approach that privileges clients' understanding and meaning.

While being reminded of the arbitrariness of categories, students can be taught, nonetheless, to see a diagnostic classification system, such as DSM-III R, as a set of ideas about mental conditions that may be useful in communicating with colleagues and in making some gross generalizations. They also learn that these arbitrary and culturally determined descriptions are developed by those in power and have powerful effects on clients' lives. Feminist critiques of conventional diagnostic categories are discussed (Kaplan, 1983) along with the political and oppressive aspects of diagnosis. Students are taught to look at the influence of more immediate contexts, such as agency policies and procedures and insurance reimbursement requirements on the use of diagnoses. They are reminded that their assessments of clients will be influenced by all of these contexts. In other words, constructivism informs the teaching of diagnostic categories by revealing the social and political contexts in which diagnostic ideas have developed and by encouraging students to understand the limitations as well as the usefulness of any system of categorization. What is different in the constructivist approach is that students are continually reminded of the philosophical assumptions that underlie their ways of understanding and working with clients.

Beginning in an inductive manner, students might be asked what they think they need to know about clients from the outset. At the same time that constructivist approaches guide them toward a concern with the *client's* definition of the problem, they will also want to be able to identify and evaluate the impact of the emotional, physiological, and social conditions (as they are currently defined) of psychosis, suicidality, depression, substance abuse, serious acute or chronic physical illness, physical disadvantages, and trauma history as well as the influences of poverty, unemployment, or immigrant status (to name just a few). Students learn to move back and forth from an awareness of signs and symptoms of more objectively defined conditions to concern with the ways these conditions are individually experienced. They learn to write diagnostic formulations using those theoretical perspectives that seem relevant and to avoid becoming overinvolved with diagnostic language and losing sight of the human aspects of clients' dilemmas.

In a role play used to demonstrate the validity of multiple perspectives and the co-construction of meaning, students are divided into teams; a student from each team interviews the same "client" in sequence (without having witnessed each others' interviews) while the class observes. At the conclusion of each brief interview the team and interviewer develop a diagnosis and formulation of the client's difficulties. When three or four interviews have been completed and formulations presented, the class compares the differences in the directions interviews took, in the interactions between "client" and "worker," and in the impact of these factors on diagnostic formulations. Recording these interviews on video or audiotape renders them available to the interviewers and provides opportunities for more detailed observation. In this exercise students are encouraged to use different theoretical perspectives and see how they influence the conduct of the interview, the view of the client, and the treatment.

Along with the diagnostic approaches to assessment, students are taught ways of interviewing that lead to more collaborative and evolving problem definitions. An effort is made to move beyond the therapist's theoretical perspectives to the unique details and meanings that each client expresses (Anderson & Goolishian, 1992). In this approach, "the meanings of words, gestures, or actions are realized within the unfolding patterns of relationship" (Gergen, 1988, p. 46). Students learn to track clients' descriptions and, through questioning, to clarify understanding and reveal deeper meanings.

I have been describing a method of teaching assessment that integrates diagnostic and constructivist approaches within a constructivist model. What is central to constructivism in the teaching of assessment is the emphasis on multiple perspectives, the recognition of the ways that therapists' theories shape and create the data, and the effort to stay as close as possible to the unique meanings that experiences have for clients. Having learned both approaches and achieved some comfort in the use of diagnostic terminology, students are helped to develop criteria for deciding on the ways they will approach assessment, such as: (1) Which theoretical concepts increase understanding of the client? (2) Which theories are useful in talking with clients and which only work when talking with colleagues? (3) Is the theory relevant given the client's cultural background and economic status? (4) Has the assessment process preserved the unique aspects of clients' experiences? Students begin to recognize that some theoretical constructs can enhance understanding while others are client blaming or devaluing. Armed with both a respect for theory and a healthy ability to question it, students are ready to learn about the treatment process.

TREATMENT

What are some of the constructivist ideas that influence ways of thinking about treatment? First, if we believe that it is not possible to know an objective reality but only our constructions of it, then it is no longer possible to define treatment as a setting in which the therapist is an expert with an objective view of the client and the situation. If knowledge is the result of interaction and not so much discovered but created, then neither the therapist nor the client holds the key to understanding. Second, the goal of a constructivist therapeutic process is for clients to become open to new ideas, new meanings, and new ways of understanding their dilemmas. Third, if assumptive frameworks are historically, socially, and culturally situated, then some clients are less free than others to change their beliefs due to the oppressive influences of political ideology and social conditions such as poverty, unemployment, racism, sexism, and abuse (MacKinnon & Miller, 1987). Students need to become attuned to the contexts in which clients' narratives are embedded and to think in terms of social and institutional as well as individual change.

These and other constructivist ideas are incorporated into teaching through a series of processes in the classroom that are themselves constructivist in nature. The teacher's art is expressed through an ability to encourage a discussion in which many different ideas are entertained, new insights occur, and there is an expansion of knowledge and understanding. This is parallel to Anderson and Goolishian's (1988) view of the therapist as a "participant manager" who "is always looking for intended meaning and creatively synthesizing information, understanding, and meaning. In doing this, the therapist takes cues and uses clues from the clients" (p. 382). Similarly, teachers, while contributing their own ideas, also draw out students' ideas, clarifying, synthesizing, and exploring these. While the teacher's expertise is available to the class, students are helped to recognize their own hunches, try out their own ideas, and find ways of evaluating their efforts. In this parallel process, the teacher models a stance that students may take with clients.

In the vignettes that follow, a series of classroom activities and exercises shows how constructivist approaches to treatment are taught in a manner consistent with constructivism. They by no means represent all that is taught but instead are intended to convey an impression of this approach.

Students learn the art of interviewing through questioning. Therapeutic action often begins with questioning. Students are introduced to different types of questions such as lineal, circular, strategic, reflexive, and others (Cecchin, 1987; Penn, 1985; Tomm, 1988). The use of questions is practiced in role plays drawn from student cases or material prepared by the teacher. Several students taking the roles of family members are interviewed by another student taking the role of the therapist. The student therapist tries to use some of the new forms of questions just learned. For example, a student asks the abusive husband in a simulated couple session if his wife would say she is afraid of him and, having obtained an affirmative answer, how her saying this would make him feel? The wife is then asked about her fear and how she thinks her husband reacts to it. (These questions can be defined as circular because they draw attention to connections and interactive effects.)

After the simulated interview has continued for a time (or when it bogs down) students in the client roles are invited to reflect on their experience and reactions to the different questions. There is a focus on whether the questions opened the conversation to new meaning or caused constriction (Anderson & Goolishian, 1988). The class members also discuss their reactions as observers. Then the "interview" is resumed, with another student serving as therapist and another series of questions initiated.

This exercise alerts students to the possible uses of different questions and encourages them to expand their own repertoires. As Anderson and Goolishian (1988) explain,

> . . . the therapist develops the art of asking questions that are not focused on discovering information and collecting data. Questions are not considered interventions, searches for preselected answers or checking out hypotheses. Questions are the tools of the therapist in a therapeutic conversation, and they are to be guided and informed by the views of the clients so that the conversation is geared toward the maximum production of new information, understanding, meaning, and interpretation. (1988, p. 383)

Students experiment with the co-creation of meaning. Divided into pairs, one student begins by explaining a concern (one that is not so personal or private that it can't be discussed in class). The other student (the interviewer) tries to ascertain the meaning of her or her partner's statement (Roth & Weingarten, 1989). When understanding is reached, they provide each other with feedback about the interview, reverse roles, and repeat the exercise. The focus is on drawing out the other person's meaning–not imposing it from outside and on avoiding "premature understanding" (Weingarten, 1992, p. 51).[4]

In this exercise students see understanding and meaning evolve through conversation. Interviewees typically discover new meanings in their concerns through the process of being interviewed. Students compare the experience of developing meaning through interaction in the interview to times when understanding is imposed from the "outside" through the application of theoretical perspectives. Both ways of achieving understanding are valued as their differences are explored.

Students learn a collaborative approach with clients. All therapists are concerned with making choices in interviews, recognizing that by picking up on some leads and ignoring others we inevitably shape the interview and the course of the treatment. This problem is especially acute for the student therapist. In a constructivist approach in which the therapist doesn't have to be the expert, it is possible to enlist clients in the process of making choices.

While reading process recording together or observing role played interviews, students are taught to recognize choice points and to say something like the following to a client: "You have brought up two important issues and I'm not sure which to pursue. What do you think?" or "You seem to have changed the subject just now; I'm not sure if we should continue in this new direction or if it would be more fruitful to return to the topic you were exploring." Or, in an example given by Irwin Hoffman (1992):

> You know when you ask for reassurance or guidance, I'm sometimes inclined to give it to you because we've developed this idea that it's something you've never had and that you really need from me. But sometimes I worry that this premise is wrong and that I'm participating with you in a way that perpetuates a kind of unnecessary dependency. (p. 300)

This is a more natural, spontaneous way of being with clients. As Hoffman (1992) points out, "Discussing such dilemmas and conflicts with patients often helps to engage them in a collaborative exploration of the various patterns of relating (rooted in various kinds of internal object relations) that are either being enacted or that are potential at any given time" (1992, p. 300). Not all clients and therapists are comfortable with more open ways of relating to one another with the accompanying feelings of exposure and vulnerability. Students are encouraged to notice the ways that clients both want to know them better and want them to remain idealized and unknown. They will also notice similar tensions in themselves between their own wishes to be known and not known. As Hoffman (1991) indicates, "The challenge is to recognize fully the complexities and problems of this approach and yet not shrink back into positions in which our own subjectivity is denied and in which any kind of spontaneous, personal participation is prohibited" (pp. 90-91).

Students learn to tolerate "not understanding." Students are introduced to constructivist writings concerning the limits of our capacities for understanding and the need to develop a tolerance for "not understanding" (Gurevitch, 1989, p. 161; Roth, 1992). They consider how efforts at understanding often cause us to emphasize things held in common, projecting from our own experiences while "not understanding" allows members of the conversation to be separate. Dialogue requires separateness; it occurs through taking the other's position and "seeing oneself through the eyes of the other" (Gurevitch, 1989, p. 163). Through an awareness of difference, it may be possible to understand. And if understanding is not possible, then at least there can be a dialogue about not understanding.

Students may need help in developing the "ability to not understand" and in recognizing an "inability to not understand" (Gurevitch, 1989, p. 164). The following exercise is used. Divided into pairs, one student role plays a client while the other student role playing the therapist tries out as many of the following positions as seem possible: (1) "I know what you mean; I can understand it based on my own understanding or experience," (2) "I don't understand your experience; what can you tell me that will help me approach it and put myself in your shoes?" and (3) "How do you (client) experience the differences between us and my inability to imagine your position?" After a short amount of time they stop the interview, give feedback, and change places.

Students learn to listen to narratives. A class watches a video-taped interview. Then they are asked to write down their idea of the client's narrative.[5] When finished, they take turns reading aloud their narratives and discovering the different ways that they experienced the client and differences in the ways they organized their presentations of the material. Then, they are sent home with a written transcript of the interview and asked to analyze the narrative they created. In a brief assignment, they examine the differences between their own version, the transcript, and the narratives their classmates generated. The teacher often needs to emphasize that there is no "correct" narrative—only different versions. Students learn that any account of a client that they develop has something of them in it and begin to see some of the ways that they shape the material. They consider how much these differences would be amplified if they were actually interacting with the client.

Students learn more about narratives by reading some of the literature on this subject.[6] They become aware of different strategies of presentation (Riessman, 1990). They listen for the plot and the underlying themes (J. Bruner, 1986). They notice the roles clients assign to themselves and others in their narratives. They consider the aspects of clients' lives that are not storied and the narratives that clients are reluctant to share (Belenky, Clinchy, Goldberger & Tarule, 1986; Laird, 1988). They learn to help clients look for exceptions to their usual stories that, according to White and Epston (1990), provide "rich and fertile source for the generation, or re-generation of alternative stories" (p. 15).

Students are invited to think about some of the important stories in their families. Are the stories about men and women different in their families and, if so, how? What aspects of their families' experience are not talked about? Students are asked to bring a family story into class that they would be comfortable sharing and analyzing together. Through this experience they are further informed of the power of narratives in shaping a family's culture and tradition and of the power of culture and tradition in shaping narratives. From here they move to consider changes in social institutions that are needed before some individuals and families can change and how to bring these changes about through social action.

Students learn to be reflective about their practice. If therapists' views are no longer privileged and clients' accounts are given credence, does this lead to an irrational atmosphere in which anything goes? According to Jerome Bruner (1990), "Constructivism's basic claim is simply that knowledge is 'right' or 'wrong' in light of the perspective we have chosen to assume" (p. 25). Giving up the idea of a single reality or objective truth by which practice can be evaluated creates the necessity for teaching students to be disciplined and reflective about practice and to make their perspectives known to themselves and others.

The following assignment promotes reflection from more than one vantage point. Students are asked to record a clinical interaction or vignette at the time of its occurrence. (They are urged *not* to use an entire interview—just an interaction.) Then they are asked to write down their understanding and impressions of this piece of clinical process. A month later, they return to the process, reread it, and record their current understanding and ideas. These later reflections may be based on further experience with the client, supervision, reading that has occurred in the interim, or additional reactions and ideas now accessible. The assignment concludes with students comparing the two accounts and writing about the learning that has accrued from this exercise. Sharing their papers with one another in class and discussing them amplifies the experience of reflection.

Through this exercise and other class discussions students see that giving up authority does not mean giving up responsibility—they are responsible for determining what works best. This is the beginning of learning to "reflect on action" (Schön, 1987, p. 25), a process whereby implicit and spontaneous aspects of practice wisdom are made explicit. Donnel Stern (1992) suggests that accepting our thoughts and the commitments they include is unavoidable.

Our thoughts occur to us. They arrive. We seldom, if ever, can describe coherently how we put them together. We may be able to claim with justification that we are thinking along the lines of certain broad intentions, such as our desire to understand some vague aspect of a patient's communication; and we may—and do, of course—evaluate our thoughts, once we have them, according to more or less objective criteria. But such evaluation occurs only after the main event, the creative portion of thinking, has already occurred. Our experience is that we receive our thoughts. (p. 332)

This awareness of the nature of clinical thought does not eliminate the need for evaluation. We act in clinical situations on the basis of the thoughts that occur to us. Then we engage in a process of evaluation, observing the effects of our actions on clients. In a constructivist model it is recognized that all forms of evaluation are value-laden and include affective commitments. Students learn that more than one view of a clinical encounter is helpful in balancing out values and personal biases. This might mean engaging the client in the evaluation process, or including supervisors, teachers, co-therapists, or other team members.

Class discussions regarding evaluation lead to the development of criteria for determining what counts as effective practice. Students are taught to consider such questions as (1) Does the clinical action cause the conversation to open up or close down (Anderson & Goolishian, 1988)? (2) Is the client's curiosity piqued? (3) Has the client's purpose in coming been served? (4) What are the signs of progress toward the client's goals? Evaluation of a clinical encounter might have to do with goodness of fit. Did the therapist and client seem to be moving along well together? Or it might be based on a therapist's sense of authenticity in the hour (Hoffman, 1992). Students and teachers can think aloud about these matters as they contemplate the complex and difficult nature of evaluation of practice and its importance. Consistent with a model of "connected learning" described by Belenky, Clinchy, Goldberger and Tarule (1986), "both teacher and students engage in the process of thinking as they talk out what they are thinking in a public dialogue" (p. 218).

In the paper thus far, a series of vignettes of teaching exercises along with the ideas embedded in these formats has been offered to convey both the content and process of a constructivist approach. We have seen how students learn to assess according to multiple perspectives, with an increased awareness of ways that theories and assumptions shape the inquiry and resulting construction of the client and situation. This led to a discussion of teaching the art of interviewing through asking questions, the co-creation of meaning through collaboration with clients, the tolerance of not understanding, the development of narratives, and the process of evaluation and reflection on action.

Much excitement is generated in this interactional and personal format for learning. Students gain confidence in their own ideas and begin to learn to use themselves creatively with clients. This is the essence of active, personal learning with students and teacher engaged in intense and lively discussions. While the benefits of this approach are many, the challenges in teaching from a constructivist position are considerable and will be discussed in the concluding section.

CHALLENGES

First, teaching a constructivist approach to treatment creates dissonance for students in a practice community in which psychodynamic and systemic models prevail and constructivism is just being introduced. Field placements (and later employment) take place in agencies adhering to realist assumptions and more hierarchical approaches to diagnosis and treatment. In keeping with the sensitivity to difference that constructivism promotes, students are encouraged to explore and consider this dissonance and are taught ways of managing differences with supervisors as well as clients. They are encouraged to listen for underlying assumptions and to weigh ideas within these contexts.

Second, the stress on teaching multiple theories and practice models places a burden on teachers and students. There is a need to assimilate larger quantities of information and to become fluent in the technical language of more than one paradigm. This is a formidable difficulty for many students–particularly those whose pre-social work training did not provide them with introductions to theories of behavior and development. Some students will accomplish this with ease, others will grasp one theory and become overly reliant on it. Frustrated by time constraints, teachers can only provide the bare essentials and, at best, a superficial understanding of different models. Despite these difficulties, the introduction of more than one model avoids students' tendencies to assume that there is a correct way to view clinical practice. Again, the students' efforts to move from one model to another may be criticized by supervisors who operate within a single model and want students to acquire a more in-depth understanding of it.

Finally, the balancing of realist and constructivist assumptions, despite the inconsistencies involved, requires a level of cognitive complexity not characteristic of all students. Some students have more difficulty than others shifting from realist to constructivist assumptions regarding diagnosis and finding ways of balancing the incompatibilities of these approaches. Additionally, there is a risk, in constructivism, of discounting the very real nature of conditions of poverty, unemployment, abuse, racism, sexism, and other forms of oppression and power. While individual and cultural constructions of these conditions are important, clients who are experiencing these conditions often need our confirmation of the unfair and oppressive realities of their lives. Students need to learn to simultaneously hold constructivist and realist positions and to manage the tension of these conflicting beliefs (Dean & Fleck-Henderson, 1992).

This capacity to move in and out of a constructivist position requires "an ironic relationship to the activity of the whole reflexive process" (Leppington, 1991, p. 99). This ironic perspective reminds us of the danger to our teaching of elevating constructivism to the position of some new "truth." As Leppington points out:

> Social Constructionism . . . provides a powerful way to describe, compare, critique, invent and to realize alternative practices in a non-equilibrium, irreversible, flow-process, mutually adaptive, evolutionary universe. And, yes, that's a reality claim–and reality claims are just so stories, and yes, that's yet another reality claim. Your turn. (p. 99)

While these conceptual challenges are formidable and create strains for teacher and student, they are intrinsic to a constructivist approach. The result, when we are lucky and it all comes together, is the development of reflective practitioners whose practice combines the use of artistic, intuitive processes with disciplined evaluation and thoughtfulness (Schön, 1983).

NOTES

1. This aspect of the exercise has been learned from Sallyann Roth through her teaching in The Program in Systemic Therapies at the Family Institute of Cambridge in 1989-1990.
2. For a discussion of additional classroom exercises associated with a constructivist approach see Dean & Fleck-Henderson, (1992).
3. As Hartman has stated, "Postmodernists believe that words not only reflect but also shape our world and that we cannot know our world except through the languages we have created to define, describe and interpret it."
4. This exercise is a variation on exercises used by Sallyann Roth and Kathy Weingarten in their teaching in The Program in Systemic Therapies at the Family Institute of Cambridge, 51 Kondazian Street, Watertown, MA 02172, 1989-1990.
5. See Dean, R. (1989). Ways of knowing in clinical practice, *Clinical Social Work Journal,* 12:2, 116-127 for additional description of this exercise.
6. See the writings of Bruner, E. 1986; Bruner, J. 1986; Gergen and Gergen, 1983; Laird, 1988; Riessman, 1990 and Schafer, 1983, to name a few.

REFERENCES

Anderson, H., & Goolishian, H. A. (1988). Human systems as linguistic systems: Preliminary and evolving ideas about the implications for clinical theory. *Family Process, 27*(4), 371-393.

Anderson, H., & Goolishian, H. A. (1992). The client is the expert: A not-knowing approach to therapy. In S. McNamee & Kenneth Gergen (Eds.) *Therapy as social construction* (pp. 25-39). Newbury Park, CA: Sage Publications.

Belenky, M. F., Clinchy, B. M., Goldberger, N. R., & Tarule, J. M. (1986). *Women's ways of knowing.* New York: Basic Books.

Berman-Rossi, T. (1988). Theoretical orientations of social work practice teachers: An analysis. *Journal of Social Work Education, 24*(1), 50-59.

Bruner, E. (1986). Ethnography as narrative. In V. Turner & E. Bruner (Eds.), *The anthropology of experience,* pp. 139-155. Chicago: University of Illinois Press.

Bruner, J. (1986). *Actual minds, possible worlds.* Cambridge, MA: Harvard University Press.

Bruner, J. (1990). *Acts of meaning.* Cambridge, MA: Harvard University Press.

Cecchin, G. (1987). Hypothesizing, circularity and neutrality revisited: An invitation to curiosity. *Family Process, 26*(4), 405-413.

Dean, R. G. (1989). Ways of knowing in clinical practice. *Clinical Social Work Journal, 17*(2), 116-27.

Dean, R. G., & Fenby, B. L. (1989). Exploring epistemologies: Social work action as a reflection of philosophical assumptions. *Journal of Social Work Education, 25*(1), 46-54.

Dean, R. G., & Fleck-Henderson, A. (1992). Teaching clinical theory and practice through a constructivist lens. *Journal of Teaching in Social Work, 6*(1), 3-20.

Epston, D., & White, M. (1992). *Experience, contradiction, narrative and imagination*. So. Australia: Dulwich Centre Publications.

Gergen, K. J. (1988). If persons are texts. In S.B. Messer, L. A. Sass, & R. I. Woolfolk (Eds.), *Hermeneutics and psychological theory*, pp. 28-51. New Brunswick, NJ: Rutgers University Press.

Gergen, K. (1985). The social constructionist movement in modern psychology. *American Psychologist, 40*(3), 317-329.

Gergen, K. J., & Gergen, M. M. (1983). Narratives of the self. In T. R. Sarbin and K. E. Scheibe (Eds.), *Studies in social identity*. New York: Praeger.

Gurevitch, Z. D. (1989). The power of not understanding: The meeting of conflicting identities. *The Journal of Applied Behavioral Science, 25*(2), 161-173.

Hartman, A. (1991). Words create worlds. *Social Work, 36*(4), 275.

Hoffman, I. (1991). Discussion: Toward a social constructivist view of the psychoanalytic situation. *Psychoanalytic Dialogues, 1*(1), 74-105.

Hoffman, I. (1992). Some practical implications of a social-constructivist view of the psychoanalytic situation. *Psychoanalytic Dialogues, 2*(3), 287-304.

Hoffman, L. (1990). Constructing realities: An art of lenses. *Family Process, 29*, 1-12.

Kaplan, M. (1983). A woman's view of DSM-III. *American Psychologist. 38*(7), 786-792.

Laird, J. (1988). Women and stories: Restorying a women's self-constructions. In M. McGoldrick, F. Walsh, & C. Anderson (Eds.), *Women in Families*, pp. 427-450. New York: Norton.

Leppington, R. (1991). From constructivism to social constructionism and doing critical therapy. *Human Systems: The Journal of Systemic Consultation & Management, 2*, 79-103.

MacKinnon, L. K., & Miller, D. (1987). The new epistemology and the Milan approach: Feminist and sociopolitical considerations. *Journal of Marital and Family Therapy, 13*(2), 139-155.

Maturana, H. R., & Varela, F. J. (1987). *The tree of knowledge: The biological roots of understanding*. Boston: New Science Library.

Penn, P. (1985). Feed-forward: Future questions, future maps. *Family Process 24*(3), 299-310.

Riessman, C. (1990). Divorce talk: *Women and men make sense of personal relationships*. New Brunswick: Rutgers University Press.

Rodwell, M. (1987). Naturalistic inquiry: An alternative model for social work assessment. *Social Service Review, 61*, 232-246.

Roth, S. (1992). Speaking the unspoken: A work-group consultation to reopen dialogue. In E. Imber-Black (Ed.) *Secrets in families and family therapy*, pp. 269-291. New York: Norton.

Roth, S., & Weingarten, K. (1989). Creating openings: Expanding and shifting meaning through language, Part I. The level of the word. Unpublished course handout, Program in Systemic Therapies, Family Institute of Cambridge, Watertown, MA 02172.

Schafer, R. (1983). *The analytic attitude*. New York: Basic Books.

Schön, D. A. (1987). *Educating the reflective practitioner.* San Francisco: Jossey-Bass.

Schön, D. A. (1983). *The reflective practitioner.* New York: Basic Books.

Scott, D. (1989). Meaning construction and social work practice. *Social Service Review, 63,* 39-51.

Stern, Donnel (1992). Commentary on constructivism in clinical psychoanalysis. *Psychoanalytic Dialogues, 2*(3), 331-363.

Tomm, K. (1988). Interventive interviewing: Part III. Intending to ask lineal, circular, strategic, or reflexive questions? *Family Process, 27*(1), 1-15.

Weingarten, K. (1992). A consideration of intimate and non-intimate interactions in therapy. *Family Process, 31,* 45-59.

White, M., & Epston, D. (1990). *Narrative means to therapeutic ends.* New York: Norton.

Family-Centered Practice:
Cultural and Constructionist Reflections

Joan Laird

SUMMARY. In this article, I describe how an interest in culture and in anthropological models for understanding merged with ideas from social constructionism to shape an approach to teaching family theory and practice. A critical stance; a search for the meanings of one's own experiences; consistent attention to issues of power, domination and the subjugation of certain "knowledges"; a sensitivity to the power of language to shape what we see and hear; and a search for collaborative and empowering approaches to work with families are some of the pervasive themes that shape the teaching-learning environment. A social constructionist metaperspective provides context and critical jumping-off place for examining prevailing models of family theory and practice.

INTRODUCTION: BEGINNING WITH THE WRITER

The lines between "knowledges," "systems of belief," "passions," and "religions" are fine ones indeed. As a college philosophy student, I remember becoming enamored of a great system of thought, of finally discovering "the truth," the answers to the great questions of the world, only, two or three weeks later, to rediscover "the truth," as Descartes gave way to Spinoza and Spinoza, in turn,

Joan Laird, MS, is Professor at the Smith College School for Social Work, Northampton, MA 01063.

[Haworth co-indexing entry note]: "Family-Centered Practice: Cultural and Constructionist Reflections," Laird, Joan. Co-published simultaneously in *Journal of Teaching in Social Work* (The Haworth Press, Inc.) Vol. 8, No. 1/2, 1993, pp. 77-109; and: *Revisioning Social Work Education: A Social Constructionist Approach* (ed: Joan Laird) The Haworth Press, Inc., 1993, pp. 77-109. Multiple copies of this article/chapter may be purchased from The Haworth Document Delivery Center [1-800-3-HA-WORTH; 9:00 a.m. - 5:00 p.m. (EST)].

to Hegel and Kant. It was a heady, liberal arts experience in the finest sense of that concept; gradually, accompanied by some despair, I learned that there was no "truth," a lesson I sometimes forgot when I began my social work journey some years later.

Similarly, as a casework student in a graduate school of social work committed, among other things, to Freudian thought, once again I discovered "the truth," always, however, somewhat uneasily. My clients–poor, oppressed, hopeless, angry–rarely resembled the rich and famous "overindulged" neurotic "patients" described by the series of analysts who taught our human behavior (in the social environment?) classes. The "knowledge" of psychoanalytic thought gave me a new sense of power and professionalism; I remember diagnosing, with great personal satisfaction, one of my clients, who could not move from her couch and was seemingly paralyzed for no good physical reason, as an example of "conversion reaction." Three weeks later, much to my chagrin, I learned she had been abusing alcohol for so many years that she had suffered severe physical and mental damage. But the "diagnosis" of "alcoholism" moved me no closer to helping her live a better life, as I placed her daughter in foster care and repeatedly sent her off for in-patient treatment.

Nevertheless, I became very proficient at "ego assessments" and at producing multiple page "psychosocials," but somehow these tools of the time were not sufficient for understanding the often large, fragmented, complex and sometimes violent families I saw every day in child welfare protective services; we only knew how to diagnose individual "pathologies" and to remove, albeit with compassion and sensitivity, children-at-risk, often to place them in other families we also poorly understood.

From a Psychodynamic to a Systemic Stance

When family systems thought appeared on the horizon, the family and ways of understanding it now "discovered" by a new generation of (white middle-class male) psychiatrists, I once again developed a new passion, I had once again found the truth, a better way of seeing the world. Attending every conference and training opportunity I could afford, I began to understand these "faulty" families in terms of their intergenerational legacies, their often bizarre systems of communication, and their dysfunctional structures; children were "double bound," "scapegoated," and "triangled" to preserve family homeostasis, couples became involved in deadly "games," families had problems in their input-output-feedback mechanisms; all were victims of unresolved losses from the past.

Gone were the myths of Oedipus and Narcissus, as we turned to the languages and metaphors of the "hard" sciences, to general systems theory, biology, and cybernetics. Ecology offered us metaphors to connect human beings with their environments, the notions of "delicate balance" (Germain, 1979) and the "patterns that connect" (Bateson, 1972); we thought we had finally solved the problem of the psychosocial interface, the person-in-environment transaction. In the decades that followed the discoveries of the pioneering "great originals" in family therapy[1] a number of schools of thought, or family theories, crystallized, becoming identified with certain leaders and major family therapy training centers. In these centers, new and exciting models of practice were developed; a professional organization was formed, and thousands of social workers flocked to the increasing number of conferences proliferating all over the country. Indeed, we seemed to have witnessed a paradigmatic revolution. For me, it was once again a heady and exciting intellectual time, although I was again uneasy.

Menacing Metaphors

For one thing, the central metaphors, both in social work and in family therapy, were troubling. One set of metaphors was clearly militaristic, as we talked of strategies, weapons, target systems, interventions; it seemed, almost, that the client was an enemy to be challenged and overcome in a battle for power. Another set of metaphors likened human beings in their natural environments to machine-like systems. These mechanistic metaphors compared family processes to hard-wired thermostatic and computer systems, and mothers to operators of complex telephone switchboards. Were these metaphors any less deadly than the medical metaphors that for so long had dominated? I fended off colleague and student suggestions that some models of family therapy seemed manipulative. Was it any less manipulative, I asked, to keep people in expensive, long-term, psychodynamic treatments where little progress or change could be demonstrated? These models, I argued, worked!

A second troubling issue was what seemed an impossible gulf between, on the one hand, the prescriptions of "science" and the growing emphasis in social work on "scientific" practice and outcome measurement and, on the other hand, the kinds of complex, measurement-defying problems and needs families bring to the helping setting. Should our models of practice be guided by the kinds of questions popular in quantitative, empirical research, by what our best practice wisdom kept telling us were often irrelevant criteria? Driven by "method" and measurement, was our work to be judged by its reliability, validity, predictability, and generalizability? To me, both individuals and families in constant interaction with their worlds seemed too changing and too complex to stand still for such linear metaphors; and our forays into their lives seemed so brief, so small a part of their total life experiences that we could never "control" or even guess at those variables that might be "significant" when things changed, let alone predict future outcomes. On the research front, the kinds of questions I was interested in pursuing, questions that had to do with pervasive intergenerational family themes and patterns, with family culture and world view, could not be approached using the tools of quantitative, positivist models, or in the terms being set forth for evaluating practice.

An Anthropological Perspective

Committed to staying in Ann Arbor, in the late 1970s I tried to locate myself in the University of Michigan's joint doctoral program in social work and social science. But the predominant interests of the sociologists of the time in large survey research and of the psychologists in experimental research, combined with a lack of interest of social scientists in the family at that time, deterred me. I had begun to believe very strongly that what families were most like were tiny societies, societies that over time seemed to develop their own systems of meaning and belief, their own mythologies and ritual practices, their own "cultures" (Laird, 1983). It seemed to me that the study of anthropology might be helpful and, knowing virtually nothing about anthropology or what anthropologists did except to go off for years at a time to exotic cultures, in the early 1980s I became the first student in the university's combined social work and anthropology doctoral program. Maybe, I thought, one could study families like Margaret Mead studied the Samoans or Elliot Liebow studied Tally's corner.

To study anthropology is not only to study the cultures of the world, I learned, but to study philosophy, history, the physical sciences, language and languages–there are seemingly few boundaries and no limits. Early on, as one begins to learn of the vast numbers of ways various peoples see the world with equally profound conviction, one learns the world can be represented in many ways; that no one has an edge on the truth, that "science" does not necessarily mean progress. To study anthropology, to the extent that one does not swear allegiance to a particular anthropological world view (e.g., cultural materialism, psychoanalytic anthropology), one begins to experience firsthand a world that is socially and culturally constructed, one comes to understand that one's own world is known or created through our words and our beliefs about it, our telling of it, our writing about it, even though the terms "constructivism" or "social constructionism" may never have been uttered. Furthermore, one comes to understand that our own seeing and knowing cannot be separated from our own story, from what some have called prior texts, codes, or forestructures of understanding (McNamee & Gergen, 1992, p. 1). It is a humbling experience to contextualize one's knowing in that way, just as coming to understand the unique and profound differences among families can be a humbling experience.

When constructivist and later, social constructionist, philosophy began to make its way into the family therapy field, the major conceptions and models that began to emerge blended comfortably with streams of thought from anthropology, with the ethnographic stance of the researcher, and particularly the work of symbolic anthropologist Clifford Geertz (see, e.g., Geertz, 1973, 1983), all of which had been stimulating my own thinking, teaching, and practice. Perhaps, I mused, anthropology, with its metaphors of culture, with its deconstruction of "expert" discourse, with its move away from a "colonialist" mentality (Clifford & Marcus, 1986), and social constructionist thought could together bring more "natural," benign, and empowering metaphors to the conception of family theory and practice.

THE FAMILY THERAPY MOVEMENT

From Sick Individuals to Sick Families

In the family therapy movement, the effort was to contextualize individual problems, to depathologize, to move away from medical or disease models of human functioning, to think in circular and recursive ways, to understand the complex relationships between people in their most intimate environments. But this movement gathered force in a context in which the "scientific" positivist paradigm was dominant. As practice creativity flourished, pushing at the boundaries of existing ways of framing human problems, researchers continued to use linear models to try to capture systemic practice. Both practitioners and researchers strove to be "objective," to stay outside of the system, to capture some empirically knowable "reality," whether it was understandable in biological, structural, or cybernetic terms. Creative as this work has been, we family therapists lacked a level of self-reflectiveness, a kind of consciousness, an ability to step outside of ourselves, to surface our own cultural biases, to examine our theory and practice in relation to the predominant sociopolitical forces of the times (MacKinnon & Miller, 1987). How were we recreating the dominant social discourse, conjuring up before our eyes what it was we expected to see in the first place? My own "take" on the movement, exciting as it was, was that it had developed its own DSM III-like language; we had moved from labelling sick individuals to labelling sick families. Furthermore, I was concerned that we were calling family actions and beliefs that we poorly understood "dysfunctional"–family myths, rituals, folklores, stories and narratives, and other cultural categories of action and belief that were universally practiced, by peoples all over the world, to give meaning to their lives.

Two shifts, two critical standpoints, both of which originated outside of but took some unique paths within family therapy, gained the force of full-blown movements in the 1980s, reshaping both epistemology and practice in the field. The first of these was the feminist critique, the second the constructivist (and more recently the social constructionist) critique.

The Feminist Critique

As family therapists, because we were "systemic," we thought we had escaped the mother-blaming, individual-blaming evils of psychoanalytic thought; we forgot, in our zeal to move from the individual to the family as the seat of understanding, that it was the family that many of the early radical feminists had seen as the central location for the forces of patriarchy. We were so intrigued by what was going on inside of families or within their immediate environments that we failed to place families themselves in an historical and sociopolitical context. We didn't notice, as family theories and therapy models proliferated, that we were *assuming* Western cultural models of the family, normative models for family life and relationships, models that were not only ethnocentric, sexist, and heterosexist but that failed to accurately describe the growing pluralism of family forms in this society.

Rachel Hare-Mustin's pioneering 1978 article, "A Feminist Approach to Family Therapy," went virtually unnoticed; it wasn't until the mid-1980s that the feminist critique began to gather momentum. Virginia Goldner's influential 1985 article in *Family Process*, "Feminism and Family Therapy" appeared about the same time a three-day conference for women in family therapy convened, organized by Monica McGoldrick, Froma Walsh, and Carol Anderson. This gathering of some 50 women leaders, followed by a second meeting two years later, made possible stronger networks of women, spawning a new and more politicized consciousness as well as an effort to take charge of our own mythmaking (Laird, 1986). Between 1986 and 1989, the field was deluged with a number of feminist family therapy books (Ault-Riche, 1986; Braverman, 1988; Goodrich, Rampage, Ellman, & Halstead, 1988; McGoldrick, Anderson, & Walsh, 1989; Lerner, 1988; Luepnitz, 1988; Walters, Carter, Papp, & Silverstein, 1988), and a large number of feminist articles were published, ushering in a new feminist awareness in the field.

Although several women leaders had left their original, male-founded training centers to begin their own programs, most of the training centers, the organizations, the journals, what we might call the rituals of the profession, continued to be male-dominated (and, I might add, psychiatrist-dominated). It was in the late 1980s that this pattern began to noticeably change; women became increasingly visible as plenary speakers at the major conferences and began to assume more leadership roles in the professional organizations. The *Journal of Feminist Family Therapy* was launched and began to be taken seriously.

The feminist movement in family therapy has gone through two stages to date. In the earlier and mid-1980s, it became a major force in opening up a new critique; the tribal elders and the canons that had become enshrined were being questioned in a way that had not heretofore been possible. This "opening up," in my view, helped to clear the way for a fresh look at what had become a relatively fixed set of truisms, of beliefs. It was a time of great tension and considerable backlash in the field. As the feminist challenge matured, it moved from critique to originality, taking up the effort to explore new approaches to work with families that would not blame and pathologize women for what they had been socialized to do and believe in, and that would begin to take account of power imbalances between men and women in the world and in the family. The family (and family therapy) became gendered.

The Constructivist Critique

Overlapping with the feminist critique, an epistemological debate began to gather force in the early 1980s, centered around re-exploration of the ideas of Gregory Bateson (1972) and led off by Bradford Keeney's (1979) article, "Ecosystemic Epistemology: An Alternative Paradigm for Diagnosis." In 1984, Paul Watzlawick published *The Invented Reality*, in which he, Ernst von Glasersfeld, and others took issue with the idea that a real world exists that we can discover, measure, or know objectively. These constructivist thinkers were not denying the existence of such a world; rather, they argued, we only ever come to know it through our bumping into it, as it is filtered through our perceptions, our languages.

As the postmodern era was ushered in across many disciplines, for example, in the fields of literary criticism, anthropology, linguistics, and psychology, and as terms like "poststructuralism" and "deconstructionism" made their way into the language and gained adherents, family therapists began to seize upon new metaphors for family theory and practice. In the mid to late 1980s, a number of creative thinkers from around the world began to take family therapy into the postmodern era.

THE EMERGENCE OF NEW METAPHORS

A number of key contributions to a radical shift in the field should be mentioned before I move to the world of teaching.

The Reflecting Team

The now famous "switching of the sound and lights" idea of Tom Andersen (1987, 1991) of Norway, a seemingly simple shift, has contributed to a reconceptualizing of the therapist-client relationship. As Andersen turned the lights off in the room where the family sat and shined them on the team behind the mirror, the balance of power shifted. Now the therapist and the therapist's ideas would be exposed, held up for scrutiny. The group, the hidden power behind the mirror became "real people," a "reflecting team" of people with ideas, stories, and biases of their own. No one's voice would be privileged as "expert" and the family would be invited to consider multiple "reflections," including their own, with no obligation to favor any. If the new idea was not different enough or too different, mused Andersen, the system, the family, would "stand still." Change would occur only when the new idea pushed for some, but not too much, difference.

Externalizing the Problem: A Therapy of Literary Merit

From "down under," South Australia and New Zealand, came Michael White and David Epston respectively, who, with a number of colleagues, introduced several intriguing sets of ideas (see, e.g., Epston, 1989; Epston & White, 1992; White, 1989a, 1989b, 1992; White & Epston, 1990). White, who had studied Foucault and had turned to anthropologists such as Edward Bruner and Victor Turner for inspiration, placed the concepts of "power," "narrative," and "social discourse" at the center of his work. The problem, White and Epston (1990) argued, was not to be located inside of people or even in the relationships between people. People had problems with a problem. And, in their "therapy of literary merit," the problem itself is often seen as a paralyzing or handicapping "story," a narrative that does not allow one to move forward. This notion of "externalizing the problem" seemed to free people from self- or other-blaming positions, to mobilize and empower people to undermine the influence of such problem narratives on their lives. A future-oriented, empowering therapy, the core of White's work, in his collaboration with David Epston, is for the client(s) to co-construct a new story, a new narrative, to escape the force of an outworn narrative that does not fit one's "lived experience."

Therapy as a Conversation in Which No One Is Expert

In this country, the work of Harlene Anderson and Harold Goolishian of the Houston-Galveston Family Institute was breaking new ground (see, e.g., Anderson & Goolishian, 1988, 1992). Drawing on postmodern theory, anthropology, and the ideas of social constructionist psychologist Kenneth Gergen (Gergen, 1985, 1991; Gergen & Kaye, 1992), among others, Anderson and Goolishian have developed a number of new metaphors for a postmodern therapeutic stance. Therapy itself is reconceptualized as "conversation" or "dialogue," drawn from the social constructionist notion that theories, ideas, concepts, memories, and so on are always mediated through language in the intersubjective spaces between people. Anderson and Goolishian have challenged the conception of mental health professional as "expert," suggesting instead that the clinician should take a "not-knowing," de-expertized position. In their most recently published work (1992), the role of the therapist is seen as akin to that of the ethnographer, an infinitely curious (Cecchin, 1987), respectful stranger, his or her voice or ideas no more privileged than any other party to the conversation.

A Collaborative Stance

In the early days of the family therapy movement, therapists saw their roles as akin to that of the orchestra conductor, helping the family to make better harmony; of the stage director, pushing the players to enact new roles; of the choreographer, suggesting new steps to the family dance while a "Greek chorus" in the background spoke to the family's unconscious. Metaphors were used powerfully, secretly, and strategically, to force the family to dislodge from its homeostatic position.

The constructionist stance is carrying with it an emphasis on collaboration, on change as a co-evolutionary process in which the therapist tries to shed power and to foster a spirit of partnership in pursuit of change. The effort is to create a more empowering context in which change can take place. In traditional psychoanalytically-informed therapies, where the clinician's narrative is reified and the goal is for the family to gain "insight" into the reasons for its dysfunction, or in some family therapies where insight is considered unimportant but rather the family is maneuvered into change, the very structure of the procedure, argue Gergen and Kaye (1992)

> furnishes the client a lesson in inferiority. The client is indirectly informed that he or she is ignorant, insensitive, woolly-headed, or emotionally incapable of comprehending reality. In contrast, the therapist is positioned as all-knowing and wise–a model to which the client might aspire. The situation is all the more lamentable owing to the fact that in occupying the superior role, the therapist fails to reveal any weaknesses. (p. 171)

In a constructionist stance, the therapist or clinician (words that clearly need re-writing), backs off from an expert position, may identify with the client's experiences, may speak her or his own uncertainties, and always offers her or his ideas tentatively, based on experience and belief rather than on truth. (This is not to say that the therapist is irresponsible or condones behavior that is harmful to self or others; it does not mean the therapist will not take a stand on issues of oppression, as I discuss below; it does, in fact, argue for a more "just" formulation and system of accountability (Waldegrave, 1990), a position in which the therapist is particularly sensitive to the ways in which narratives are shaped in a context of power relationships.)

In the context of a dialogical, conversational, collaborative model for helping, the therapist becomes a "conversational artist" whose expertise lies in the ability to keep the conversation going long enough so that a new and more potentiating narrative can take shape (Anderson & Goolishian, 1992).

Power and Domination: Subjugated Knowledges

There has been a tension in the field between those who believe that the social context is embedded in the individual narrative and will emerge in the conversation (that is, that the therapist should not take a "political" stance on any issue), and those who believe that the therapist has a responsibility to in some way bring her or his understanding of relevant power imbalances in the world or in the family to the client's or family's attention. Hoffman (1992), representing the former group, in a stance that seems to pit her against the feminist movement in family therapy, argues for neutrality and suggests that all therapeutic discourses, like those of Marxists or feminists, "can contain the same colonial assumptions as medical approaches . . . they can all offer the client a savior to help them" (p. 14), presumably simply substituting another powerful, privileged discourse for the eschewed therapeutic discourses. Others (e.g., Efran and Clarfield, 1992), argue that

> constructionists are obliged to take responsibility for being advocates of particular positions. They are not enjoined from having them. Constructionists are even allowed to test their hypotheses using the canons of science, provided they keep in mind that science itself is a tradition involving a dialectic between the observer and the observed. It never yields value-free observations. (p. 201)

My own position is that, while ethnographic and constructionist metaphors are extremely useful, we are not simply philosophers or anthropologists, we are not neutral observers. Many of our clients have been excluded from certain kinds of "knowledges," their ways of knowing disparaged, their voices silenced, their experiences invalidated. Many have been taught to blame themselves for their "symptoms," they have learned that their cultural beliefs and practices are "lower class" or that their lack of efficacy in a techno-logical society is a result of their own ignorance. Some women have been so silenced that they cannot story their own experiences of sexual and physical violation even to themselves (Laird, 1992).

What *is* the responsibility of the constructionist clinician, I be-lieve, is to be "expert" on relationships of power and domination, on the social construction of social discourses that shape individual meanings, and, when necessary, to make those worlds of meaning accessible to our clients. Feminism, for example, is not just another dogma, it does not mean having to privilege a particular political belief anymore than does sensitivity to the society's messages about culture. It is *about* relationships of power and domination, about how "knowledge" is constructed in particular sociopolitical con-texts; at that level, it is about social discourse, which is exactly what social constructionism is about.

Crossing Boundaries

Many others are expanding on the fundamental ideas of social constructionism and deconstructionism, including William Lax and his colleagues at the Brattleboro Family Institute in Vermont (see, e.g., Lax, 1989, 1991, 1992; Miller & Lax, 1988) and Sallyann Roth, Kathy Weingarten and others at the Family Institute in Cam-bridge (see, e.g., Weingarten, 1991, 1992).

My own work combines ideas from anthropology, postmodern theory, and feminist theory, using linguistic and cultural metaphors (e.g., story, myth, narrative, ritual) to explore the gender story in this society, particularly how men and women "story" their lives, and to draw implications for practice (Allen & Laird, 1990; Laird, 1983, 1988, 1989, 1992, in press). Cultural metaphors, which in my view come closer to the social categories human beings themselves have drawn upon to define and describe their lives, themselves, their soci-eties, and their meanings, hold promise for getting us closer to what White calls "lived experience." These metaphors seem to me more people-friendly, less distancing, less hierarchical, and less abstract than the psychological/medical deficit-describing metaphors that have dom-inated clinical practice in the mental health professions. The inner, psychological experience is negotiated in social and cultural worlds of meaning and might better be named in those terms.

Up to now, I have been describing the shifts in context and in my own thinking that are shaping what I define as a social constructionist perspective in teaching and learning family theory and practice. Before I go on to describe how these ideas are reflected in the classroom, one more point should be made. In the emerging social constructionist models, the boundaries around individual, family, couple, group become irrelevant, for neither theory nor method is related any longer to the system level one is thinking about or working with. Since meaning is always shaped in dialogue, inter-subjectively, social constructionist metaphors for practice bridge practice with individuals, families, groups, and larger systems. Problems are located in social discourse, in language, and in the relationships of power and domination that shape problem definition, ideas relevant to work with any size system.

Our curricula in schools of social work are still, to a large extent, organized by method, theory and/or system level. At Smith, for example, psychoanalytic theories dominate most of the required practice and theory courses, which are oriented toward work with individuals. Family theory is allotted one required course, and practice with families may be found in three or four elective courses. While efforts are made to blend the psychological and the social in other courses, these two dimensions of human life are kept relatively separate, with social theories taught in their own required courses. The psychological and the social finally come together again most strongly in a third-summer course entitled "From Private Troubles to Public Issues," described by Phebe Sessions elsewhere in this volume. It is clear, however, that constructionist ideas are burrowing into all of the courses, as the postmodern revolution begins to infiltrate even those social work programs dominated by a single strong system of beliefs. What a social constructionist stance demands, even for the most passionate proponents of particular bodies of theory, *is* that we begin to contextualize our own thinking, to recognize our favorite theories *are* sets of beliefs shaped in particular historical, cultural, political, and social times. It is in this sense that it is not just another body of theory coming down the road; it is more accurately a stance, a meta-perspective, a theory about theories, as Hoffman (1990) puts it, a lens through which to view other lenses. The challenge, of course, is to *not*, in turn, reify social constructionism itself, to keep "meta" to this metaperspective.

TEACHING FAMILY THEORY AND PRACTICE

I teach both a required foundation course on family theory and a two-semester elective course on clinical practice with families. The latter course moves from introductory to advanced practice. The organizing conception for both courses is similar, leaning on the organization of family-centered practice presented in Hartman and Laird (1983), which is used as a basic text. The conception is presented in Figure 1. Families are explored along four major dimensions: (1) Ecologically, in sociocultural context and in terms of

FIGURE 1. The family in space and time. (Source: *Family-centered Social Work Practice*, by Ann Hartman and Joan Laird. Copyright © 1983 by the Free Press, a Division of Macmillan, Inc., Reprinted with the permission of the publisher.

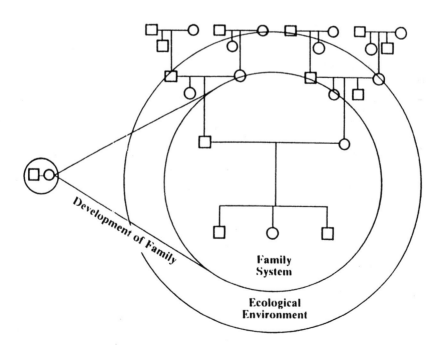

their transactions with their environments; (2) Intergenerationally, in terms of the patterns and "cultures" they have developed over time; (3) Developmentally, in terms of the experiences and shifting patterns of the family at hand over their time together as a family; and (4) Internally, that is, in terms of the meanings, relationships, and patterns that describe the current family. Students learn early on that these boundaries are arbitrary and imaginary, that all of these dimensions are present, interacting, moving, and shifting all of the time, and that we are using the framework for its heuristic value.

Both courses are "historical" in the sense that, as we move through these dimensions, through space and time, various family theories, models, ideas, and concepts are explored roughly in the order they emerged in the field. In the practice course, the major models are applied and tried in various ways, through video, role play, experiential exercises, and so on. For example, in the ecological segment, the ideas of Auerswald (1985), Aponte (1976), Imber-Black (1988) and other family theorists whose work has been particularly sensitive to context, are featured. In the intergenerational segment, the ideas of Bowen (1978), Boszormenyi-Nagy and Spark (1973) and others occupy center stage. In the developmental segment, the work of Carter and McGoldrick (1980, 1988), Combrinck-Graham (1985), and others help us examine shifts in family needs and tasks over time and in how the family constitutes itself in shifting contexts. The works of the structural (e.g., Minuchin, 1974; Minuchin & Fishman, 1981), strategic (Haley, 1987, Madanes, 1981; Watzlawick, Weakland, & Fisch, 1974), and the systemic (e.g., Selvini-Palazzoli, Boscolo, Cecchin, & Prata, 1980) family therapists are also studied through class discussion of their writings, through viewing videotaped examples of their practice, and through experiential exercise.

Several additional themes and stances are threaded throughout this basic pattern of organization. Taking a "pivoting the center" or "standpoint" stance (see, e.g., Collins, 1990; Hartsock, 1983), I do not assume the two-parent, white, heterosexual middle-class family as the normative family against which all others are contrasted. While we do carve out special time for examining ethnicity and race, gender, sexual orientation, issues of social class and economic privilege, and particular family "structures," these themes are present in every class. The lesbian family, the Southeast Asian-American family, the poverty-stricken single parent family, and even the two-parent, heterosexual, white middle-class family with mother at home and 2.4 children all become part of ordinary conversation about families and, indeed, we look at the social construction of "normative" ideas about family and family constellation.

Since our semesters last for five weeks and are extremely fast-paced and intense, courses must be carefully planned in advance, books and articles pre-ordered, and so on. The students do not have time to do extensive, independent, research-based papers. I have not thought it feasible in this program to "co-construct" the class in the way I would like; that kind of approach requires time for group development, for a growing trust on the part of students in their own ideas and those of their peers, for a slower, more democratic and less hierarchical approach to teaching and learning in which the teaching-learning medium better mirrors the practice models emerging from a constructionist stance.

The focus is, however, on providing a teaching-learning context in which students learn to critically examine their own pre-packaged assumptions, to welcome the "foreign," to enhance their sensitivity to the power of the social context and of social discourse to shape individual meanings and experiences, in other words to foster their critical faculties at every turn. In the pages that follow, I describe how these goals are approached.

The Social Construction of "Family"

In the first class of both the theory and practice classes (itself an arbitrary boundary, for theory and practice are closely interwoven in both courses), the students introduce themselves by sharing something about their families. Some mention sibling systems and their own "place" in the family or talk of their "only child" experience, some describe turning points or crises, some offer a metaphor they think communicates the family paradigm, others share how they themselves are "storied" in the family as the "caretaker," the "family clown," or whatever. As this exercise is processed, students usually remark that they are amazed at the new pictures they have of their peers and friends, people they thought they had come to "know" quite well. This discussion leads, then, to consideration of what "context" has to do with "who we are," with the notion of "self" or "identity"–it is a different cut, a new set of meanings, than they have experienced in their personality theory classes. They begin to have an idea of the intersubjective quality of a self-in-construction.

In the theory class, my next step is to show a seven-minute segment of a videotaped interview with a family.[2] In this case, the eldest of three daughters, married, with children of her own, and concerned about her parents' marriage and the degree of argument, tension, and strife in the family, has urged them to come for counseling. She and one of her sisters, both in their 30s, and the older couple, both in their late 60s, are present for the first interview.

After the eldest daughter tells why she has asked for this family meeting, the older couple is invited to share their perspectives. The wife begins, summarizing her life as a mother and as a wife, as a woman whose early aspirations to be an artist and then a clothing designer were transformed into making clothes for her children. She goes on to describe something of how her life has changed since her husband retired; a story that seems to suggest that she feels intruded upon, monitored.

The husband continues, beginning by indicating that he has come to help his wife in whatever way he can; he describes her discontent and we learn that he, at least, has storied his wife as "mental patient," that she, indeed, suffered some years ago from "involutional depression" (his term), and that part of the reason he retired from a satisfying career as a college professor was to be more available to her. He understands that retired husbands are sometimes seen as "in the way," but doesn't understand why he has become such an object of resentment; he wonders whether it could have something to do with all of these "women's lib" ideas she has heard about, that she now sees her life as a failure.

The students are asked to listen very carefully to each person's narrative, to try to enter each of their stories, to search for their meanings. The ensuing discussion is always very lively, with a great many differences of opinion, and what I call "multiple reflections." Since the great majority of our students are strongly feminist, they hear in her story a series of losses and disappointments related to patriarchal definitions for womanhood; they find it much more difficult to "hear" the possible meanings in *his* story, pointing out that his story seems more about her.

The possible learning edges provoked by this tiny segment of tape are many and can only be partially described here. For example, students begin to think about the social context of depression, the meanings for men and for women of coming for help and what that has to do with male and female socialization and the social discourse surrounding "helping" and "getting help." The discussion surfaces multiple "life cycle" issues, the meanings of retirement for men and for their wives in traditional marriages in this society, the experience of children leaving home and its meanings for mothers and fathers, of how men and women mark the courses of their lives. One of the things the couple argues about, for example, is where they will live–he wants to move to Florida for the weather and the golf and she wants to stay in the North near their children and grandchildren. Again, the different meanings of "family" to the family's members begin to surface.

It is significant that, in this point in their learning, the students for the most part fail to recognize the changing social and historical contexts in which the couple's narratives have been shaped and have shifted over time, even though the husband himself comments on the influence of "women's lib." As I raise this issue, students begin to consider how the social messages for women's lives have changed, how women no longer seem to "have" involutional depression in such great numbers, how the leaving home of children has become not only loss but new opportunity. It is more difficult for them to consider what the impact of this changing story for women on *his* life and on his marriage might be. After all, I point out, he has done very well what the larger social discourse prescribed as successful career for husband and father, a career and a view of the family later found wanting by the women's movement. Students begin to consider how history itself may consist of an ever changing narrative about the same events, a recasting, a re-experiencing.

In the family practice course, I often begin with an exercise that creates a context for a similar learning experience, using an exercise developed early in the family therapy movement. Students are asked to stand, to mill around the room, and to choose some one other person with whom to engage in conversation, someone they could see as "being in their family." After the dyads have had a brief time to become acquainted, they are instructed to mill about and to choose another twosome they could imagine as part of their family. These new groups are given time to become acquainted. Then they are asked to assign formal "roles" to themselves/each other (child, parent, sibling, etc.). In the next phase, the "families" are asked to assume informal roles and to assign someone in the family the "problem," something for which they might seek family counseling. Once they have completed that task, they are asked to elaborate among themselves about this beginning construction of "family" and problem.

In the processing of this exercise, students are asked to talk about their reasons for choosing family members, how these people fit into their ideas of "family," to describe how they went about assigning various roles, and how they came to define "the problem" and who would be identified as "having" it. Within-family differences in the experience, as well as student impressions of other families, are discussed. What becomes clear is that there are certain social stories about families, certain "forestructures of meaning," that foster some commonality in the group, as well as powerful differences which they begin to link to their own family experiences. We begin to wonder, as a class, how these individual and social narratives, which so clearly are implicated in how we interpret what we see, will affect what we see and do in our practice.

These "families" are then used in a variety of ways in the early weeks of the class. For example, in a segment on "getting started," someone in the family makes an initial call to a family agency, child welfare services, or a mental health clinic, and a student worker begins to elicit the family's story over the telephone. Students learn how even the face sheet or the way a referral is taken or the way the agency describes its functions or one's own "prior texts" about identifying problems or whom one encourages to come in begins to shape an ongoing narrative that will give shape to the relationship and to the work together.

Rules for feedback are established, which mirror some of the same conventions that have become common in offering reflections to families, which the students will practice later on. The student interviewer and family members are invited first to comment on their experiences and observations. Comments/reflections on role playing "conversations" by them and by all of the observers are offered tentatively, respectfully, positively, and are limited to what has been said in the room, or are offered speculatively and have to do with the future, the hypothetical, what Peggy Penn (1985) has called "feed-forward" questions (e.g., I wonder what would happen if Bill were to ask the family about Lisa's birth parents; if Angela were to say more about her worries about her father).

Two additional learning edges should be mentioned at this juncture. First, by this time students are learning that there are no "right" answers, no "correct" or "accurate" ways to proceed; they are beginning to understand that the same conversation may be heard very differently by various members of the class, that each will see and hear differently, that a multiplicity of ideas may be useful, that the ideas they think are most useful may not be those that are most meaningful for the client family. We begin to talk about how it is that many of us seem to see different dimensions, what that may have to do with the social contexts in which our ideas have been shaped, an exploration that leads us to a second learning edge, that of a constant critical stance toward one's own ideas as well as those embedded in the formal theories and practice models they are studying and will be using. They begin to understand that all of our theories, our "texts," our "codes," our languages, contain built-in biases, that our own narratives have been shaped in social meaning-making contexts that differ from each other and that we assume these narratives are correct. Students begin to probe how their own gendered senses of self, their ethnicities, social class backgrounds, and so on influence their pictures of the world. Similarly, they wonder about the "masters" (an interesting, gendered, hierarchical term popular in the field)–what were the worlds that created their words and how are their words in turn creating what it is they are seeing and hearing? Do these ideas/languages work as well or will they have the same meanings in work with an inner city black single-parent family in which the mother has AIDS? With a lesbian couple in a heterosexist suburban environment? With a French-Canadian farm family struggling with alcohol and incest problems? We begin to listen carefully for the world views embedded in our commonly used "expert" terms to describe individuals and families, gradually exploring whether there are other languages that may be less toxic, less hopeless, closer to people's life experiences and the ways *they* might describe themselves and those experiences.

Both Ruth Dean and Ann Fleck-Henderson (this volume) mention that they find some students to be anxious with this kind of uncertainty, students looking for "how to" answers. I wonder if this burden may become lighter as students begin to construct a view of themselves as other than "expert," as not pressured to have the "right" answers. My experience is that students do not have as much difficulty with uncertainty and ambiguity as they do with the rigid certainty in some agencies, where they are constrained from trying out new ideas or even from seeing all of the members of a family together in one room.

In the classes that follow, as we explore ecological, intergenerational, systemic and other "schools" of family theory and therapy (always trying to use examples and contexts relevant to the settings where social workers are most likely to be employed), we maintain this critical stance. This positioning, when combined with a "reflecting" rather than a "dissecting" approach, allows students to be more forgiving not only of their own work and each other's but also the work of the "experts" whom we read and whose videotapes we watch, always alert to the narratives the "masters" bring to the conversation and, where possible, the contexts in which those narratives have been shaped.

The Student's Own Narrative

There are a number of ways throughout both the theory and practice courses that the students' own life experiences become grist for the learning mill, a common practice in family therapy training and one I find extremely valuable in the teaching-learning context. Perhaps most importantly, it helps students become ethnographers in search of their own narratives and it gives them a kind of respect for the narratives of others in a way that seems to me more powerful than any other kind of experience. Much of this work is done in dyads and in small groups; much of it is voluntary and any sharing with the larger group is always voluntary.

These experiences include:

1. Student pairs interviewing each other about their family-of-origin "ecologies," drawing eco-maps of how they think their family-in-environment was constituted at some point during their childhood or adolescence. Many say it gives them a much altered, much enriched sense of their childhoods, a better sense of what the world was like for their parents.
2. Students in small groups working together on one student's intergenerational family narrative, using a genogram and exploring the family's heroes and heroines, legacies, loyalties, stories, myths, occupational patterns, and so on–or an "intergenerational interview" conducted before the entire class.
3. Family sculpting, using a student's own family, choreographing changes over time (e.g., when a new child was born, when the student went away to college, when mother went to work or father remarried) or imagining the future (e.g., How will a son's lover, a foster child, or an aging grandparent in need of care enter the family.)
4. Sharing family rituals or stories. In these exercises, in which I may use guided imagery with the whole class or have the students meet in small groups, students reach for special ritual times or a particular story that has become part of the family's folklore. These categories of life experience are very powerful windows into family culture and socialization, into family prescriptions and proscriptions for behavior. Sometimes I ask them to tap into the times and ways ethnicity is expressed in the family through ritual or story; other times we look at gender, for the ways in which the family, through ritual and story, taught the student to be male or female.

In the processing of these experiences, those who share an eco-map, a genogram, a story, a ritual, or a sculpture are asked first if they would like to share any meanings the particular story or experience holds for them. They are then asked if they are open to having the class ask questions about what has been offered, or whether they are willing to invite class members to "reflect" on what they have seen and heard, what meanings they make of it, what ideas they might have. These exercises tend to deepen student empathy for all families, to understand that the themes in their families are common to all families; furthermore, in a most "near-experience" way, to understand the power of family culture in shaping how we think and act and to respect the fact that it is extremely difficult to re-write a family narrative about how things ought to be.

REVISIONING "ASSESSMENT" AND "INTERVENTION"

As we work our way through intergenerational, structural, strategic, and systemic models of family theory and therapy, we look at the "what" that is seen as the focus of assessment and intervention in each major model. That is, what theory of change is driving this view, where is the location for change, and what are seen as the most effective paths to change? In each case, we use our own families/experiences, watch videotapes of practice from the model at hand, and/or read case materials. In the practice class, we frequently use role play to practice assessment and intervention strategies, "entering the model" and enacting family interviews. We try to include a range of kinds of families and problem situations, enacting the diversity in the wider society.

Students are encouraged to ask certain questions of each approach. These include:

1. What world view drives this model? What are the prior assumptions, texts, biases, sets of meanings? How are they obscured or made manifest in the work? Are the worker's assumptions/ meanings shared with the family, or are they "secret?"
2. What is the role of the therapist in this model? What is the nature of the relationship between the worker and client(s)?
3. How is "power" viewed and where is it located (in the system, couple, or family, in particular members of the family, in the worker, in systems outside of the family, in certain social discourses)? Is this approach empowering for this family? Why or why not? Is it subjugating? Does it privilege particular points of view?
4. In what ways is the theory/the model sensitive to cultural diversity? Economic diversity? Issues of gender? Is it heterosexist?
5. Even if its biases are rampant, are there good ideas here that should be retained? Can some of these ideas be transformed in a

way that may render the work more empowering, more collaborative, less subjugating, less pathologizing, less "truth"-oriented? Can the same "interventions" be used in a more collaborative, power-sharing way? (For example, the eco-map, genogram, and family sculpting are reconceptualized, not as maps of what really happened, but as pictures in time, stories; students are asked to consider how collaboration can be maximized in using them.) Or with structural, strategic, or systemic interventions, students imagine how they can be used in more empowering ways. (Can a couple be told by the worker that sometimes "reversing roles" for a week seems to help some couples who feel very stuck? Would they be interested in trying that out?)

6. Can we together suggest any new language that might capture the spirit of the ideas but be, for example, less hierarchical, less objectifying, closer to natural experience?

Finally, we move to a social constructionist stance, the final stance to be considered more formally as a model (although, as I have described, a constructionist critique and readings have been threaded throughout the course). Now we move actively and consciously to revisioning the concepts of "assessment" and intervention." The very words conjure up an image of an expert seeking truth and "objectively" analyzing what is wrong with someone else (albeit according to widely-accepted social and professional "stories" or "languages") and then planning a series of strategies or maneuvers designed to "attack" the problem. In my experience, these assessments and strategies, even when workers carefully contract, are rarely openly shared with clients. We do not tell individuals or families, usually, presumably for their own peace of mind, that we see them as "borderlines," "sociopaths," "narcissistic personality disorders," or "self-defeating personality disorders," as enmeshed, disengaged, dysfunctional, manipulative, and so on. Instead, we plan strategies to shift their self-concepts, their boundaries, their coalitions, their intergenerational patterns, often without sharing our thinking.

What might assessment and intervention mean in a more collaborative approach? Students are invited to explore this question, as we move to reading, viewing, and considering the emerging "social constructionist" ideas and practice approaches of Tom Andersen, Harlene Anderson and Harold Goolishian, Michael White and David Epston, Bill Lax, Charles Waldegrave and his colleagues, Kathy Weingarten, and others.

For one thing, it is clear that "assessment" and "intervention" as we know these terms, are ceasing to have the same meanings. These thinkers/practitioners do not assess people, and they do not usually even assess relationships. What is assessed is the history and the current story of the problem, as well as the influence this story/problem is having on their lives (Andersen, 1990; Lax, 1992; White & Epston, 1990). As Epston, White, and Murray (1992) frame it:

> a story can be defined as a unit of meaning that provides a frame for lived experience. It is through these stories that lived experience is interpreted. We enter into stories; we are entered into stories by others; and we live our lives through these stories. (p. 97)

These stories are not seen as mirroring "reality," but in the shared space of therapeutic conversation, no matter how seemingly bizarre, "each discourse is considered relevant if the participants consider it so, with the context of the conversation given an equal value to the content" (Lax, 1992, p. 79).

People perform their lives through these stories. In the conversation, they are invited to share how these performed stories impact on their well-being, their ideas about themselves, on their relationships inside and outside of the family, and to consider how they might change these stories so that they are more potentiating.[4] Anderson and Goolishian (1988) suggest that, since problems exist in language, problems become "dis-solved" when they are no longer "languaged" as problems by the group concerned, not according to some set of "objective" criteria. White (1988), White and Epston (1990), and Epston, White, and Murray (1992), in their "therapy of literary merit" see change as a process of "re-authoring."

> A re-authoring therapy intends to assist persons to resolve problems by (1) enabling them to separate their lives and relationships from knowledges/stories that are impoverishing; (2) assisting them to challenge practices of self and rela-

tionship that are subjugating; and (3) encouraging persons to re-author their lives according to alternative knowledges/stories and practices of self and relationship that have preferred outcomes. (Epston, White, & Murray, 1992, p. 108)

In this segment, in addition to reading descriptions of cases and seeing videotaped examples, class members serve as "reflecting teams" themselves, reflecting on each others' reflections in a recursive, dialogical process. In the practice class, which is a 10-week course, we often have time to take one special kind of problem of the students' choice (e.g., family violence, incest, alcohol or drug abuse, AIDS) to read about and to revision assessment and intervention from a social constructionist stance. Lively dialogue ensues, especially when some students who have worked in settings with impassioned political stances (e.g., battered women's shelters) begin to examine their own prior assumptions. Can we bring in alertness to power imbalances, to gender oppression, to irresponsible behavior without making pre-packaged treatment prescriptions and interventions? Can we "hear" everyone's story? Can we, for example, hear the paradox of "love and violence" in the same conversation (Goldner, Penn, Sheinberg, & Walker, 1990)?

We also consider "real world" barriers to integrating and using some of the approaches we have considered and discuss what possibilities exist for our own "unique outcomes" (Bruner, 1986), how we can better potentiate ourselves in agencies and settings that have not yet adopted a postmodern perspective.

CONCLUSION

In the final stage of this course, the social constructionist critique must be turned back upon itself; this is clearly a critique in its infancy. How can we ward off the reification of *this* story?

Moving one level up, or once again trying to stand "meta" to the meta-perspective, students are encouraged to think about the social and political context in which social constructionism itself, the conservative postmodern era of the 1970s and 1980s, has taken shape. What risks does this stance generate? What are its possible shortcomings? If "objective" criteria for the evaluation of ourselves and the families we work with are problematic, do we move ahead with *no* criteria, no way to hold ourselves or our clients responsible for their actions?

Minuchin (1991b) argues against the tendency, in postmodern thought, to "concentrate overmuch on the idiosyncratic 'story' of the individual family and ignore the social context that may actually dictate much of the 'plot' of their lives" (p. 49). In another cautionary tale (1991a), he warns:

> When the constructivists equate expertise with power, and develop a new technology of interventions that avoid control, they are only creating a different use of power. Control does not disappear from family therapy when it is re-named "cocreation." All that happens is that the influence of the therapist on the family is made invisible. Safely underground it may remain unexamined.

Minuchin goes on to wonder if postmodern theory rescues us from having to think about the evils and hopelessness in the world around us in an era when our government rechanneled resources to the rich and destroyed most of the programs we cared about.

Students consider these kinds of criticisms in the context of the mission of social work. Clearly, poverty, hopelessness, wife abuse, child sexual abuse, and other ills endemic in modern society and in the family, cannot be "storied away" or "languaged away" in conversation, however collaborative. We cannot become so infatuated with the beauty of the narrative metaphor that we ignore or fail to hold accountable the institutions and other forces that are powerful co-authors of the stories of these families. All stories are not equal. We can never allow the authors of those stories to become invisible, and we must continue to interrogate both the story-making context and the story metaphor itself. Furthermore, beyond such interrogation, as social workers we are in unique positions to serve as ethnographers of our own society; we hear every day the experiences and stories of people in pain in a way many people are insulated from. As clinicians, it is our responsibility to take these stories beyond the therapeutic context, to bear witness to them in public places, and to work to shape contexts in which more empowering stories may become possible.

On the clinical level, some beginning criteria for the evaluation of individual and family "stories" and "re-storying" are emerging in the literature and are implicit in the works we read. Gergen and Kaye (1992), for example, argue that we must move beyond a notion of narrative which simply suggests learning new meanings, to "developing new categories of meaning, to transforming one's premises about the nature of meaning itself" (p. 182). Clients need to be invited to "adopt multiple perspectives and accept the relativity of meaning itself" ". . . [in the] relational context in which behavior is situated" (p. 183). They go on to suggest

> the troubled person can be invited . . . to find exceptions to their predominating experience; to view themselves as prisoners of a culturally inculcated story they did not create; to imagine how they might relate their experience to different people in their lives; . . . to consider how they would experience their lives if they operated from different assumptions—how they might act, what resources they could call upon in different contexts, what new solutions might emerge; and to recall precepts once believed, but now jettisoned. (p. 183)

White (1992), who describes therapy as the generation of "alternative" or "preferred" narratives, leans on Derrida's deconstructionist approach in helping people to challenge and subvert "failure" stories, to bring forth the hidden contradictions in their stories, to ferret out repressed or oppressed or subjugated knowledges that have been considered "secondary, derivative, or worthless" (p. 136), to "appreciate the degree to which these narratives may have been impoverishing, to explore the nature of local, relational politics, and to deconstruct the ruses and practices of power and challenge inequities."

This is perhaps a lofty and difficult goal, to ask students to critique the critique. In a way, however, it is no more difficult than asking families to stand outside of their own stories long enough to consider more empowering stories. Can we do any less? In my experience our students are equal to the challenge and can, indeed, help us to co-construct more empowering languages for what we do.

NOTES

1. The term "great originals" was used by Lynn Hoffman (19) to describe, at least in one version of the family therapy field's his-"story," the men identified with founding the various "schools" of family therapy. Hoffman also describes the contributions of Virginia Satir, a social worker whose work was often disparaged in public gatherings of the "founders."

2. I am indebted to JoAnn Allen of Ann Arbor Center for the Family for sharing her work with me, and to the family who has allowed their story to be shared in professional education and training.

3. The first three of these exercises are described in some detail in Hartman and Laird (1983).

4. White (1988), in an article reprinted in White (1989) entitled "The Process of Questioning: A Therapy of Literary Merit," offers an extensive list of what he calls "unique outcome," "unique account," "unique redescription," and "unique possibility" questions. These are enormously useful for conceptualizing how the constructionist conversation may proceed.

REFERENCES

Allen, J., & Laird, J. (1990). Men and story: Constructing new narratives in therapy. *Journal of Feminist Family Therapy, 2*(3/4), 75-100.

Andersen, T. (Ed.). (1991). *The reflecting team: Dialogues and dialogues about the dialogues.* New York: Norton.

Andersen, T. (1987). The reflecting team: Dialogue and meta-dialogue in clinical work. *Family Process, 26*(4), 415-428.

Anderson, H., & Goolishian, H. (1992). The client is the expert: A not-knowing approach to therapy. In S. McNamee & K.J. Gergen, *Therapy as social construction* (pp. 25-39). Newbury Park: Sage.

Anderson, H., & Goolishian, H. (1988). Human systems as linguistic systems: Preliminary and evolving ideas about the implications for clinical theory. *Family Process, 27,* 371-394.

Aponte, H. (1976). The family school interview: An eco-structural approach. *Family Process,* 303-312.

Auerswald, E. (1985). Thinking about thinking in family therapy. *Family Process, 24,* 1-12.

Ault-Riche, M. (1986). *Women and family therapy.* Rockville, MD: Aspen Systems.

Bateson, G. (1979). *Mind and nature: A necessary unity.* New York: Dutton.

Bateson, G. (1972). *Steps to an ecology of mind.* New York: Ballantine.

Bowen, M. (1978). *Family therapy in clinical practice.* New York: Jason Aronson.

Boszormenyi-Nagy, I., & Spark, G. (1973). *Invisible loyalties: Reciprocity in intergenerational family therapy.* New York: Harper & Row.

Braverman, L. (Ed.). (1988). *Women, feminism, and family therapy.* New York: The Haworth Press, Inc.

Bruner, J. (1986). *Actual minds, possible worlds.* Cambridge, MA: Harvard University Press.

Carter, B., & McGoldrick, M. (Eds.). (1988). *The changing family life cycle: A framework for family therapy.* New York: Gardner Press.

Carter, B., & McGoldrick, M. (Eds.). (1980). *The family life cycle: A framework for family therapy.* New York: Gardner Press.

Cecchin, G. (1987). Hypothesizing, circularity, and neutrality revisited: An invitation to curiosity. *Family Process, 26,* 405-413.

Clifford, J., & Marcus, G. (1986). *Writing culture.* Berkeley, CA: University of California Press.

Collins, P.H. (1990). *Black feminist thought: Knowledge, consciousness, and the politics of empowerment.* London: Harper Collins.

Combrinck-Graham, L. (1985). A developmental model for family systems. *Family Process, 24,* 139-150.

Efran, J., & Clarfield, L. (1992). Constructionist therapy: Sense and nonsense. In S. McNamee & K.J. Gergen (Eds.), *Therapy as social construction* (pp. 200-217). Newbury Park: Sage.

Epston, D. (1989). *Collected papers.* Adelaide, So. Australia: Dulwich Centre Publications.

Epston, D., & White, M. (1992). *Experience, contradiction, narrative and imagination: Selected papers of David Epston & Michael White, 1989-1991.* Adelaide, So. Australia: Dulwich Centre Publications.

Epston, D., White, M., & Murray, K. (1992). A proposal for a re-authoring therapy: Rose's revisioning of her life and a commentary. In S. McNamee & K.J. Gergen (Eds.), *Therapy as social construction* (pp. 96-115). Newbury Park: Sage.

Geertz, C. (1973). *The interpretation of cultures.* New York: Basic Books.

Geertz, C. (1983). *Local knowledge.* New York: Basic Books.

Gergen, K. (1991). *The saturated self.* New York: Basic Books.

Gergen, K.J. (1985). The social constructionist movement in American psychology. *American Psychologist, 40,* 266-275.

Gergen, K.J., & Kaye, J. (1992). Beyond narrative in the negotiation of therapeutic meaning. In S. McNamee & K.J. Gergen (Eds.), *Therapy as social construction* (pp. 166-185). Newbury Park: Sage.

Germain, C.B. (1979). *Social work practice: People and environments.* New York: Columbia University Press.

Goldner, V. (1985). Feminism and family therapy. *Family Process, 24,* 27-31.

Goldner, V., Penn, P., Sheinberg, M., & Walker, G. (1990). Love and violence: Gender paradoxes in volatile attachments. *Family Process, 29,* 343-364.

Goodrich, T.J., Rampage, C., Ellman, B., & Halstead, K. (1988). *Feminist family therapy: A casebook.* New York: Norton.

Haley, J. (1987). *Problem-solving therapy.* San Francisco: Jossey-Bass.

Hare-Mustin, R. (1978). A feminist approach to family therapy. *Family Process, 17,* 181-194.

Hartman, A., & Laird, J. (1983). *Family-centered social work practice.* New York: Free Press.

Hartsock, N. (1983). The feminist standpoint: Developing the ground for a specifically feminist historical materialism. In S. Harding & M.B. Hintikka (Eds.), *Discovering reality; Feminist perspectives on epistemology, metaphysics, methodology, and philosophy of science.* Boston: D. Reidel.

Hoffman, L. (1990). Constructing realities: An art of lenses. *Family Process, 29*(1), 1-12.

Hoffman, L. (1981). *Foundations of family therapy.* New York: Basic Books.

Hoffman, L. (1992). A reflexive stance for family therapy. In S. McNamee & K.J. Gergen (Eds.), *Therapy as social construction* (pp. 7-24). Newbury Park: Sage.

Imber-Black, E. (1988). *Families and larger systems.* New York: Guilford.

Keeney, B. (1979). Ecosystemic epistemology: An alternative paradigm for diagnosis. *Family Process, 18*, 117-129.

Laird, J. (1984). Sorcerers, shamans, and social workers: The use of ritual in family-centered practice. *Social Work, 29*, 123-129.

Laird, J. (1988). Women and ritual in family therapy. In E. Imber-Black, J. Roberts, & R. Whiting (Eds.), *Rituals in families and family therapy* (pp. 331-362). New York: Norton.

Laird, J. (1986). Women, family therapists, and other mythical beasts. *American Family Therapy Association Newsletter*, No. 25, Fall, pp. 32, 35.

Laird, J. (1989). Women and stories: Restorying women's self-constructions. In M. McGoldrick, C. Anderson, & F. Walsh (Eds.), *Women in families: A framework for family therapy* (pp. 422-450). New York: Norton.

Laird, J. (1992). Women's secrets–Women's silences. In E. Imber-Black (Ed.). *Secrets in families and in family therapy.* New York: Norton.

Laird, J. (In press). "Thick description" revisited: Family therapist as anthropologist-constructivist. In E. Sherman & W. Reid (Eds.), *Qualitative research in social work.* New York: Columbia University Press.

Lax, W. (1992). Postmodern thinking in a clinical practice. In S. McNamee & K.J. Gergen (Eds.), *Therapy as social construction* (pp. 69-85). Newbury Park: Sage.

Lax, W. (1991). The reflecting team and the initial consultation. In T. Andersen (Ed.), *The reflecting team: Dialogues and dialogues about the dialogues.* New York: Norton.

Lax, W. (1989). Systemic family therapy with young children in the family: Use of the reflecting team. *Psychotherapy and the Family, 5*(3/4), 55-73.

Lerner, H. (1988). *Women in therapy.* Northvale, NJ: Jason Aronson.

Luepnitz, D. (1988). *The family interpreted: Feminist theory in clinical practice.* New York: Basic Books.

MacKinnon, L., & Miller, D. (1987). The new epistemology and the Milan approach: Feminist and sociopolitical implications. *Journal of Marital and Family Therapy, 13*, 139-155.

Madanes, C. (1981). *Strategic family therapy.* San Francisco: Jossey-Bass.

McGoldrick, M., Anderson, C., & Walsh, F. (1988). *Women in families: A framework for family therapy.* New York: Norton.

McNamee, S., & Gergen, K.J. (1992). *Therapy as social construction.* Newbury Park: Sage.

Miller, D., & Lax, W.D. (1988). Interrupting deadly struggles: A reflecting team model for working with couples. *Journal of Strategic and Systemic Therapies, 7*(3), 16-22.

Minuchin, S. (1974). *Families and family therapy.* Cambridge, MA: Harvard University Press.

Minuchin, S., & Fishman, H.C. (1981). *Family therapy techniques.* Cambridge, MA: Harvard University Press.

Minuchin, S. (1991a). The restoried history of family therapy. Unpublished paper.

Minuchin, S. (1991b). The seductions of constructivism. *Family Therapy Networker, 15*(5), 47-50.

Penn, P. (1985). Feed-forward: Future questions, future maps. *Family Process, 24,* 299-311.

Selvini-Palazzoli, M., Boscolo, L., Cecchin, G., & Prata, G. (1980). Hypothesizing–circularity–neutrality: Three guidelines for the conductor of the session. *Family Process, 19,* 3-12.

von Glasersfeld, E. (1984). An introduction to radical constructivism. In P. Watzlawick (Ed.), *The invented reality* (pp. 17-40). New York: Norton.

Waldegrave, C. (1990). *Social justice and family therapy.* Entire issue of *Dulwich Centre Newsletter,* No. 1, 5-47.

Walters, M., Carter, B., Papp, P., & Silverstein, O. (1988). *The invisible web: Gender patterns in family relationships.* New York: Guilford.

Watzlawick, P. (Ed.). *The invented reality.* New York: Norton.

Watzlawick, P., Weakland, J., & Fisch, R. (1974). *Change: Principles of problem formulation and problem resolution.* New York: Norton.

Weingarten, K. (1991). The discourses of intimacy: Adding a social constructionist and feminist view. *Family Process, 30,* 285-306.

Weingarten, K. (1992). A consideration of intimate and non-intimate interactions in therapy. *Family Process, 31,* 45-59.

White, M. (1992). Deconstruction and therapy. In D. Epston & M. White, *Experience, contradiction, narrative & imagination: Selected papers of David Epston & Michael White, 1989-1991* (pp. 109-151). Adelaide: So. Australia: Dulwich Centre Publications.

White, M. (1989a). The process of questioning: A therapy of literary merit. In M. White, *Selected papers* (pp. 37-46). Adelaide, S. Australia: Dulwich Centre Publications.

White, M. (1989b). *Selected papers.* Adelaide, So. Australia: Dulwich Centre Publications.

White, M., & Epston, D. (1990). *Narrative means to therapeutic ends.* New York: Norton.

Private Troubles and Public Issues: The Social Construction of Assessment

Phebe Sessions

SUMMARY. This paper describes a course for clinical social work students which presumes social work's core commitment to work at the psychosocial interface, but addresses this commitment using the conceptual tools of social constructionism. The course is based on social constructionist interests in the social and historical construction of professional knowledge; the value of multiple lenses to understanding any clinical phenomenon; and the inclusion of the position of the subject in the disciplined examination of any theory. We look at the social construction and location of commonly encountered psychiatric diagnoses; at the same time, we use these tools to examine the construction of the professional identities of the course participants.

INTRODUCTION: CONTEXT AND RATIONALE

In this paper I describe a course for advanced master's level social work students which has been designed both to teach and to embody constructivist principles for clinical practice. The course is offered to seniors in their final term of a 27-month program. Over the past three years, approximately 175 students have completed it. I describe, in the following pages: (1) the context and rationale

Phebe Sessions, PhD, is Associate Professor at the Smith College School for Social Work, Northampton, MA 01035 and is in private practice in Amherst, MA.

[Haworth co-indexing entry note]: "Private Troubles and Public Issues: The Social Construction of Assessment," Sessions, Phebe. Co-published simultaneously in *Journal of Teaching in Social Work* (The Haworth Press, Inc.) Vol. 8, No. 1/2, 1993, pp. 111-127; and: *Revisioning Social Work Education: A Social Constructionist Approach* (ed: Joan Laird) The Haworth Press, Inc., 1993, pp. 111-127. Multiple copies of this article/chapter may be purchased from The Haworth Document Delivery Center [1-800-3-HAWORTH; 9:00 a.m. - 5:00 p.m. (EST)].

leading to its development; (2) the constructivist perspective and its relationship to social constructionism and critical theory; (3) the course design; and (4) student and instructor experience of the course.

During the 1980s, the Smith College School for Social Work, known historically for its clinical specialization, began an intensive study of the courses, Sociocultural Concepts and Racism. Between these courses and required courses in personality theory, students were exposed to some balance between psychological and social theories on the foundation level. Practice instructors teaching foundation content could rely on both theoretical streams in order to develop a psychosocial synthesis in case analysis. As students moved into the advanced level of clinical specialization, however, they were no longer required to study social theories. As a result, the study of the various models of clinical social work practice, whether based in psychodynamic or systemic theories, became increasingly decontextualized as one "advanced" in the curriculum. The implicit message of this design is that social content, which might provide an enriched or even an alternative explanatory perspective on human issues, becomes increasingly irrelevant as one "advances" in the profession. Since many psychodynamically-trained clinicians, as well as family therapists, do use practice models which fail to make explicit their social assumptions, it is perfectly understandable that social work students can identify with and incorporate such beliefs without experiencing them as foreign.

As we re-examined our curriculum, we began to realize that our silence on social theory, our unstated assumptions, spoke volumes, constituting a most powerful learning experience. The acknowledgement of the importance of social variables in classroom discussions of cases had an "add on" and superficial quality, inadvertently communicating that social factors were ancillary rather than fundamental to analysis and clinical intervention. To include social theory in an integrated, meaningful way would require social science knowledge at an advanced level, skills in applying social concepts to clinical cases, and a willingness to live with the uncertainty which comes from attempting to forge awkward syntheses not well developed in the clinical literature.

As we confronted this educational challenge, we sought to understand the interests of the various groups with a voice or a stake in the educational experience of our students, including the profession of social work, the field of clinical practice, our students, and our faculty. The profession, as represented by the Council on Social Work Education, has clearly stated in its curriculum policy standards that material on oppression and on a range of cultural and socially stigmatized groups must be infused throughout the curriculum. This is a useful standard to inspire reflection and action. However, these guidelines are somewhat vague about the specialization level in social work education and quite deliberately leave much discretion to the programs. Therefore, the professional standards in social work education gave us no specific guidelines for what would constitute social theory at the advanced level or how a consideration of social issues should be different at the foundation and specialization levels.

As we examined the context of the field of clinical practice, we discovered contradictory pressures on social work education. On the one hand, the increasing use of managed health care settings mandated that students become more technically proficient in brief treatment models which demand rapid focus and delineation of a problem-to-be-solved. The brief therapy models available to clinical practitioners, however, are for the most part devoid of considerations of social context. Pressure to intervene in a technically precise manner seems to imply a narrowing of focus in social work; it represents a moving away from complexity, from consideration of the wide range of meanings and experiences which might help us better understand the relationships between people and their environments.

At the same time, unrelenting pressure to embrace the certainty of brief problem-solving and more technical models was being countered by a growing discourse among both psychoanalytic and family therapy theorists in which the scientific and humanistic claims of positivist mental health models were being challenged. The spread of a constructivist epistemology among theorists and practitioners from both psychoanalytic and family systems traditions signalled a radical shift in ideas about change. For one thing, no longer would particular theoretical constructs be superimposed upon client experience. Rather, the client's perspectives would be considered as important if not more important than that of the clinician; change would be co-constructed, emanating from the evolving dialogue between client(s) and clinician. Such a stance requires that clinicians avoid translating clients' experience into the terms of a favored theoretical framework; instead clinicians are enjoined to elicit a phenomenological description of clients' lives and experiences. The process of clinical intervention is then reconceptualized as a lifting of unnecessary restrictions on ways of understanding the client's problems and a liberating of the realm of possibilities which might allow for healing and the creation of alternative stories. Openness to a greater range of explanatory stories or discourses for understanding individuals or the "psychological," suggests the possible significance of alternative stories grounded in "knowing" about the social and the cultural. Understanding how society is structured, how discriminatory processes operate, and how cultural allegiances lead to alternative conceptualizations of problem construction and solution become a central part of the co-evolving discourse between client and clinician.

Although students have shown confidence in the profession by applying to schools of social work in increasing numbers, they have responded to these developments in the mental health field with a mixture of worry and interest. At the same time, clinical social work students express increasing concern about the conditions of clinical practice in the public agencies in which they work. The recession has led to severe cutbacks in state-supported community mental health programs, a major setting for clinical social work practice, and strict limitations on the length of treatment available to individual clients and families. Managed care has led to severe time restrictions in both psychiatric and medical in-patient care. Social work students are concerned about whether they will in fact be able to practice the clinical models they have worked so hard to learn, concerned that they will have to base their interventions on the requirements of the third-party reimbursers rather than what might be most helpful for the client. The pressure for specific outcomes restricts the range of explanatory variables that can be considered and leads to more standardized procedures, signalling a trend away from meaning-centered models of practice to problem-centered models.

At the same time, social constructionist inquiry based on a constructivist epistemology appears to students to provide some balance to the positivist, objectifying medicalized models they have learned (Atwood & Stolorow, 1986; Spence, 1982). Social constructionists advocate the use of multiple lenses to examine the same phenomenon, providing a metaperspective and rationale for the inclusion of seemingly irreconcilable points of view. A social constructionist stance appears to open the door to a new form of psychosocial synthesis. Social variables do not have to be reduced to the domain of the psychological; nor do they need to be "tagged on" awkwardly. Psychological and social discourses exist as separate but related and complementary linguistic conventions, as different conversations which vary in their power to establish meaning with every situation. When applied as lenses through which to view the same situation, they allow for depth perception.

Finally, the particular life stage and career position of the instructor were significant in the development of this course. Following nine years of clinical practice in well-funded community mental health settings which included much outreach into low income-communities, I had moved to social work education and had been teaching required practice for several years, like most faculty struggling to respond to student concerns and educational needs. Because of my continued interest in issues of practice in low-income communities, I completed my doctoral work in social policy rather than in clinical theory and practice. This course of study, which I completed during our self-study and reaccreditation process, enhanced my understanding of and appreciation for current social theories, including structural-functionalism, conflict theories, critical theory, and social constructionism. Furthermore, as a family therapist and classroom teacher, I had also developed the skills for eliciting multiple points of view, and had come to enjoy the process of developing depth perception in conversation through the layering of perspectives and stories.

CONSTRUCTIVISM, SOCIAL CONSTRUCTIONISM, AND CRITICAL INQUIRY: AN EPISTEMOLOGICAL FRAME

Many forces stimulated and shaped the development and direction of this course. These included: (1) A knitting together of what the faculty understood as the educational needs of our students for a reformulation of the psychosocial synthesis at an advanced level; (2) the continuing demand of the social work profession to find new ways of understanding this synthesis; (3) the emerging discourse of constructivism, with its valuing of multiple perspectives; and (4) the particular resources and interests of the faculty.

To help anchor our ideas and provide a link between past and present, I borrowed a phrase from C. Wright Mills (1959), "private troubles and public issues," a concept elaborated in the social work literature by William Schwartz (1974). During the 1960s, Mills had eloquently expressed his concern that American society greatly favored individually-oriented solutions to various forms of human suffering, at the expense of attention to the social conditions which create them. Psychological accounts of painful personal history are "privileged" over narratives in which, for example, personal history might be seen as a particular manifestation of a social dynamic. When sorrow is understood only as a personal or individual story generated by painful interactions among intimates, the solutions become individual ones too. Refocusing on the social dynamic would generate a call for political solutions in the public domain, rather than psychotherapeutic solutions in the private domain.

Mills' alternative formulation suggests ways in which current social theories can be used to provide an important context for understanding clinical theories, a set of ideas that seemed to me congruent with and supportive of emerging ideas in social constructionist epistemology. In a social constructionist stance, attention is drawn to the historical circumstances which shape the ideas that achieve prominence in a particular era. Clinical ideas are fundamentally rooted in the social discourses of the historical times in which they are generated. For example, both ego psychology and the early stages of family therapy were developed principally during the 1950s and 1960s when structural functionalism was a dominant way of understanding social processes. Neither the psychodynamic nor the family literature of the era makes much reference to the most central American structural-functional thinker of the times, Talcott Parsons. However, an analysis of the assumptions and basic tenets of structural-functionalism and the dominant clinical theories of the period indicate significant overlap and interpenetration of ideas (Sessions, 1991). Informing clinicians about these links helps them to understand, for example, that ego psychology did not develop simply in reaction to and as an elaboration of Freudian drive theory, but was also an expression of the interest in processes of accommodation central in Parsonian theory.

Moving to another level of inquiry, we might seek to understand why the decade of the 1950s produced such a priority. Social constructionism and critical theory provide a framework for addressing this problem, for us to explore such questions as: Who gets to determine the agenda for intellectual inquiry? Who benefits from the prominence of certain ideas and who loses? How does the social position and interest of the theoretician influence the theories espoused? Some critical theorists analyze the social dynamics of power in the evolution of ideas and include the self interest of those who control the flow of ideas as a fundamental part of their analysis. By exposing what is hidden in the negotiation of ideas, they seek to change both ideas and practices (Freire, 1974; Held, 1980).

Social constructionism and critical theory seemed to me to be two significant social currents, or in constructivist terms, discourses, it might be useful to bring to an examination of Mills' problem of the dynamic tension between private troubles and public issues. They provide the rationale for locating clinical theories in their historical context and seeking alternative explanations which might yield a broader and more penetrating analysis. By including the dynamics of power in understanding the construction of professional knowledge, they pierce the illusion of the neutrality of the detached observer. Though there are many critical theorists who do not subscribe to a constructivist epistemology, the generation of these questions about the context of professional knowledge is similar to the constructivist commitment to such ideas as: the need to include the observer in an understanding of the phenomena observed, the need to apply multiple lenses to the same phenomena for richer descriptions, and the significance of understanding that "truth" is a product of dialogue. The social theories used to analyze mental health models are epistemologically congruent with the constructivist metatheoretical perspective currently generating new approaches in clinical practice.

COURSE DESIGN

The course begins with an examination of its history and the perspectives and assumptions described above. I define my position and some of the interests that led me to develop the course, so that at least part of my stance is open for observation and negotiation. I then try to elicit their interests in taking on the dynamic of private troubles and public issues as a problem. What stake might they have in this inquiry as they approach graduation and assumption of a full professional role? While the plan of the course has been formulated out of my dialogical history in diverse professional settings, from dialogue with previous students, out of my clinical and policy educational experiences, from conversations with my clients, in concert with the standards of my profession and with my employer, the School for Social Work, the course can only be actualized in the present in conversation with the particular group of students who have elected to be there. Their participation is shaped not only by the stimulus of the course plan, but especially by all of the professionally-related conversations which affect their interests and concerns. Thus, we attempt to develop a contract which is within the parameters of our shared purpose and yet responsive to the actuality that what is most significant about what will occur cannot be pre-planned; it will evolve in our conversation.

The first topic to be considered after the development of the contract is the social location, significance, and meaning of professional knowledge, particularly clinical knowledge. Ideas developed by Michel Foucault (1984) about the relationship of power and knowledge, and by Barbara Ehrenreich (1989) about the professional-managerial class and the anxieties of middle-class life are used to help students to extend their understanding of their own professional self-interest. For some, they are perhaps considering the topic for the first time. We use Michael Lerner's (1986) extremely useful book, *Surplus Powerlessness: The Psychodynamics of Everyday Life and the Psychology of Individual and Social Transformation*, as a primary text. Lerner helps students to think about the relationship between the circumstances of work and the experience of well-being. The use of segments of documentary films which highlight the perspectives and interests of different social classes helps to bring the social class experience out of the obscurity in which American culture generally keeps it. Students are asked to share both their most demeaning and their most dignifying work experiences. The themes that emerge are then linked to ideas about the relationship between power and knowledge, the desire to be in charge of one's own self-definition, and the seductive hazards of taking charge of the self-definitions of others. Students have an opportunity to explore the responsibility which accompanies the power to delineate and provide names to others' experience.

THE SOCIAL CONSTRUCTION OF DIAGNOSIS

From there, we move to examine several diagnostic categories in historical context, focusing on the personality disorders and using the tools of social constructionism and critical theory. We use student case studies and systematically enter different "discourses," both psychological and social. The aim in discussion is to help students experience the explanatory power of different lenses. We also continually try to relate these case-centered discussions to the themes the class has identified early in the term as being significant for professional development and the choices they will confront in the field.

The personality disorders lend themselves to this kind of analysis because they are labels which are used in a manner which implies scientific reliability and validity, yet they are "disorders" which are quite specific to this culture (Kleinman, 1988). While the major mental illnesses may also be analyzed as social constructions, they occur cross-culturally in rather similar forms, suggesting a powerful biological and genetic substrate. The personality disorders, in contrast, seem to define and categorize behaviors that people in our society find offensive and unproductive. They provide the clearest examples of psychiatric diagnosis as social construction. The personality disorders are also significant because of the intensive interest which psychoanalytic theory has directed towards them in recent decades. Much of the elaboration of both object relations theory and self psychology within psychoanalysis has centered around efforts to understand the personality disorders. Until recently, however, there has been virtually no reference to the demographics or social contexts of the people examined and treated, using models grounded in these theories. For this paper, I will give examples of how we try to contextualize narcissistic personality disorder and borderline personality disorder. In the course, we also examine "acting out" behavioral diagnoses in terms of social processes of oppression and alienation.

Deconstructing Narcissistic Personality Disorder

"Narcissistic Personality Disorder" has been called by some social critics "the disorder of our times" (Lasch, 1979; Wachtel, 1983). For the most part, psychiatric and psychoanalytic discussions have failed to address the social contexts which have impacted on the personal and family experiences of the clients seeking help with this "disorder." Similarly, social critics have tended to use the diagnosis superficially and pejoratively to decry some aspects of our culture, without much reference to the now extensive psychoanalytic literature on the experience of pathological narcissism.

As with other personality disorders, the DSM-III-R lists the traits and behaviors which characterize Narcissistic Personality Disorder without attention to causality. It describes this "illness" as a profound disturbance in the ability to regulate self-esteem, which leads to grandiosity and aloofness in interpersonal relations as well as a tendency to either idealize or grossly devalue others.

Self-psychology has used what it has discovered from the analysis of persons with this symptom picture to reconstruct what it considers to be causative circumstances and interpersonal events. Through an appreciation of what has been missing from the early lives of these clients, self-psychology has provided an elaborate description of the kinds of early life experiences which seem to be necessary for people to develop a cohesive sense of self. Two kinds of experiences in early development appear to be critical: the experience of idealization of another, a caretaker from whom one can borrow or share in a sense of power and efficacy, and the experience of mirroring in which a more powerful caretaker appropriately and realistically responds to one's skills and capacities.

In self-psychological theory, it has been increasingly recognized that critical psychological processes of development are negotiated in not only an interpersonal but also an intersubjective field. Complete autonomy and insulation of the subject is an illusory goal; human beings, in a process that seems fundamental to psychological well-being, not only are reliant on each other most obviously in early childhood, but throughout the life span need others to function at least temporarily in affirming and admirable ways. Knowledge of another is most powerfully gained through empathy rather than objective observation, which presumes detachment of subject and object. With insufficient experiences of idealization and mirroring from an empathic other, people are left to compensate for deficits in self-structure by searching for the missing pieces in others while simultaneously disguising their own need.

Self psychology at the very least offers to clinicians a powerful model to explain poor self-esteem and vain grandiosity. It presents rich descriptions of exquisitely sensitive clinical interventions; its emphasis on empathy as both a way of knowing and as the critical experience which propels therapeutic change resonates with social work's humanistic orientation; and its increasing focus on intersubjectivity links it to constructivist epistemology. However, like other clinical models, it does not contextualize itself by asking questions about its own success in the competition of ideas, a process that would require social explanations.

Assuming that clinicians are correct in their observations that their caseloads are crowded with people who suffer from extreme over-sensitivity and vulnerability to slights, and who attempt to manage their images in the eyes of others by detachment and contempt, we then can ask two kinds of contextual questions. What about our social arrangements produces families and other intimate relationships which so frequently fail to provide the specific developmental experiences which self psychologists describe as necessary? Secondly, why are clinicians so focused on this problem that it should be described as "the disorder of our times"? Both the clinical phenomena which are categorized as a "disorder" and the discourse about the disorder are social constructions and can be analyzed using social theories. This requires that clinicians be able to step outside of their immersion in the clinical theory while using its terms and concepts to make links with social theories.

Lerner's (1986) book, *Surplus Powerlessness*, helps to provide some useful perspectives on the first question, as does *Habits of the Heart* (Bellah, Madsen, Sullivan, Swidler, & Tipton, 1985). These social commentators describe and analyze the breakdown of community in American life and the overvaluation of individualism as a cultural norm. American society distinguishes itself from both traditional as well as other highly industrialized societies by its disparagement and disavowal of human interdependence. Bellah and his colleagues show how the withdrawal from civic interests has led to an intensification of focus on the need to derive all of life's satisfactions within intimate relationships. As these relationships become overburdened with desire in a context in which it is shameful to admit need, relational success becomes even more difficult to achieve.

Lerner presents a somewhat similar analysis but focuses on the redirection of energy from the frustrating and disqualifying experiences of labor to the family; his conclusions are similar. He describes the intrusion of market place thinking, where the value of exploitation of resources is prominent, into the intimate domain of family life. In the context of these cultural analyses, narcissistic personality disorder begins to look less like a distinct psychopathological syndrome and more like an exaggeration of what American culture asks its citizens to do: to conceal their vulnerabilities behind a mask of arrogance and indifference and to get what they need from others without revealing much about themselves. This is a culturally adaptive but profoundly disappointing strategy.

To offer answers to the second question of why this discourse about narcissistic personality disorder has gained such prominence in the mental health field at this time is more difficult, in part because clinicians, like other professionals, avoid acknowledgement of the power/knowledge nexus. They tend to describe relationships of ideas to each other, rather than to show how ideas emerge from negotiations of power and influence. Since I have not done a full analysis of the historical development and context of self psychological ideas, I can only make suggestions about the kind of questions which should be addressed. What is known about the demographics of the client population about whom this clinical theory was developed? In what kinds of settings were they seen? We know that self psychological ideas were originally developed within the framework of psychoanalytic treatment; however, more recently self psychologists have been penetrating the full range of public and private mental health settings and working with a wide range of clientele. How has this affected the content of their theory? Why has the mental health field been so receptive to this set of ideas during this period? With its emphasis on empathy, self psychology has sometimes been accused of being too "soft" and "supportive" (perhaps "feminine") a practice model, too enthusiastically embraced by social workers. How can our understanding of gender and class dynamics in the evolution of professional knowledge deepen our appreciation of this model?

These kinds of contextual questions may seem to frontline clinicians to be too removed from the decisions they have to make to be useful in practice. However, I have found that when students use social theories to contextualize clinical theories they acquire an important critical perspective which they report makes them feel they are both thinking and practicing at a deeper level. It affects how flexibly they use the practice model and the extent to which they can recognize any theory as one explanatory model among many. Clinicians who hold and apply theories rigidly tend to encourage the expression of some aspects of their clients' experience and to ignore the communications which fall outside the purview of their preferred theory. A multitheoretical capacity, on the other hand, has the potential to allow clinicians to include a much wider range of experience as fundamental to the clinical task.

The Social Construction of Borderline Personality Disorder

A second personality disorder which we subject to social analysis is "Borderline Personality Disorder" (BPD). The DSM-III-R provides a description of traits and behaviors of "borderlines." They are seen as desperately frightened of abandonment, alternatively clinging to and disparaging or attacking a succession of significant others in relation to whom they play out their internal dynamics. Their fear of aloneness repeatedly drives them into unstable attachments where they experience dramatic shifts in mood. They also are thought to be confused about their identity so that their images of themselves change with their context.

Object relations theorists, especially in the United States, have often focused on the borderline experience in order to develop their ideas about the nature of secure attachments and the negotiation of a distinct self, separated from fusion with the environment. Borderline Personality Disorder is seen in psychoanalytic theory as fundamentally a problem of secure attachment and failure to negotiate individual identity due to threats of abandonment from the significant others who are perceived to be essential to existence.

In recent years, some social perspectives have been brought to bear on this diagnosis via feminist theory and trauma theory (Herman, 1992; Herman & VanderKolk, 1987). First, it was discovered that over two thirds of people hospitalized with this diagnosis are women. Like depression, BPD is a category much more frequently applied to women. Other studies subsequently indicated that a significantly higher percentage of people diagnosed with BPD in inpatient settings have suffered from sexual abuse than the rest of the patient population (Herman & VanderKolk, 1987). Therefore, we may reasonably ask: Why do women more commonly show the set of behaviors called "borderline?" What meanings do these behaviors have for various professionals and why has this diagnosis become so central to the development of psychoanalytic theory? If the diagnosis were to be reconceptualized as a response to, or residue of, trauma, how would that affect not only clinical practices, but how people diagnosed with BPD are valued in the mental health culture?

The history of ideas about women and trauma appears to be fertile ground for understanding the political and ideological context that shapes psychiatric theory. In recent years, there have been different accounts and interpretations of the changes in Freud's thinking, from his first observation that his hysterical women patients appeared to have been sexually traumatized by trusted male adults, to his revocation of the seduction theory and exclusive focus on the intrapsychic world of internal drives and psychological defenses (Herman, 1992). Controversy about the actuality of traumatic events has shifted from the focus on hysteria, which has disappeared from official psychiatric nomenclature (though not from analytic theory), and resurfaced around BPD and the dissociative disorders.

In this course, we help students broaden and deepen their thinking about this clinical phenomenon. The psychological literature about women's development (Jack, 1991; Jordan, Kaplan, Miller, Stiver, & Surrey, 1991) and literature about the dynamics of gender oppression (Benjamin, 1988; Collins, 1990; Okin, 1989) are important to the deconstruction of women's "disorders." "Self-in-relation" theorists challenge the emphasis of some developmental theories on the central importance of separation and individuation processes in the psychological health of women. They see models which prioritize autonomy as synonymous with health as failing to understand the essential continuity of relationships in women's lives and relying on a model of development which privileges male values. Using a theoretical model which emphasizes relational continuity as essential to health to reexamine the plight of the women experiencing symptoms designated as "borderline" casts a different light on the condition. It shifts the focus from the failure to develop autonomy to the continuity of effort, however awkward and frustrating, of these women to do what they understand as women they need to do. They perform certain aspects of a gendered role in a highly exaggerated form. An empathic understanding of their efforts and frustrations requires use of a gender-informed theory.

Theories of gender oppression examine the effects of women's relative lack of power in every area of social life: personal relationships between men and women, the generation and acceptance of knowledge claims; and institutional authority. An understanding of gender oppression is critical for understanding common "borderline" symptoms, particularly the tendency to direct aggression against the self. It also is useful for understanding the low regard for borderlines among mental health professionals who share in the general cultural distaste for interpersonal demandingness, displays of intense affect, and neediness in women.

The increasing acceptance of trauma theory will probably remove substantial numbers of women from the category of borderline personality disorder altogether. Clinicians treating women with trauma histories seek to uncover the silenced stories which have been concealed by social as well as personal dynamic processes. In many clinical programs for trauma survivors, there is a strong emphasis on the need to connect with others with similar experiences in order to destigmatize the problem and empower the clients. A trauma focus not only changes the understanding of the problem, it also adds a vital social dimension to the therapy.

EXPERIENCING THE COURSE:
A BIRD'S-EYE VIEW
FROM STUDENTS AND INSTRUCTOR

Students have seen this course as a model for psychosocial integration and an important experience in their professional development. They have particularly valued the process of including their professional concerns in the development of the educational contract and integrating a consideration of these concerns throughout the course. Students have expressed appreciation for what they experience as the parallel process of the course, a synchrony between the course content and process. The core ideas and values of the course were enacted as well as analyzed. For a final assignment, students are asked to develop a five-year plan for their professional development and reflect on their plan using the social theories with which they have been working during the course. This assignment generates a fair amount of anxiety. Students are accustomed to analyzing what has already transpired in their lives and the lives of others. Imagining themselves into a future for which they are responsible yet cannot entirely control, and clarifying the social importance of their choices, is a challenging task. However, students approach the assignment very seriously and use it as an important termination experience from the School for Social Work.

As an instructor, I have greatly enjoyed teaching this course. Though I have always tried to work collaboratively with students in an educational contract, I have observed that the subject matter of this course reduces the usual hierarchy between teacher and students, the sense that the teacher mostly "knows" and the students mostly "receive" and try to duplicate the teacher's knowledge. I have a greater sense of reciprocity in the experience. Finally, I find myself reading widely and far afield for this course. Most of this reading never leads to direct classroom assignments. But it continues a dialogue which I have in my mind with the students who have been in this course and which I find professionally enriching and valuable for me as a teacher and learner.

REFERENCES

Atwood, G. and Stolorow, R. (1986). *Structures of subjectivity.* Hillsdale, NJ: Analytic Press.

Bellah, R., Madsen, R., Sullivan, W.M., Swidler, A., & Tipton, S.M. (1985). *Habits of the heart: Individualism and commitment in American life.* Berkeley: University of California Press.

Benjamin, J. (1988). *Bonds of love: Psychoanalysis, feminism and the problem of domination.* New York: Pantheon.

Collins, P. (1990). *Black feminist thought: Knowledge, consciousness, and the politics of empowerment.* New York: Routledge.

Ehrenreich, B. (1989). *Fear of falling: The inner life of the middle class.* New York: Pantheon.

Freire, P. (1974). *Education for critical consciousness.* New York: Seabury Press.

Foucault, M. (1984). Truth and power. In P. Rabinow (Ed.), *The Foucault reader.* New York: Pantheon.

Gergen, K. (1985). The social constructionist movement in modern psychology. *American Psychologist, 40,*(3), 317-329.

Held, D. (1980). *Introduction to critical theory.* Berkeley: University of California Press.

Herman, J. & VanderKolk, B. (1987). Traumatic antecedents of borderline personality disorder. In B. VanderKolk (Ed.), *Psychological trauma.* Washington, DC: American Psychiatric Press.

Herman, J. (1992). *Trauma and recovery.* New York: Basic Books.

Jack, D. (1991). *Silencing the self: Women and depression.* Cambridge: Harvard University Press.

Jordan, J., Kaplan, A., Miller, J., Stiver, I., & Surrey, J. (1991). *Women's growth in connection.* New York: Guilford Press.

Kleinman, A. (1988). *Rethinking psychiatry: From cultural category to personal experience.* New York: Free Press.

Lasch, C. (1979). *The Culture of narcissism.* New York: Norton.

Lerner, M. (1986). *Surplus powerlessness: The psychodynamics of everyday life and the psychology of individual and social transformation.* Oakland, CA: Institute for Labor and Mental Health.

Mills, C.W. (1959). *The sociological imagination.* New York: Oxford University Press.

Okin, S. (1989). *Justice, gender, and the family.* New York: Basic Books.

Schwartz, W. (1974). Private troubles and public issues: One social work job or two? In P. Weinberger (Ed.). *Perspectives on social welfare,* 2nd edition. New York: MacMillan.

Sessions, P. (1991). *Family therapy and urban poverty.* Unpublished dissertation.

Spence, D. (1982). *Narrative truth and historical truth.* New York: Norton.

Wachtel, P. (1983). *The poverty of affluence: A psychological portrait of the American way of life.* New York: Free Press

So Much for the Bell Curve: Constructionism, Power/Conflict, and the Structural Approach to Direct Practice in Social Work

Ruth R. Middleman
Gale Goldberg Wood

SUMMARY. This essay presents our understanding of construction-ism, our structural approach to practice, and what we consider important issues of power and conflict in the United States. One practice activity–consciousness-raising–is used to illustrate what practice informed by these three perspectives looks like. Some ways to help students understand social constructionism are elaborated.

"Ah! Here is a subject," exclaimed the king, when he saw the little prince coming. And the little prince asked himself: "How could he recognize me when he had never seen me before?" He did not know how the world is simplified for kings. To them, all men are subjects.

St. Exupery, *The Little Prince*, p. 41.

Ruth R. Middleman, EdD, MSW, is Professor, Raymond A. Kent School of Social Work, University of Louisville, Louisville, KY. Gale Goldberg Wood, EdD, MSW, is also Professor at the Kent School of Social Work in Louisville.

[Haworth co-indexing entry note]: "So Much for the Bell Curve: Constructionism, Power/Conflict, and the Structural Approach to Direct Practice in Social Work," Middleman, Ruth R., and Gale Goldberg Wood. Co-published simultaneously in *Journal of Teaching in Social Work* (The Haworth Press, Inc.) Vol. 8, No. 1/2, 1993, pp. 129-146; and: *Revisioning Social Work Education: A Social Constructionist Approach* (ed: Joan Laird) The Haworth Press, Inc., 1993, pp. 129-146. Multiple copies of this article/chapter may be purchased from The Haworth Document Delivery Center [1-800-3-HA-WORTH; 9:00 a.m. - 5:00 p.m. (EST)].

129

INTRODUCTION

From a constructionist perspective, understanding is a matter of interpretive construction by the experiencing person (von Glasersfeld, 1984). The king orders and organizes his world in terms of his position in it. For a king all others are subjects, which in another sense renders them objects.

Constructionist thinking appears in philosophy, psychology, anthropology, and other social sciences. Certain scholars in these disciplines are embracing an epistemology that claims there is no reality apart from one's construction of it in dialogue with others. Since the content of social work is the experience of the other, apprehending the elusive meaning of another's life experiences with some degree of fidelity becomes *the* challenge–the stuff of observation, definition, and interpretation.

But it is hard to allow other persons to have their own experience. The all too human tendency is to presume the other's situation is similar to something in one's own life or the lives of other clients, and to try to speed up the process of understanding by telling oneself, "I know about this," and telling the other, "Yes, yes, I understand." In so doing one takes away the experience of the other. In one's eagerness to connect with the other, one may transform and distort the other's message by making it into something that fits with what one has known. It is imperative that social work professionals and students learn to suspend understanding deriving from their own preconceptions (previous understandings) as others describe their experiences and the special meanings they have for them.

In our book, *The Structural Approach to Direct Practice* (Goldberg Wood & Middleman, 1989; Middleman & Goldberg, 1974), we weave together social constructionist and power/conflict perspectives. In the latter perspective, society is seen as a complex of conflicting and competing groups. In this chapter, we present our understanding of constructionism, our structural approach to practice, and what we see as important issues in a power/conflict perspective. One practice activity–consciousness raising–is used to illustrate what practice informed by these three perspectives looks like. Finally, some ways to help students understand social constructionism are elaborated.

CONSTRUCTIONISM

Constructionism is about perception, and thus perspective. It is about how people look at things, seeing them differently, and how their individual interpretations merge into their ways of understanding the world (Goldberg & Middleman, 1980; Middleman & Goldberg, 1985). It is about the ways in which they talk to each other about it, creating through such talk with others an agreement about how things are. It is through such dialogues or conversations that meaning is socially constructed (Berger & Luckmann, 1967). Meaning is therefore local (Geertz, 1983), not universal; and historically situated, not timeless.

In the last decade these ideas have crept into the literature that informs social work. Family theory has been one rich source of constructionist ideas (see, e.g., Goolishian & Anderson, 1987; Hoffman, 1990; Mittleman & Friedman, 1991; Tomm & Lannamann, 1988; Watzlawick, 1984; and Weingarten, 1991). Constructivist thinking has also begun to appear in the more general social work literature (see, e.g., Dean, 1989; Dean & Fenby, 1989; Dean & Fleck-Henderson, 1992; Goldstein, 1990; Hartman, 1991; Middleman & Goldberg Wood, 1991b; Witkin, 1990; and Witkin & Gottschalk, 1988).

Some key aspects of constructionism are: All knowledge is constructed and the knower is an intimate part of the known (Goodman, 1984); language creates reality (Bruner, 1986); people are historically situated when they construct their views of reality; thinking and understanding change in relation to the shifts of social processes (Gergen, 1985; Witkin & Gottschalk, 1988); objectivity is impossible in the human sphere (Gergen, 1991); people are the final arbiters of the meaning of their own experiences (Weick, 1991); these experiences are expressed in narratives or stories (Bruner, 1986, 1990; Gergen & Gergen, 1986; Hartman, 1990; Laird, 1989); and "there exist as many . . . constructions as there are individuals . . . science itself is such a construction. . . ." (Guba & Lincoln, 1989, p. 43), one among many intellectual activities alongside of, but not above, literary criticism, jurisprudence, history, and so forth (Brown, 1992). And no one is an expert on another's situation (Hoffman, 1990).

From a constructionist perspective, truth is nothing more than an agreement among self-other(s) to see things in a particular way, not the only possible way. Each like-minded group[1] has its own truth which comes out of its own experience. There are many groups and there are many truths. But some group's truths are given more credence than others because they have the power to impose their constructions on those with less power. Most often, the so-called truth of the dominant group becomes THE TRUTH, determining what is normative, and thus right. Such truths are taught and passed on by the family, the peer group, the school, the church, and the popular media. A memorable Pfeiffer cartoon captures the impact of the power elite on subordinates. An old man sitting in a chair muses through several frames: "I used to think I was *poor*, then they told me I wasn't poor, I was *needy*. Then they told me it was self-defeating to think of myself as needy, I was *deprived*. Then they told me deprived was a bad image, I was *underprivileged*. Then they told me underprivileged was overused. I was *disadvantaged*. I still don't have a dime. But I have a great vocabulary" (Pfeiffer, 1965).

For any given group, the environment is composed of other groups and the institutions that have been created and operate to maintain the power of the dominant groups, thus preserving the status quo. Consideration of this status quo must transport one's thinking into the political/economic realm–a construction of a reality created and perpetuated by the interests of Western white males (Gatens, 1991; Hekman, 1990), a construction which Miller calls "patriarchal necessity" (1990, p. 8).

THE STRUCTURAL APPROACH

The structural approach is a model of practice for direct work with clients and others that is centrally focused on the needs of people who are powerless, stigmatized, and oppressed. The term structure refers to *social* structures, such as the local school, the welfare office, or the public transit system. The structural approach presupposes that clients are not necessarily the cause of their problems and therefore not always the appropriate targets for change efforts. Institutionalized bias, as expressed in such forms as racism, classism, or sexism, produces obstacles that are rampant in clients' social worlds; thus environmental constraints need to be dealt with first.

The environment is neither neutral nor passive. Nor is it mere context for the thinking and acting of the assumedly autonomous individual(s) posited by liberal humanists, including those within social work's tradition whose humanistic assumptions accent client autonomy and self-determination, as if the sociopolitical environment were merely the stage for life's dramas. Rather, the environment is an active and often oppressive performer that constrains one's actions, especially the freedom of any non-dominant group (e.g., women, persons of color, elderly people, lesbians and gay men), to make a consequential impact on society. If clients do gain the opportunity for self-determination, it is usually because of the courage and commitment of the social worker, as the following excerpt from a structurally-oriented social worker in a nutrition program illustrates:

> I worked with an older woman who received Meals-on-Wheels in a second story apartment. She used a wheelchair and had taken in a young, homeless man for companionship and also as "bodyguard." One night the apartment was gutted by fire. The young man was able to carry the woman to safety and neither was injured. The woman made it clear to both the police and Adult Services that what she needed was an apartment for two. Separate living arrangements could be made immediately for them at shelters for the homeless. The woman refused to go and the young man would not leave her. Instead, the two of them lived in the shade of a tree during the day and slept in the young man's disabled van at night. It was August.
> Was the woman competent to judge that her housing needs would be safely met outside? Was it okay for her to exercise her right to self-determination? Discontinuing the woman's meals would have forced a decision against her will. Adult Services did not seek a mental inquest warrant and we continued to deliver her meals each day–under the tree. This continued for seven days, until an apartment was found and the two moved in.
> All of the workers, volunteers, and the landlord were upset by the less than adequate living arrangements during the interim. If the story had not had a "happy ending," there may well

have been justifiable charges of criminal neglect lodged against the police, Adult Services, and the Nutrition Program.

A client's right to self-determination is a difficult thing to accept and respect in the face of your own feelings and those of the community that the client is making what appears to be a crazy choice. But this challenge–to respect the right of self-determination–is not an option; it is a professional obligation.

This approach to direct practice emphasizes power and empowerment: helping people connect with needed resources, changing social structures that limit them, and negotiating problematic situations. The structural approach offers a socio-economic/political explanation for social problems, an explanation that does not blame the victims for the pain they suffer. As Mirowsky and Ross (1989) found, conditions such as joblessness, homelessness, lack of education, and barriers of class and status cause acute distress because these social factors prevent people from having a sense of control over their lives. Their despair "is deeply personal. Their problems are deeply social . . ." (1989, 3). Unfortunately, research with this slant remains largely ignored today in favor of individual and psychological factors.

CONSTRUCTIONISM AND THE STRUCTURAL APPROACH

Constructionist thinking plays a significant role in structural social work, for the practice hinges on attention to perceptual differences and differences in frames of reference. A central tenet of both constructionism and the structural approach is the belief that *clients* are the experts on their own pain. Students must therefore learn to listen to their clients, to learn from *them* about their pain, and to explore together ways to alleviate it. But they must be taught to listen as *conferees*–not as therapists or counselors.

The structural approach accents the term "conferee," a term which notes a collaborative, non-hierarchical worker-client relationship dynamic through which the work begins. The terms "therapist" and "counselor" (occupational titles) produce hierarchy and power differentials. These titles proclaim that the social worker is privileged/privy to expertise, a great knower who will diagnose and treat. We prefer to conceptualize the relationship of social worker and client(s) as a partnership where both parties, as conferees, have a conference, are active, "diagnostic" equals, and are capable of the task of finding or inventing ways to relieve some of the problems.

A key principle in the approach is to look beyond the client to see if others are in the same fix. If there are others, then a structural change must be attempted, that is, a change in whatever community structures are exacerbating the client(s') problems, and/or not alleviating the pain they are supposed (mandated?) to ease. If no such structure exists, then worker and client(s) are asked to invent one, such as a self-help group or a "trade unit" (e.g., bartering child care for transportation to the grocery). Some situations call for advocacy (Goldberg Wood & Middleman, 1991a) and the creation of new programs.

POWER/CONFLICT

One reason structural social work is important is because the majority of clients seen by social workers are poor and powerless. They are forced to accept the meanings given to their situations by powerful others who label them and try to regulate their behavior through schools, courts, and elsewhere. The ignored meanings of these non-dominant groups, with their poignant and painful experiences, are also highlighted in postmodern feminist thought in which the deconstruction[2] of literature and history texts is used to uncover the suppressed voices of the silenced, marginalized, and excluded populations (Hutcheon, 1989; Weedon, 1987). Similarly, deconstruction of American history surfaces a "reality," a set of meanings that differs from that promoted in school texts–a history of oppression of slaves and serfs, of women, and of racial and ethnic minorities (Searle, 1990). Deconstruction has contributed to a growing skepticism of the written word with its biasing time and place aspects that affect meanings and messages. Recently, deconstruction was used to analyze the DSM-III, exposing the problems of meaning loss that accompany any effort to develop comprehensive category schemes (Cutler, 1991).

While the social constructionist recognizes that there are multiple views of reality, all constructions are not equal. One of the reasons they are not equal has to do with power, a dynamic generally neglected in social work practice (Hasenfeld, 1987). As the deconstruction of literature and the social sciences has begun to show, society is a complex of conflicting groups competing for access to scarce opportunities, resources, and rewards. Social order is founded on force and constraint, on the domination by some and the subjugation of others. Because of cultural valuation, some groups are ascribed greater power, giving them greater access to these resources than other groups. In our society, white males control the political and economic spheres, as well as the schools, the churches, and the media, thereby ensuring that their voices are heard. Their history is learned in the school and their construction of reality is projected through television, radio, and newspapers while the voices of the subjugated are all but silenced.

We are not living in a culturally plural society. *Cultural pluralism* "implies a universalist democratic culture of taking in, respecting, and integrating into itself various ethnic cultures" (Lippert, 1991/2, p. 379). This is a rosy view that does not fit with the experiences of oppressed and marginalized peoples. And it does not reflect the politics of domination and suppression. *Multiculturalism* is a term that better fits the client's experience of how things are: a complex of disparate groups that struggle with each other for their own differing interests and power.

Foucault (1977) recognized that power is exercised for political and economic advantage and that "we . . . must base our analysis of power on the study of the techniques and tactics of domination" (p. 102). His understanding of power dynamics grounds the power/conflict world view that is central to the structural approach. He saw power and knowledge as inseparable. "Power produces knowledge. . . . There is no power relation without the correlative constitution of a field of knowledge, nor any knowledge that does not presuppose and constitute at the same time, power relations" (1979, pp. 27-8). Thus he spoke of power/knowledge.

Foucault described three different ways in which power/knowledge is used to transform people into objects and thereby control them. One means of objectification involves *the creation of disciplines* which study the individual "scientifically." Each discipline has its own regimes of power and truth, within which matters of what constitutes the normal and the deviant, the acceptable and the extraneous, are determined. And each discipline establishes a means of inquiry which gives it status as a "real" science. Examples include the transformation of geography from a grade school subject to an erudite doctoral level discipline (Goodson & Dowbiggin, 1990), and the effort of social workers to pursue predictive, statistical research at the expense of descriptive, qualitative methods of study in order to be considered a profession in Flexner's (1915) terms and to gain university acceptance.

Another means of objectification and control involves *classifying and dividing practices*. Often, in terms of discipline-defined categories, people are labeled, distributed, and manipulated. A clear example of this affecting social work practice is the DSM-III-R which, as Kirk and Kutchins (1992) point out, shows how a small group of researchers in the name of psychiatric reliability were able to promote their beliefs about mental illness, thus dominating the mental health establishment.

Thirdly, people become objects through *the voluntary study of one's self* with a legitimized other, for example, through confessions with clerics where the authority prescribes, appreciates, and intervenes in order to judge, punish, forgive, and console; and through discourse with psychotherapists (Rabinow, 1984).

CONSCIOUSNESS RAISING

The structural approach has a "minimax principle" for times when needed resources are not forthcoming and neither mediating nor advocacy by the worker will suffice. This principle directs the worker to raise consciousness. As a constructionist would suggest, people act in the world as they perceive it. Their actions are heavily influenced by an environment where power is reserved for and preserved by those who have it. For many people, especially women and minority groups, their cultural surround is stacked against them. They are other. They are the non-wealthy, the non-white, the non-male. They have been socialized to expect fewer opportunities and rewards, lesser jobs, and less adequate education; and they believe that they are, in fact, inferior. This is what Jones

(1971) meant when he told black people "the problem isn't Mr. Charlie; it's what Mr. Charlie has done to your mind" (p. 4)–convinced you to accept less. It accounts for the belief among women and minority groups that they are the source of their own problems. And in believing it, they blame themselves for their plight and become partners in their own oppression. This is what makes consciousness-raising in structural social work necessary.

Consciousness-raising is necessary "when people present problems that obviously incriminate structural conditions . . ." (Longres & McCloud, 1980, p. 275). In such instances the personal is political, and oppressed persons need to understand this. They need a new perspective on the problem; they need to learn that they are not to blame for it.

Consciousness-raising is not an effort to deny the experience of oppressed people. To the contrary, it speaks to the development of a more empowering narrative. It helps clients expand their narratives (the stories they tell themselves) to include an understanding of their personal experiences in terms of the political experience of all those in their ascribed category. This expanded awareness is a "critical" consciousness, one which submits their experience to analysis, one which involves collaborating with others to work against the vested interests of more powerful groups. It is not a "naive" consciousness, one which locates the blame in individual inadequacy, nor a "magical" one that accepts what is as fate or God's will (Friere, 1974).

The ideal medium for consciousness-raising is the small group, which is known to offer the opportunity for mutual support and to provide an intimate situation for helping people deal with the traumas they have suffered, moving beyond them to political action. The structural approach's directive to "look beyond the client" often leads to working with groups toward social and political action rather than treating client "inadequacies." In these groups it is essential that participation be voluntary, non-hierarchical, and non-coercive (Hawkesworth, 1990). In a group, people can move toward freeing themselves from self-blame and the definitions foisted upon them by the power-holders. Ultimately they can engage in collective attempts to change those environmental structures that impact negatively on their lives. Parsons' (1991) work with Head Start mothers provides an example: Group members confronted the housing manager, intervened with the school and the recreation director, led a boycott of the local grocery store when the owner refused to lower his check-cashing price, and organized transportation to a supermarket. They ultimately joined a citizens' action council to work on broad community issues.

Sometimes consciousness-raising is necessary and a group experience is not possible or indicated. No matter. The client still needs to know that the problem is not inside her, that she deserves better even though nothing better will be given to her. Such is the situation below, taken from a structurally-oriented social work student record:

> Mrs. Lopez had just received a cut-off notice from the gas and electric company and she was very upset. "I've never gotten this far behind before. I just had to repair the car so we could have reliable transportation to the hospital for my husband's treatments. I'll have to do better but I don't know how."

> "You sound like you're mad at yourself," I said. She said, "You bet I am. You know he needs electricity to keep his heart monitor going." "It's not your fault," I replied. "I see a lot of people who get cut-off notices. It happens at one time or another to practically everyone trying to live on AFDC. Hardly anyone can make ends meet while trying to pay high utility bills." "I know I can't," she replied. I said, "The electric company wants to make all the money they can and they're allowed to get away with it because they have a monopoly." She replied, "That makes me angry." "Yes. You and a lot of other people," I said.

At times the consciousness that needs raising is that of co-workers. Structural social work guides practice within the organizational context as well as with clients. Organizations, like any subculture, "socialize their members into the norms of the organizational subculture and thus into defining reality in the light of the overt and manifest functions of the organization" (Scott, 1989, 45). Often the realities defined by the organization are at odds with client realities and the preferred practices of social workers. This creates conflict and tension for the worker. To reduce the felt tension, workers may adapt to the agency's way of seeing things. Over time, these workers forget that they adapted. This is what makes consciousness-raising with co-workers necessary.

TEACHING

Students need to know that, within a constructionist framework, there are many knowings and that ambiguity is here to stay. They need to learn that meanings are multiple, that theories are metaphors, that meaning making is local and contextual. They need to learn that they will have to make many decisions with no one to tell them that they are right. And ultimately they have to accept that this is how professional life will be.

The teacher can encourage students to examine the underlying assumptions of the practice one teaches as well as those that underlie other approaches to practice they may also be learning. She can also encourage students to examine the language in which any practice is packaged, to appreciate the ideologies hidden in the words–to deconstruct.

Although students cannot totally escape their frames of reference, they can become consciously aware that these limit their perspectives, and they can deliberately force themselves to move outside of them at times.

One way to help students realize that they invent their own experiences is through the use of colors. Students are shown a poster with five bands of color: green, white, orange, red, and black. They are asked to take away any two colors that do not belong and write down the reason for eliminating the two. From these seemingly neutral stimuli come an awesome diversity of responses. Some eliminate the two colors they like least. Some eliminate black and white but for different reasons–because black is the absence of color and white is the combination of all colors, because nothing is black or white, because racism is abhorrent. Still others experience the Italian flag, the Irish flag, the Black African flag. They see their different "seeings," and more, they see what they ignored.

Another way to help students explore the biases in their meaning making involves presenting the class with a list of words such as the following: triangle, pyramid, orange, green, rectangle, cherry, sphere, circle, yellow, square, plastic, oval, cube, blue. Students are then asked to make lists of those words that belong together and to tell why they belong together. Students can make as many lists as they want, and may use the same word in as many different lists as they choose. They are asked to report their different lists and the rationale for each grouping.

After this, attention is directed to similarities and differences among lists, indicating that what each student just did was receive an array of stimuli and organize some of the stimuli into an experience by fitting them into categories, or concepts. Referring to the lists, the teacher can demonstrate that some students experienced one-dimensional shapes while others experienced two- and three-dimensional shapes. Some students experienced color; some experienced fruit. Still others experienced building materials, roundness, and so forth.

The teacher can then point out that the experience each student had was not part of the words on the board. That is, they each *invented* their own experience. They actively structured what they saw in order to make sense out of it for themselves. Each student gave parts of the list meaning, and different students chose different stimuli to concentrate on, organized the stimuli differently, and therefore had different experiences. Concepts like shape and color were not there. Only the stimulus words were there. And people do not always have the same experiences because they choose what to see and because they invent different categories to explain what they see.

This discussion often leads students to express the highly charged excitement of the "aha" that accompanies sudden insight. But hidden in and overshadowed by the excitement is a deep sense of inadequacy that lingers long after the excitement subsides. The coldness of exposure is terrifying as the students resign themselves to their human limitations. They ask, "Biased as I am, how can I possibly be a social worker?" And the long, hard process of learning to suspend knowing and get outside one's frame of reference begins.

The academic atmosphere should not be chilly for anyone (Sandler, 1986). Perhaps too, teachers have to give up their reliance on lecture, let the students in on the action of learning, and devise deliberate approaches for student involvement.

The use of the small work groups in the classroom can also

enhance students' appreciation of multiple meanings, especially when students remain in the same small group throughout the semester. In these work groups, the students engage in various learning tasks: reviewing assigned readings, applying content to particular situations (fieldwork settings, knowings from prior life and work), role playing and so forth. Because individuals bring their own frames of reference to any given task, in the group situation, it is common for multiple meanings to collide. Thus the teacher must help the students in each work group live with the conflict, appreciate that it is natural and inevitable and try to reach out of their personal frames to hear and connect with each other. Over time, they learn to check out their inferences, observe and restrain their own urges to dominate, and value each other's knowings. In this messy process, they gradually construct a narrative separate from the individual ones with which they came.

Students start out believing that doing is talking, planning, and problem-solving, not listening, reflecting, and encouraging others to say more. Eventually they learn that listening is also a doing, and a doing they have to be taught, a kind of doing with impactful consequence in their work with each other and especially in their work with clients. Such teaching is highly interactional. Students learn interaction through interaction (Goldberg Wood & Middleman, 1991b; Middleman & Goldberg, 1972; Middleman & Goldberg Wood, 1991a).

CONCLUSION

Constructionism encourages awareness of multiple realities and hidden meanings. It reduces the distance between teacher and student and between practitioner and client. It tames the practitioner's (and teacher's) desire and need to be the expert. It demolishes the claim of objectivity–by practitioners and researchers. It suggests that categories are and should be suspect.

Constructionism also strongly suggests that we never assume normative is good and non-normative is bad (so much for the Bell Curve). Constructionism is most helpful to the extent that it raises a critical consciousness in both practitioners and clients. It does not necessarily determine what the practitioner looks at and listens to, although it does raise the practitioner's desire to understand the client's situation from the client's point of view which, once done, reinforces her commitment to structural social work. Social workers are expected to work within the broader system of human welfare which is *not* constructed to promote human well-being nor prevent human misery. The structural approach to social work practice recognizes this and is designed for use by practitioners to challenge and change oppressive policies and procedures despite the socio-economic/political pressures against such a stance.

NOTES

1. We use Derrida's (1976) method ("under erasure") to indicate that *group* most closely approximates our meaning of persons who share a common perspective; yet it is also inaccurate, for members may or may not see each other face to face. So we cross it out, yet leave it legible.

2. Deconstruction is a method of analysis in which the dominant ethos is decentered, and the interrupted and marginalized perspectives are given centrality. The aim of deconstruction is to recover the interrupted and ignored meanings in any social and political context at any time in history. There are always many realities, but only some are recorded.

REFERENCES

Berger, P., & Luckmann, T. (1967). *The social construction of reality*. London: Penguin.

Brown, R.H. (1992). Poetics, politics, and truth: An invitation to rhetorical analysis. In R.H.Brown. (Ed.), *Writing the social text* (pp. 3-8). New York: Aldine de Gruyer.

Bruner, J. (1990). *Acts of meaning*. Cambridge, MA: Harvard University Press.

Bruner, J. (1986). *Actual minds, possible worlds*. Cambridge, MA: Harvard University Press.

Cutler, C. (1991). Deconstructing the DSM-III. *Social Work, 36*(2), 154-157.

Dean, R. (1989). Ways of knowing in clinical practice. *Clinical Social Work Journal, 17*(2), 116-127.

Dean, R., & Fenby, D. (1989). Exploring epistemologies: Social work action as a reflection of philosophical assumptions. *Journal of Social Work Education, 25*(1), 46-54.

Dean, R., & Fleck-Henderson, A. (1992). Teaching clinical theory and practice through a constructivist lens. *Journal of Teaching in Social Work, 6*(1), 3-20.

Derrida, J. (1976). *Of grammatology*. Baltimore: Johns Hopkins University Press.

Flexner, A. (1915). Is social work a profession? *Proceedings* (pp. 576-590). National Conference of Charities and Correction.

Foucault, M. (1980). *Power/knowledge*. New York: Pantheon.
Foucault, M. (1979). *Discipline and punish*. New York: Vintage.
Freire, P. (1974). *Education for critical consciousness*. New York: Seabury.
Gatens, M. (1991). *Feminism and philosophy*. Cambridge: Polity Press.
Geertz, C. (1983). *Local knowledge*. New York: Basic Books.
Gergen, K. (1991). *The saturated self*. New York: Basic Books.
Gergen, K. (1985). The social constructionist movement in modern psychology. *American Psychologist, 40*, 266-275.
Gergen, K., & Gergen, M. (1986). Narrative form and the construction of psychological science. In T. Sarbin (Ed.), *Narrative psychology* (pp. 22-44). New York: Praeger.
von Glasersfeld, E. (1984). An introduction to radical constructivism. In P. Watzlawick (Ed.), *The Invented Reality* (pp. 17-40). New York: Norton.
Goldberg, G., & Middleman, R. (1980). It might be a boa constrictor digesting an elephant: Vision stretching in social work education. *International Journal of Social Work Education, 3*(1), 213-225.
Goldberg Wood, G., & Middleman, R. (1991a). Advocacy and social action: Key elements in the structural approach. In A. Vinik & M. Levin (Eds.), *Social action in group work* (pp. 53-65). New York: The Haworth Press, Inc.
Goldberg Wood, G., & Middleman, R. (1991b). Principles that guide teaching. In R. Middleman & G. Goldberg Wood. *Teaching secrets: The technology in social work education* (pp. 111-116). New York: The Haworth Press, Inc.
Goldberg Wood, G., & Middleman, R. (1989). *The structural approach to direct practice in social work*. New York: Columbia University Press.
Goldstein, H. (1990). The knowledge base of social work practice. *Families in Society, 71*(4), 32-43.
Goolishian, H., & Anderson, H. (1987). Language systems and therapy: An evolving idea. *Psychotherapy, 24*, 529-538.
Goodson, I., & Dowbiggin, I. (1990). Docile bodies: Commonalities in the history of psychiatry and schooling. In S. Ball (Ed.), *Foucault and education* (pp. 105-129). New York: Routledge.
Goodman, N. (1984). *Of mind and other matters*. Cambridge, MA: Harvard University Press.
Guba, E., & Lincoln, Y. (1989). *Fourth generation research*. Newbury Park, CA: Sage.
Hartman, A. (1992). Enriching our profession's narrative. *Social Work, 37*(2), 99-100.
Hartman, A. (1991). Words create worlds. *Social Work, 36*(1), 275-276.
Hasenfeld, Y. (1987). Power in social work practice. *Social Service Review, 63*(3), 468-483.
Hawkesworth, M. (1990). *Beyond oppression*. New York: Continuum.
Hekman, S. (1990). *Gender and knowledge: Elements of a postmodern feminism*. Cambridge: Polity Press.
Hoffman, L. (1990). Constructing realities: An art of lenses. *Family Process, 29*(1), 1-12.

Hutcheon, L. (1989). *The Politics of postmodernism*. New York: Routledge.
Jones, R. (1971). Proving blacks inferior. *Black World*, 4-19.
Kirk, S., & Kutchins, H. (1992). *The selling of DSM*. New York: Aldine.
Laird, J. (1989). Women and stories: Restorying women's self-constructions. In M. McGoldrick, C. Anderson, & F. Walsh (Eds.), *Women in families* (pp. 422-450). New York: Norton.
Lippert, P. (1991-2). The semantics of multiculturalism. *Etc, 48*(4), 363-374.
Longres, J., & McLeod, E. (1980). Consciousness raising and social work practice. *Social Casework, 61*(6), 267-275.
Middleman, R., & Goldberg, G. (1972). The interactional way of presenting generic social work concepts. *Journal of Education for Social Work, 3*(1), 213-225.
Middleman R., & Goldberg, G. (1974). *Social Service Delivery: A Structural Approach to Social Work Practice*. New York: Columbia University Press.
Middleman, R., & Goldberg, G. (1985). Maybe it's a priest or a lady with a hat with a tree on it. Or is it a bumble bee?! Teaching group workers to see. *Social Work with Groups, 8*(1), 3-15.
Middleman, R., & Goldberg Wood, G. (1991a). Helping students learn from each other. In R. Middleman & G. Goldberg Wood, *Teaching Secrets* (pp. 31-40). New York: The Haworth Press, Inc.
Middleman, R., & Goldberg Wood, G. (1991b). Seeing/believing/seeing. *Social Work, 36*(3), 243-246.
Miller, D. (1990). *Women and social welfare*. New York: Praeger.
Mirowsky, J., & Ross, C. (1989). *Social causes of psychological distress*. New York: Aldine de Gruyer.
Mittleman, C., & Friedman, S. (1991). The Rashoman effect: A study in constructivist conversation. *Family Therapy, 18*(1), 17-36.
Parsons, R. (1991). Empowerment: Purpose and practice principle in social work. *Social Work With Groups, 14*(2), 7-21.
Pfeiffer, J. (1965). Pfeiffer's fables. *Magazine: The Philadelphia Bulletin*.
Rabinow, P. (1984). *The Foucault reader*. New York: Pantheon.
St. Exupery, A. (1943) *The little prince*. Harcourt, Brace and World.
Sandler, B. (1986). *The campus climate revisited: Chilly for women faculty, administrators, and graduate students*. Washington, D.C. Association of American Colleges.
Scott, D. (1989). Meaning construction and social work practice. *Social Service Review, 63*(1), 39-51.
Searle, J. (1990). The storm over the university. *The New York Review of Books*, December 6, 34-42.
Tomm, K., & Lannamann, J. (1988). Questions as interventions. *The Family Therapy Networker*, Sept./Oct., 38-41.
Watzlawick, P. (1984). *The invented reality*. New York: Wiley.
Weedon, C. (1987). *Feminist practice and poststructuralist theory*. New York: Basil Blackwell.

Weick, A. (1991). The place of science in social work. *Journal of Sociology and Social Work, 18*(4), 13-33.

Weingarten, K. (1991). The discourses of intimacy: Adding a social constructionist and feminist view. *Family Process, 30,* 285-305.

Witkin, S. (1990). The implications of social constructionism for social work education. *Journal of Teaching in Social Work, 4*(2), 37-47.

Witkin, S., & Gottschalk, S. (1988). Alternative criteria for theory evolution. *Social Service Review, 62*(2), 211-224.

Feminism and Constructivism:
Teaching Social Work Practice with Women

Liane V. Davis

SUMMARY. In this article, I explore the tensions between constructivism and feminism in teaching a course on social work practice with women. Drawing on modernist feminist theory, I examine the conflict between validating the stories that women construct for themselves, while raising women's awareness of the difficulties in constructing liberated stories in an oppressive society. I discuss strategies I have used in the classroom to address, albeit not resolve, these tensions.

INTRODUCTION

From the earliest days of the second wave of the feminist movement, feminists have relied heavily on constructivist notions. While not labeling them as such, consciousness-raising groups rested on the assumption that reality was socially constructed (Bricker-Jenkins & Hooyman, 1986). Women came together in these groups to share and give new meanings to the stories of their lives.

Embedded in these early groups were the seeds of the challenges that confront me today as I, a feminist social work educator, introduce new generations of social workers to what I believe it

Liane V. Davis, PhD, is Associate Professor, School of Social Welfare, Twente Hall, University of Kansas, Lawrence, KS 66045.

[Haworth co-indexing entry note]: "Feminism and Constructivism: Teaching Social Work Practice with Women," Davis, Liane V. Co-published simultaneously in *Journal of Teaching in Social Work* (The Haworth Press, Inc.) Vol. 8, No. 1/2, 1993, pp. 147-163; and: *Revisioning Social Work Education: A Social Constructionist Approach* (ed: Joan Laird) The Haworth Press, Inc., 1993, pp. 147-163. Multiple copies of this article/chapter may be purchased from The Haworth Document Delivery Center [1-800-3-HAWORTH; 9:00 a.m. - 5:00 p.m. (EST)].

147

means to be a feminist social work practitioner. How do I affirm the individual realities that women construct for themselves and simultaneously raise their awareness of the many ways in which disempowering realities continue to be imposed on them? How do I help them see the many ways in which our gender makes a difference? How do I convince them that feminism is still necessary for analysis and action? How do I allow them their own reality while exposing them to mine? How do I expose them to my reality without imposing it on them? How do I prevent myself from believing that my way of looking at the world is the only correct way? My explorations in feminist theory have offered some guidance as I have struggled with these questions. They have, at a minimum, enabled me to see that I am not alone in confronting these questions.

A Brief Overview of Feminist Theory

In recent years, feminist scholars (and social workers, too) have become fully engaged in ongoing philosophical discussions centering on postmodern theory (e.g., Nicholson, 1990; Sands & Nuccio, 1992; Weedon, 1987). Unfortunately, as Sands and Nuccio observe, too often these writings are obtuse, creating unnecessary obstacles for even the most intellectually curious. In my attempts (and struggles) to understand and apply these exciting ideas in my role as social work educator, my attention has been drawn repeatedly to one overarching question: To what extent is the social construct of women [as in "women's ways of knowing" (Belenky, Clinchy, Goldberger, & Tarule, 1986) and "women's voice" (Gilligan, 1982)] still viable and necessary?

As I have interpreted the arguments, the dialogue centers on the extent to which gender (or any similar category) is, can, and should remain a staging point for future thinking and action. Some feminists, in their embrace of postmodern theory, have criticized as exclusionary the tendency to generalize about *women* and have advocated the need to speak in many voices; others have as vociferously argued that, despite the vast differences among women, there remains a strong need to speak in one voice. The issue, it seems is one of timing (and strategy) rather than of substance.

To capture complex arguments in only a few paragraphs always risks oversimplification. With that caveat I will try to define what I perceive to be the debate (or, perhaps, dialogue). On one side are those who have come to be called feminist standpoint theorists (e.g., Alcoff, 1988; Hartsock, 1990; Stanley & Wise, 1990). The concept of standpoint assumes that all persons see the world from the place in which they are objectively situated. For feminist standpoint theorists, it is *gender* that firmly grounds the reality of women's lives. Regardless of the relative inputs of biology and socialization, being a woman-in-society gives women a shared place from which to look out upon the world and their lives in that world. As Aptheker (1989) has so graphically written, the "dailiness of women's lives" (p. 37), cleaning the toilets and nurturing the children and men in private and in public, leads women to a different understanding of the world than men.

There are clearly differences among women. Women differ on the basis of race, class, sexual orientation, culture, and religion. Not all women share the same standpoint; not all women have the same view of reality. Some women are more privileged than others when it comes to sharing in the material riches that power bestows. But overriding these differences is the oppression that all women experience because of their shared sex.

I am reminded of a very proud woman. She had been born to a Southern family whose ancestors came to this country even before the Mayflower, as she frequently reminded her guests. When I met her, she was living in a semblance of wealth. And yet, the veneer was thin. The dark, rich curtains and muted lighting prevented the visitor from seeing the worn carpets, the fraying furniture, the well-worn clothing. The occasional dinners out in stylish restaurants, which she insisted on paying for, came at the expense of too many days of barely eking by. She had lost, through divorce, the money to support the only lifestyle she had ever known. She had helplessly watched as her ex-husband, who had claimed poverty at the time of the divorce settlement, regained his former wealth. And so when she remarried, a very wealthy and respectable lifelong acquaintance, perhaps she knew her new husband was a violent man. But the occasional nights under the dining room table, protected from his blows, seemed a small price to pay for a return to her former status.

It is experiences such as battering, economic marginalization, and psychological disempowerment, that give women the shared perspective that

> provides an edge, an advantage. . . . Women's oppression gives them fewer interests in ignorance . . . and fewer reasons to invest in maintaining or justifying the status quo than the dominant group . . . thus, the perspective from their lives can more easily generate fresh and critical analyses. (Harding, 1991, p. 126)

Those who are oppressed (whether they be women, people of color, or gays and lesbians) need dual vision for their survival. They must see through their own lenses; they must see through the lenses of their oppressors. And, if they are multiply oppressed (as are women of color or lesbians), their need for dual vision is magnified. As Collins (1989) writes, "Black women cannot afford to be fools of any type, for their devalued status denies them the protections that white skin, maleness, and wealth confer" (p. 759).

Early feminists had overgeneralized, ignoring the different realities of women's lives. In their eagerness to establish a common bond among all women, they assumed that all women share the same standpoint. But

> as new narratives began to be produced, telling the story of the diversity of women's experiences, the chief imperative was to listen to become more aware of one's own biases, prejudices, and ignorance, to begin to stretch the borders of what Minnie Bruce Pratt calls the 'narrow circle of the self.' (Bordo, 1990, p. 138)

As feminists have opened themselves to the diversity among us, other questions necessarily arise. How many different standpoints can there be before the construct of women loses all meaning? How many different perspectives can there be for gender itself to remain a useful and usable construct.

To correct the false generalizations made from the lives of a select few to the totality of women, some feminists have turned to postmodern theory. Holding that each individual, situated in her own time, her own place in history, and in society, constructs her own reality, they argue that searching for commonalities among women provides further ammunition for our oppressors (see, for example, Flax, 1990; Nicholson, 1990). Accepting the category of the female, of woman, of gender itself, means embracing a way of looking at society and our place in it that has been imposed on us and has contributed to our oppression. Postmodern theorists privilege all perspectives equally, holding none out as the absolute standard against which to judge truth and fiction. They allow no universal claims. In their commitment to hearing multiple voices, they seek to dismantle and deconstruct all categories, including that of woman (e.g., Nicholson, 1990).

As I have searched for ways to translate these heady intellectual arguments into the teaching of social work practice, I have found myself asking such interrelated questions as: Is it time, as Friedan (1986) has argued, for us to move from a concern with women's issues to a concern for human issues? Is it time to move beyond gender? Is it time to give up the deeply held belief of many feminists that some constructions of reality are "better" than others?

My answer to these questions is always "No." I listen to the stories that students tell of their clients: the women in public housing, on AFDC, in the health, mental health, child welfare, or corrections systems. I listen for, but rarely hear, an appreciation of the depth of the patriarchal oppression that keeps women in their place. I listen for, but rarely hear, the stories of women's survival and their strength despite their oppression. Instead, I hear the labels the students so eagerly apply: "co-dependent," "manipulative," "dependent personality disorder." As I work with students and directly and indirectly with women clients, I am continually reminded of the power that others have to write our stories for us. I am reminded how difficult it is to write and believe in our own stories after so many years of being silenced, so many years of having our reality continually negated. I have come to share Christine Di Stefano's (1990) concern that:

> in our haste to deconstruct hierarchical distinctions such as gender as harmful illusions we may fail to grasp their tenacious rootedness in an objective world created over time and deeply resistant to change. (p. 78)

I experience the constant tension of wanting women to name their own reality (and experiencing the personal empowerment that accompanies such actions), while wanting them to understand the realities of their oppression (and joining in action with other women whose lives are similarly affected). It is in this tension that my conflicts with constructivism are most acute and unresolved. While I hope that in telling their own stories women can come to understand the shared socio-political realities of their lives, as did so many women in the early consciousness-raising groups, I know that too frequently the realities that women construct for themselves remain tales of individual pathology and self-blaming. I am aware that in my desire for all women to understand their historic and continuing oppression, I may be imposing my reality on them, inadvertently recreating the very oppression I am seeking to obliterate. That is where the delicate balance between constructivism and my own feminism may be upset. And yet, I am willing to repeatedly face this challenge, convinced as I am that it is not coincidental that

> just at the moment when so many of us who have been silenced begin to demand the right to name ourselves, to act as subjects rather than objects of history, that just then the concept of subjecthood becomes problematic. Just when we are forming our own theories about the world, uncertainty emerges about whether the world can be theorized. Just when we are talking about the changes we want, ideas of process and the possibility of systematically and rationally organizing human society become dubious and suspect. (Hartsock, 1990, pp. 164-165).

So what do I make of all of this as I teach social work practice with women to a new generation of women. I believe that the concept of women is a viable and necessary political position from which to teach and from which we as social workers must be prepared to act. I no longer hold a simple notion of gender duality. *Women* is not a unitary construct; it must take into account the diversity among us. Further, as a social work educator, I have a responsibility to teach about the concrete realities of women's lives. While women can construct (and be empowered by validating) their own realities, they also need to be reminded that women perform two-thirds of the world's work, receive five percent of the world income, own less than one percent of the world land; in the United States every seven minutes a woman is raped, every eighteen seconds a woman is battered; and women and children in female-headed households are estimated to comprise almost all of the population in poverty by the year 2000 (Allen, 1989, pp. 41-42).

Social Work and Women: Beyond the Mandate

Since 1977 the Council on Social Work Education (CSWE) has mandated that content on women be included in all social work curricula. In addition to content on women, its current accrediting guidelines require that social work programs make "continuous efforts to ensure the enrichment of the educational experience it offers by including women in all categories of persons related to the program . . ." (Council on Social Work Education, 1991, p. 67).

Over the past 15 years, this mandate has been fulfilled by what has been aptly called the "just add women and stir" approach (Bunch, 1987, p. 140). Women have been added to faculties; material on women has been added to already existing courses; and new courses dealing specifically with women have been added to the curriculum. In a recent survey, Knight (1991) found evidence that these efforts have, at least partially, succeeded. Schools of social work now give moderate attention to a range of women's issues. Yet, as Knight's data further illustrate, there are certain inherent limitations to just adding content on women to the curriculum. The "women's issues" covered tend to be problems women face because of their oppression: sexism/sex discrimination; feminization of poverty; domestic violence; gender discrimination in the delivery of social services; sexual assault; and sexism in social work itself. Although these are indeed problems that women face, this approach gives a negative valence to "women's issues" and women's lives. While the curriculum may be "enriched," it is not transformed (see Minnich, 1990 for a compelling case for curriculum transformation). There is little impetus to rethink women's (and men's) lives nor the society in which we live. Abramovitz (1987), in an earlier article on bringing feminism into the social work curriculum, wrote that the task for social work is to "ask questions that bring women into view and create new ways of thinking about women and other underrepresented groups" (p. 29). Adding women's issues to the curriculum does little to create these new ways of thinking, to decenter "malestream" thinking, to move women from margin to center (hooks, 1984).

A number of years ago, when I was beginning to seriously struggle with the role that gender plays in the social construction of reality, I had the privilege of seeing Lily Tomlin. I will never forget sitting in the theater in New York and hearing her say: "REALITY IS A COLLECTIVE HUNCH!"

Her words came at a critical moment in my life. I was becoming conscious that I was looking at the world, and especially the actions and beliefs of social workers, through a different lens, a gender lens. I was also realizing that few of my colleagues, those with whom I worked most closely, even those I considered feminists, saw the world through the same lenses. Throughout the next few years, as my scholarship increasingly challenged the reality that others imposed on us (as women) and as I battled unsuccessfully to achieve tenure (not unrelated occurrences), I was strengthened by Tomlin's words. They reminded me that, even if I saw a different reality, I was not crazy. I just wasn't a member of the collectivity that had defined *the* reality that was daily imposed on me.

In 1991 these feelings came pouring back as I watched this nation transfixed by Anita Hill and Clarence Thomas. At one level this high order spectacle seemed to be about truth-telling and fact-finding. Motives were examined, witnesses paraded before the white men assembled in judgment. At a deeper level, this was about socially constructing reality. "They just don't get it," reverberated throughout the year and the country as women (especially older women), responding to Anita Hill's challenge, began to openly acknowledge how much they (men) just don't get the realities of women's lives. And at another level, this was about power and how those in power get to impose their reality on the rest of us.

TEACHING SOCIAL WORK PRACTICE WITH WOMEN

It is in teaching a course on social work practice with women that all of these notions (of social constructivism, of power and powerlessness, of marginalization and privilege) come together. I have taught, periodically, a course on social work practice with women since 1987. It is never the same, always influenced by my evolving and everchanging feminist awareness and by the students who participate.

The beginning. I began teaching the course at a university in upstate New York. I indicate where because, as I have since discovered, there are significant regional differences influencing what occurs in this course. When I began, I knew that I not only wanted to teach content on women, but wanted to do so using what I had come to think of as feminist pedagogy. To this day I am not certain what that means exactly, but I knew that I wanted to achieve congruence between the teaching/learning model of the classroom and my vision of feminist social work practice [see Luke & Gore (1992) for a discussion of feminist pedagogy].

Five concerns were most prominent as I developed and structured the course: power, valuing experience, developing a cooperative environment, building on diversity, and getting the message across that the personal is the political. With each of these I experience the tension of wanting women to name their own reality while wanting them to understand the realities of their common oppression.

Power. Power is always present. I wanted us to discuss and grapple with how power affected us in the classroom and to analyze and grapple with its effect in our work with clients. As a teacher, I held power over the students. I wanted to share that power (by sharing knowledge, by sharing responsibility), while being honest about the existence of my (objective) power.

I invited all interested students to meet with me to discuss what they wanted from the course. I wanted to be clear that this was their course as much as it was mine. I let them know that I had ideas that I wanted to share with them, but I also respected their ideas about what they wanted to share with me. Because this was the first time I had taught the course, I was able to walk into this meeting without a predeveloped syllabus and was able to build a syllabus around these ideas.

I felt (and still do) that I held some real power over the students. Even if I had told them at the beginning that they would all get A's, the power of my approval still would have been there. I do believe that, while we can work to equalize the power, there is always the impediment of evaluation. While I am aware of ways around evaluating students, I have never been comfortable, in my role as a gatekeeper of the profession, circumventing the issue. I am, however, comfortable sharing responsibility for grading. Since much of what we were going to be doing in the class was in the form of group projects, we decided that we would all participate equally in the grading.

I tried to give up the expert power that comes from being the professor. I am usually very much in control, having a great deal of information and strong opinions to share. I want to teach to them. This class made me confront the inconsistencies between that teaching style and feminist empowerment. I was (and remain) up front with students about how sharing my knowledge with them in a traditional pedagogical style might undermine their willingness to delve into their own wisdom and knowledge. I participated (almost) as a peer, sharing my experiences and my knowledge with them. I refused, however, to be THE EXPERT, refused to be the authority. I waited for them to take over, to provide direction, to pull things together. That was (and remains) difficult for me (as it was for students), but I have learned to trust the students (just as they learn to trust clients).

I made explicit the common power dynamics in the teacher-student and social worker-client relationship. Just as I had the power to impose my reality on them, they had the power to impose their reality on clients. It was only by demystifying the power dynamics that students (and their clients) could feel empowered to challenge the realities constructed by others.

Validating experience as a knowledge source. I wanted to create an environment in which personal experiences and personal wisdom were valued as knowledge sources and where students were encouraged to bring themselves as women into their practice as social workers. I shared how my own personal experiences had enhanced my practice as a social worker and as a social work educator.

Students kept journals in which they reflected upon their personal and professional lives, where they began to see how their experiences were all interconnected. I encouraged them to focus on the interconnections between their diverse worlds, to share the intellectual and emotional changes they were experiencing. I encouraged them to read the papers, to watch and listen to television, to listen to their families and friends, as well as other instructors. The journals provided an opportunity to pull it all together. This was (and remains) a highly successful learning mode. Since I expected that students might share a lot of very personal material, I told them that I didn't feel comfortable grading the journals. Instead, I entered into a conversation with them. The journals provided students a rich opportunity to shape and share the construction of their own reality; the journals provided me with a non-threatening, non-confrontive vehicle for suggesting alternate realities. In the absence of grades, students and I could engage in a mutually affirming dialogue.

Cooperative environment. Together we co-created a cooperative learning environment. They were held responsible for the group product, for working together, for building a coherent whole. I encouraged them to focus as much on the group process as on the product.

One group used this as an opportunity to switch their group project midstream. They began to do a group project on social work practice with lesbians. Being confronted (by one group member) with their own homophobia, they chose to present the class with a video of their own group process as they struggled with their homophobia.

These smaller groups provided a further opportunity for students to give voice to and get support for their own unique realities, while sharing the commonalities of their experiences.

Diversity. I wanted to create an environment which valued diversity. Although there was little racial diversity amongst the students, there was considerable ethnic diversity, with broad representations of Italian-American, Jewish-American, and Irish-American students. There were also a number of lesbians, many of whom were out to their classmates. We built on this diversity, using it as an opportunity to share different perspectives with one another, and to openly acknowledge the richness this gave to us all. Acknowledging our diversity freed us to see our commonalities.

The personal is the political. I wanted to provide an environment where the personal and the political merged with social work. In many ways this was the primary way in which I conveyed what was important to me. I wanted them to have a framework for seeing the many

ways in which our personal lives are constructed by the larger sociopolitical environment, and the ways in which we as social workers can
co-construct new meanings for ourselves and our clients.

One of the tools for this was something we did early on in the
semester. I sent the students to the bookstore or local library self-
help shelf and asked them to critique one of the books they found.
Laughing about how self-help books taught women how to fix
themselves, while self-help books taught men how to fix their cars
or their houses, provided an effective way to get at this powerful
tool of women's oppression.

We all brought to class the newspaper stories that documented
women's oppression as well as stories of the growing visibility and
power of women's activism. I liberally shared with the class my
own social work activism and encouraged them to do likewise.
Throughout I clearly explicated the direct linkages between social
work practice and policy, emphasizing the need to always look
beyond the individual client (see Davis & Hagen, 1992).

FURTHER DEVELOPMENT (AND, PERHAPS, SOME REGRESSION)

That first class, I have since discovered, was unique. The students thrived. They used the class as an opportunity to discover how
alternative modes of expression (poetry, song, art) could be incorporated into social work. They had vivid dialogues with one another, often straying far afield from where we were supposed to be. I let
it go, uncomfortable at first (we were not accomplishing our goals),
but finally learned to trust in the process (especially when I read the
journals, discovering the depth of their learning).

Since moving to the Midwest, this has been more difficult. Students seem more used to structure, more willing to be passive
learners, more eager to learn the right way to do things. They
experience discomfort with multiple realities, discomfort without
an authority figure.

There was another way in which the first class was unique. There
was a critical mass of lesbian students and, perhaps more importantly, a critical mass of out lesbians. This provided an opportunity for
other women to come out as lesbians to themselves and to the class

during the semester. It was a sharing environment in which people felt few constraints. It was also an all-women class. This made it easier to talk about sensitive issues. Students felt freer to speak about the homophobia that they experienced from other students and from faculty. They felt freer to express anger (often against male society and sometimes against specific men).

I have struggled with the issue of men in the class. I know, all too well, that the presence of men changes the classroom dynamics (see Hall & Sandler, 1982). I have tuned into and share with the class my own feelings about men in the class. I find myself alternately feeling guilty if the women express too much anger (knowing that these are the "good men") and responsible for protecting the men (because they are students and because women frequently protect men). I always begin the class with a clear message to male students: It is their responsibility to take care of themselves here. While that may sound harsh, it is the only way I know to free the women to focus on themselves, to take care of themselves. Most often the class ends up being all women. A few men might enroll, but they quickly withdraw. They often make disparaging remarks outside the class ("It's a group of dykes." "It's a group of angry women").

This first class raised what was to be a central and ongoing tension for me. How could I achieve a balance between what *I* wanted students to know and what *they* wanted to know? How could I achieve a balance between my construction of reality and theirs? How could I *guide* them to construct a reality that affirmed their experience and was grounded in the common oppression of all women? This has become even more important in the Midwest. Here I have found students far more caught up in what I perceive to be the pathological construction of women's lives. Many of the students come into the class having already taken on the "damaged" identities that society has constructed for them. Eager for answers to their own pain and confusion, they latch on to answers I perceive continue to oppress women. They define themselves and their women clients as "co-dependents," "enablers," "dependent personality disorders," "borderline personality disorders." They uncritically buy society's new labels that "privatize, individualize, and pathologize 'women's problems,' rather than understand these difficulties as a natural outgrowth of inequality and the socially constructed fabric of work and family roles" (Lerner, 1990, p. 15). The challenge is to encourage them to adopt a view of reality that empowers them while simultaneously encouraging them to critique what has been imposed upon them. That is the same challenge that they will face when working with clients. How can they affirm what the client brings, including the client's perception of her world and herself, while simultaneously opening up new vistas that allow her to see the ways in which a world has been imposed upon her?

I continue to send each new class to the self-help sections of the bookstore. We talk about the messages that women are given and how difficult it is to fight them. I now have them do genograms, but restrict them to unearthing the (too frequently untold) stories of the women. I ask them to discover what has enabled women to survive. Often the students do genograms on their own families, discovering hidden tales of strong women. It is a joy in the Midwest to learn about the pioneer women, the grandmothers and great grandmothers of the students. As they do this assignment, many build new connections or repair old ones.

I challenge them to see as strengths what have too frequently been seen as pathologies, to look differently at what have been labeled enabling or codependent behaviors, to begin to understand and value the caring of women, seeing that such caring can get women into difficulty, but that it is also a powerful force for good.

Students are eager for different ways of looking at themselves and others. While hesitant to call themselves feminists during the first few weeks, many proudly claim the term by the end of the semester. They are creative in conveying their new-found awareness.

One group of students, doing a presentation on single mother families, made a video.[1] A social worker at a mental health clinic was interviewing a young single mother who came in complaining of depression. As the worker and client engaged in a traditional medical model assessment (similar to what they were expected to do in their practicum), assessing symptoms of depression, suicidal ideation, self-talk, medication, and so on, the other students surrounded them, holding up bold signs of all the "women's issues" to which the worker was blind: no child-support; low paying, dead-end job; no job benefits; inadequate childcare; the lack of family and medical leave; the lack of affordable housing. It was a powerful, if humorous way, to get the message across.

Cutting across these classroom experiences is the delicate balancing act: affirming and validating the stories that women construct for themselves while raising womens' awareness of how difficult it is to construct liberated stories in an oppressive society.

DIFFICULTIES

Their new (and in some instances renewed) awareness places added stress on the students. These new ways of looking at things often are not affirmed in other classes or in their agencies. It is a pleasure for me when students begin to challenge malestream thinking, yet I know it can come at a cost to them. The cost, however, is one the students appear willing to pay.

I have had to fight the tendency to institutionalize the course. I no longer meet with the students during the preceding semester to ask for their input in developing the syllabus. I rationalize this by saying that I now have a keen sense of what it is that students want. While I hand them a pre-determined syllabus on the first day of class, I tell them that it is certainly open for change. I worry that I have taken over too much, that in the interest of efficiency I have taken back the power. I now grade their journals, evaluating them on how able they are to engage in a conversation with themselves and with me. This year, for the first time, I have moved away from group projects. This is partially in response to the difficulties that students have had getting together, as so many of them travel long distances and their time at school is limited (so many of them, like women around the world, are balancing too many roles with too few resources.) In part, however, it is because I want to bring more outsiders in, more community people, both practitioners and clients. I want to expose the students to more diversity than exists in the classroom. It remains the most vital class that I teach, always presenting me with new challenges and new learning. I continue to talk explicitly about power, sitting back to allow students to discover the wisdom and strength within themselves. In that regard the class has changed little. Students have difficulty at first, being used to teacher-as-expert. They quickly adapt, meeting the challenge of sharing themselves and their expertise with others.

NOTE

1. We learn to label things for what they are and, therefore, construct more affirming representations. See Abramovitz (1991) for a discussion of language.

REFERENCES

Abramovitz, M. (1987). Making gender a variable in social work teaching. *Journal of Teaching in Social Work, 1*, 29-52.

Abramovitz, M. (1991). Putting an end to doublespeak about race, gender, and poverty: An annotated glossary for social workers. *Social Work, 36*, 380-384.

Alcoff, L. (1988). Cultural feminism versus post-structuralism: The identity crisis in feminist theory. In E. Minnich, J. O'Barr, & R. Rosenfeld (Eds.), *Reconstructing the academy: Women's education and women' studies*, pp. 257-288. Chicago: University of Chicago Press.

Allen, J. (1989). Women who beget women must thwart major sophisms. In A. Garry & M. Pearsall (Eds.), *Women, knowledge, and reality: Explorations in feminist philosophy*, pp. 37-46. Boston: Unwin Hyman.

Aptheker, B. (1989). *Tapestries of life: Women's work, women's consciousness, and the meaning of daily life*. Amherst, MA: University of Massachusetts Press.

Belenky, M.F., Clinchy, B. M., Goldberger, N.R. and Tarule, J. M. (1986). *Women's ways of knowing: The development of self, voice, and mind*. New York: Basic Books.

Bordo, S. (1990). Feminism, postmodernism, and gender-scepticism. In L. J. Nicholson (Ed.), *Feminism/postmodernism*, pp. 133-156. New York: Routledge, Chapman, and Hall.

Bricker-Jenkins, M., & Hooyman, N. R. (1986). A feminist world view: Ideological themes from the feminist movement. In M. Bricker-Jenkins & N.R. Hooyman (Eds.), *Not for women only: Social work practice for a feminist future*. Silver Spring, MD: National Association of Social Workers.

Bunch, C. (1987). *Passionate politics: Essays 1968-1986: Feminist theory in action*. New York: St. Martin's Press.

Collins, P. H. (1989). The social construction of Black feminist thought. *Signs, 14*, 745-773.

Council on Social Work Education (1991). *Handbook of accreditations standards and procedures*. Alexandria, VA.

Davis, L. V., & Hagen, J.L. (1992). The problem of wife abuse: The interrelationship of social policy and social work practice. *Social Work, 37,* 15-20.

Di Stefano, C. (1990). Dilemmas of difference: Feminism, modernity, and postmodernism. In L. J. Nicholson (Ed.), *Feminism/postmodernism,* pp. 63-82. New York: Routledge, Chapman, and Hall.

Flax, J. (1987). Postmodernism and gender relations in feminist theory. In L.J. Nicholson (Ed.), *Feminism/postmodernism,* pp. 39-62. New York: Routledge, Chapman, and Hall.

Friedan, B. (1986). *The second stage* (Revised Edition). New York: Summit Books.

Gilligan, C. (1982). *In a different voice: Psychological theory and women's development.* Cambridge: Harvard University Press.

Hall, R.M., & Sandler, B.R. (1982). The classroom climate: A chilly place for women. *Project on the status and education of women.* Association of American Colleges.

Harding, S. (1991). *Whose science? Whose knowledge?: Thinking from women's lives.* Ithaca: Cornell University Press.

Hartsock, N. (1990). Foucault on power: A theory for women? In L.J. Nicholson (Ed.), *Feminism/postmodernism,* pp. 157-175. New York: Routledge, Chapman, & Hall.

hooks, b. (1984). *Feminist theory from margin to center.* Boston: South End Press.

Knight, C. (1991). Gender-sensitive curricula in social work education: A national study. *Journal of Social Work Education, 27,* 145-155.

Lerner, H. G. (1990). Problems for profit? *Women's Review of Books, 7,* 15-16.

Luke, C., & Gore, J. (Eds.) (1992). *Feminisms and critical pedagogy.* New York: Routledge.

Minnich, E. K. (1990). *Transforming knowledge.* Philadelphia: Temple University Press.

Nicholson, L. (1990) Introduction. In L. J. Nicholson (Ed.), *Feminism/postmodernism,* pp. 1-16. New York: Routledge, Chapman, & Hall.

Sands, R. G., & Nuccio, K. (1992). Postmodern feminist theory and social work. *Social Work, 37,* 489-494.

Stanley, L., & Wise, S. (1990). Method, methodology, and epistemology in feminist research processes. In L. Stanley (Ed.), *Feminist praxis: Research, theory, and epistemology in feminist sociology,* pp. 20-60. New York: Routledge.

Weedon, C. (1987). *Feminist practice and poststructuralist theory.* Oxford: Basil Blackwell.

Field Education for Reflective Practice: A Re-Constructive Proposal

Howard Goldstein

SUMMARY. The author traces the history of the shaping of the discourse that came to define the field component in social work education. It is then argued that the emphasis of education for practice be shifted from the class to the field, since it is primarily direct experience that fosters the talent of reflective thinking.

If recent constructionist theories have anything to tell us, it is to alert us to the powerful ways our language and concepts govern our schemes of living. Even the clear-thinking scientist is not immune to the limits of language. Over a half-century ago, when physicists futilely attempted to adapt classical Newtonian laws of objective and linear causality to the indeterminate nature of quantum mechanics, at least one among them (Heisenberg, 1958) anticipated what social science constructionists now advise: The concepts we inherit and value may have little applicability to experiences we are trying to understand. Putting this in constructivist terms, our endeavor to describe, explain, or account for our world is restricted by the language that is bequeathed us (Gergen, 1985). The words we use to map our reality are social artifacts having their own historical ori-

Howard Goldstein, DSW, is Professor Emeritus, Case Western Reserve University.

[Haworth co-indexing entry note]: "Field Education for Reflective Practice: A Re-Constructive Proposal," Goldstein, Howard. Co-published simultaneously in *Journal of Teaching in Social Work* (The Haworth Press, Inc.) Vol. 8, No. 1/2, 1993, pp. 165-182; and: *Revisioning Social Work Education: A Social Constructionist Approach* (ed: Joan Laird) The Haworth Press, Inc., 1993, pp. 165-182. Multiple copies of this article/chapter may be purchased from The Haworth Document Delivery Center [1-800-3-HAWORTH; 9:00 a.m. - 5:00 p.m. (EST)].

165

gins. But they also have a serious social purpose: They allow for social discourse and so serve the purpose of maintaining stability and continuity in social life.

What does this commentary on language have to do with the issue of field education noted in the title of this essay? There are specific connections. First, as I want to show, the terms, words, and concepts that order and define the profession as a whole also serve to maintain its stability, continuity, and resistance to change. Thus any proposal that suggests redefinition and change–that imperils stability–will either be treated with caution or incorporated and compromised within the existing order.

The history of field education in social work is a good example. Over time, the field component has been renamed, lengthened, squeezed, and otherwise experimented and tampered with in countless ways. Yet we can count on it to pop back into something resembling its original shape as subsidiary to the university-based, academic program.

It would be visionary on my part to propose any substantial changes in the role of field education in preparation for professional practice without first considering this component (as well as the whole of social work) as a consensual, historically-situated construct. If the field component is granted the status of a conditional social construct rather than that of an established, hardened precept, then perhaps my proposal will invite further discourse and debate. Specifically, I will propose (1) that the emphasis of education for practice be shifted from the class to the field because (2) it can be argued that effective learning for practice is gained from the kind of direct experience that fosters the talents of reflective thinking.

CONSTRUCTS SHAPING SOCIAL WORK

As monolithic and enduring as a profession appears to be, it may seem odd to speak of such an institution as a "social construct," as a social invention or cultural artifact. Yet a reading of the history of most professions will tell a story of the social origins and definitions of the profession, of the effects of political intrigue, and of the many contingencies and accidents bearing on the profession's quest for the demarcation of its authoritative domain.

Although patterns of emergence vary considerably, Ben-David and Collins (1966) offer a rational outline of the progressive stages of a profession's ascent. First, for a profession to come into being, ideas related to its need must already have been available for some time in several segments of society. Second, as the embryonic profession begins to take shape, only a few of the ideas originally available are selected. The reasons for this selection are various and at times arbitrary. In addition to theoretical and technical considerations, selection often expresses the interchange of ideological, political, and economic forces. And third, the growth of the profession is further animated when these ideas are seized by or become identified with particular individuals.

A cursory review of social work's roots and beginnings shows that they conform to the developmental stages noted above. Just a few of the available ideas that presaged the beginning of social work as a profession included Judaeo-Christian precepts of responsibility and caring and a commitment to social reform, ideas linked with society's aims for improving the economic and moral qualities of the lives of the poor and disenfranchised.

These ideas were narrowed and refined once services were established by social agencies and organizations, particularly when social work opted to lend its weight to casework and individualized approaches. Further distillation of the design of social work occurred when educational programs were created to produce and define professional people. In many ways, this was a process of "natural selection," analogous to the Darwinian motif: the ideas that persisted served to ensure the relevance, authority, and status of the profession and its continuity over time. In constructivist terms, the result, as Siporin (1975, p. 9) suggests, was "a societally prescribed system" whose work is carried on by "socially authorized personnel." These ideas became personified and imprinted into the canons of the profession by the works and writings of illustrious forbears of the profession, among them Mary Richmond, Jane Addams, and the Abbotts, Edith and Grace. The resulting constructs finally became regulated and codified when formally enunciated in the requirements for the accreditation of educational programs.

FIELD EDUCATION AS A CONSTRUCT

Of special interest is one longstanding educational construct, which may be phrased as follows: In addition to foundational academic education, students of social work should spend some part of their formal education in the field where they will have first hand opportunity to observe and participate in selected forms of professional practice. This slice of education for the profession is variously–and often interchangeably–called "field placement," "field instruction," or the "practicum." In their ordinary or casual usage, these constructs refer to the "doing" component of the educational plan. Although "integration" is a prime value, the field experience exists somewhat outside and apart from the classroom, which is primarily concerned with "knowing." The distinction is even more telling when we look at what these terms imply. "Field placement" is geographical in its connotation, referring to a site, typically outside the academy, in a social agency or other organization that provides social services. "Field instruction" or "field supervision" is more specific: These terms connote the giving of direction, guidance, or information by an expert authority to a novice. "Practicum" implies some linkage with the academic base. The learner, again under authortative guidance and in an external setting, is expected to undertake "the practical application of previously studied theory" (Websters Third New International Dictionary, 1971). I might add that the term "internship" also has been applied to field education with its intimations of the hierarchy involved in medical training. However this segment of learning is defined, the field experience is regarded as different, separate from and subordinate to the classroom.

To be sure, many educational programs, past and current, ambitiously strive to attain an increased measure of integration or consonance between class and field, an endeavor usually initiated and managed by the university program. But for many practical reasons, integration is difficult to attain. Geographical separation is an obvious reason. Field teachers are likely to be diverse as far as their skills, backgrounds, interests and connections with the school are concerned. And often, the disparity between the general and broad objectives of the school and the field organization's immediate priorities or pressures can also impede the route to coherence.

Roslyn Chernesky (1986), in her contribution to the book *Feminist Visions for Social Work*, proposes a more fundamental reason for the lack of integration. Critical of the traditional forms of supervision in social work that have not changed over the past century, she claims that the hierarchical, patriarchal, and ambiguous disposition of supervision fosters dependency, inhibits workers' use of knowledge, experience, and creativity, and in other ways hinders professional growth and maturity. I agree and would add that integration also is thwarted by the ambiguity of the field teacher's pedagogical role. Having been assigned the responsibility for the student's field education, often that role is diffuse and undefined.

A specific answer to this question is not evident in the meager reference given to the "field practicum" in the recent Curriculum Policy Statement of CSWE. Its purpose is to provide "the practical experience in the application of the theory and skills acquired in the foundation areas"; "each educational program must establish standards for field practicum settings"; and, "the instructional focus . . . must be consistent with the professional foundation curriculum." Absent in this explicit mandate, however, is a pedagogical rationale for this arrangement or guidance for how this form of instruction should be implemented.

ORIGINS OF FIELD EDUCATION
AS AN EDUCATIONAL CONSTRUCT

The complexion of field instruction has, over time, taken on a variety of tinges, tones, and shapes. We see variations in such aspects as the role of the instructor, the use of concurrent and block plans, types of group or peer supervision, and methods of recording. But, extending the metaphor a bit, these changes are largely cosmetic. The field experience, although an educational imperative, remains ancillary to the prominence of the classroom as the primary source of learning and preparation for practice.

Stepping back in time, we find that this educational doctrine is not, as is the case with social constructions in general, preordained, but a tentative idea selectively influenced by permutations in context, culture, power, and discourse. As was noted at the outset, the origin of a particular construct is the result of a process of selection among other ideas and constructs.

The links between practical and theoretical forms of education trail back to the medieval craft guilds when apprentices gained their skills by working with a master. With the emergence of the major professions–most noteworthy, law and medicine–the period of apprenticeship remained indispensable to the attainment of professional status.

And so at the turn of this century, the first deliberations about the nature of educational preparation for social work not only included but gave primacy to the need for a period of apprenticeship. The budding field was receptive to Anna Dawes' advice that there was much to be gained by making it possible for practitioners to "transmit to their successors what they had learned during their years of service . . . to save him [sic] from the needless repetition of mistakes" (Bruno, 1948, pp. 138-139). Mary Richmond's plan for the first training school included Dawes' recommendation; it also insisted that the curriculum should emphasize "practical work rather than academic material" and that students should have the opportunity to "observe social work practice under the supervision of their instructors" (Bruno, 1948, p. 138). A final recommendation that heralds a major proposal of this essay was that the responsibility for teaching social work methods should be the responsibility of the field component; the classroom was to concern itself only with the general principles governing all social work (p. 139). In any case, the construct of the field segment as discrete mode of instruction, separate from the classroom, was accepted by the incipient institutional structure of social work.

Although this separation from the classroom persisted, the primacy of the field as the center for learning practice was short lived. With Abraham Flexner's imputation that social work was not a profession–he could not identify a method that was unique to the practice nor were its techniques intellectually communicable–the weight of the responsibility for education shifted from the agency to the university. The pedagogical gene that shaped the figure and form of professional education in the years to follow was now viable and the distinction between education and training was made even more explicit. In somewhat elitist terms, the head of the Simmons College School of Social Work in 1911 made this distinction: Training was the acquisition of experience under leadership; education was the acquisition of knowledge (Bruno, 1948, p. 143). The field was designated as the practical subsidiary to the intellectual authority of the academic classroom.

THE CHICAGO ALTERNATIVES

A reading of history can leave one with a sense, perhaps Utopian, that it might have been different. What I have in mind is the possibility that, if things had worked out in other ways, professional education could as easily have adopted an alternative construct about the nature of experiential learning. Specifically, this alternative embraces the educational principles advanced by Jane Addams and John Dewey during the same early years of social work. Although these ideas did not survive the selection process, they are more than merely historical curiosities. They remain, as I will explain, serious and useful foundations for a sound approach to field education.

In those early years when Mary Richmond and other key East Coast educators were beginning to sketch out the identity of the profession, movements were afoot in Chicago that spoke to a more balanced partnership between field and class. For example, Sophonisba Breckenridge and Edith Abbott, the founders of the School of Social Service Administration at the University of Chicago, argued that education for social work should be rigorous and multidisciplinary, combining theory, research and practical experience in the field (Altany, 1992). Taking the higher intellectual ground, they regarded field work as essential, "but only to the extent that it embodied carefully planned and supervised learning experiences in selected agencies" (Costin, 1983, cited in Altany, 1992).

Complementing this position was another that maintained that knowing and doing, knowledge and experience (and, one might add, valuing) were inseparable and interdependent. In this view, the field was not considered as subordinate or dependent on knowledge generated and taught in the academy. It was, instead, regarded both as the source of experiential wisdom and the site where the validity of the scholarship of the academic center might be tested and implemented.

It was the "Chicago School," the sociology and education departments of the University of Chicago, that generated these ideas about learning and doing. Dynamic and innovative, these departments were deliberately involved in community affairs including welfare reform, the public schools, and the settlement movement. At the forefront was John Dewey whose bond with Hull House's Jane Addams was especially significant. Dewey, among his many other community commitments, served as a trustee of Hull House while actively engaged in the daily life of the immigrants, the citizens and the working people who benefitted from the democratic and collegial climate of the settlement house. As Bernstein (1966) recalls, "Dewey was welcomed by the Jane Addams circle because he could bring the theory and methods of social philosophy to bear on the concrete facts" (p. 37).

The settlement movement began to wane in the early 1920s as did its influence on the embryonic profession. The settlement was, after all, a philosophy and a program that did not employ a specific method. Thus it failed to conform to the construct of professionalism advocated by Flexner and popularly adopted by the growing number of social work education programs across the country.

FOUNDATIONS OF A REFLECTIVE, CRITICAL MODEL

Nonetheless, John Dewey's ideas about learning persist. Germinated in his alliance with Hull House, his enduring wisdom is acknowledged by modern scholars in the fields of education. And they are equally germane to our interests in optimal preparation for professional practice and the problems of the hierarchical relation of classroom to field. Let us consider how these ideas might be shaped into an alternative construct for professional education that might enhance the potential for integration between the conceptual and operative dimensions of the curriculum.

What Dewey called a "pedagogical fallacy" dismissed the idea of the hierarchical relationship between classroom and field. This "fallacy" refers to the error in assuming that previously acquired knowledge and theory (classroom content) will prepare the learner for eventual practice in the field. Quite simply, the rational and systematic organization of knowledge taught in the classroom cannot prepare the learner for the unforeseen contingencies and irrational demands of actual practice. The most effective learning is gained in the immediate, vital experience–where meaning is directly located–not in a setting that promises to prepare one for something that may happen in the future (Dewey, 1938, pp. 48-49). More important, the dynamics of experiential learning are more likely to encourage critical thinking.

Recently, Robert Bellah and his associates (Bellah, Madsen, Sullivan, Swidler, & Tipton, 1991) eloquently expressed their disquiet about the fundamental shift in our culture toward an exclusively scientific paradigm of knowledge that supports the separation of learning and doing. They transposed Dewey's premises in these terms:

> . . . one learns, not through accumulating tested propositions about the objective world, but through participation in social practices, by assuming social roles, by becoming familiar with exemplary narratives and with typical characters who illustrate a variety of patterns of behavior. One does not feel like an autonomous subject learning facts about an objective world out there. One becomes what one knows. (Bellah et al., p. 158)

To "become what one knows," to be able to participate in the social world of our clients, however, requires the learner to develop the ability to use critical reasoning or reflective thinking.

Kitchener (1983) contends that Dewey's seminal work on critical inquiry is only the starting point since his work is limited to stages of problem solving concerned only with objective problems that do have an attainable and correct solution. This is not the case in social work practice. A single correct or objective solution does not exist for the human problems encountered in the field by social workers. Consider only the bare facts of a fairly common scenario. Mrs. Roy is depressed, frustrated about her failure to curb her daughter's use of drugs. Her husband is of little help since he is more concerned with the possibility of losing his job. What is to be done? The problems are serious enough; the absence of a reasonable solution is even more disheartening.

If, in a better world, there was a possible solution to such griev-
ous problems, uncertainty would still prevail. For one thing, the
consequences of any choice or decision cannot be known until some
future time and even then only through subjective interpretation.
And not the least, we find that the consequences we are trying to
evaluate inevitably are enmeshed in a web of other conditions,
influences, and contingencies that muddle the connections between
the solution and the outcome. If Mrs. Roy chose or was helped to
become more confident and assertive, there is no way of being
certain that her actions, any more than, say, her daughter's maturation, change of friends, the economic picture, or even more subtle
catalysts had something to do with how things turned out.

To put it directly, the student (and the seasoned practitioner) must
contend with complex, ambiguous human circumstances for which
there are no prescriptions, equations, recipes, or dependable guidelines that will ensure one predictable solution. As Gitterman and
Miller (1991) point out, it would be a mistake to place "the worker
front and center as the maker, shaker, breaker and doer" in the
helping process that, as they define it, is "analogous to a joint
venture characterized by mutuality, shared goals, and openness
about means and ends" (p. 282). To be sure, foundational frameworks and theories gained in the classroom serve as a lens that may
help the learner get a better likeness of the particulars and perhaps
distinguish between the ground and field of the problem. But this
knowledge cannot anticipate the ever-changing experiences that
will be encountered in the untidy and inconstant context of field
practice.

Many students suffer frustration and disappointment when they
begin to comprehend that diligent study will not be rewarded with a
dependable kit of techniques to fit all occasions. They need to be
helped to understand that uncertainty is part of the knowing process
and that, as I will show, this process of knowing calls for their
ability to engage in reflective thinking and judgment.

Educating for Reflective Thinking: Some Examples

To set the scene for some thoughts about the talents of reflective thinking, what they entail and how they can be developed, it
is useful to cite the few current examples of educational schemes

and experiments designed to foster reflective and critical reasoning. Although these educational plans are pertinent to the field practicum, they are now being used in practice classrooms by educators who acknowledge the signal role of reflective thought in practice.

An ambitious project, located at the University of Bristol, employs a program called Enquiry and Action Learning (Burgess & Jackson, 1990). The program is based on knowledge about adult learning and responsibility and respect for the wealth of knowledge and skills that students possess. Actual scenarios, problems of practice, are presented to a group of students. Study groups of students explore the problem, decide their learning priorities, and consult a broad range of resources available. They confer with each other, consult with a facilitator and constantly engage in processes of evaluation. The primary aim is constructive integration of theory and practice along with closer relationships with agencies, the creation of adult learning environments, and preparation for team collaboration.

The theory of constructivism expressly supports the teaching of Dean and Fleck-Henderson (1991). Based on the assumption that the meaning of a problem is located within the client's understanding of her experience, students are first exposed to exercises designed to awaken their understanding of how they and others define and construct their personal realities and premises. When they move on to decompound case material and grasp its narrative nature, critical reasoning is stirred by comparative analyses of how various theories might define the problem in contrasting ways and how different modes of intervention would differentially affect the helping process. Also subject to scrutiny are the effects of agency policy, and political, cultural and ethical implications.

Cossom's (1991) educational plan to develop critical thinking brings reality into the classroom by using a carefully selected case to keep "the discussion grounded upon some of the stubborn facts that must be faced in real life situations" (p. 140). This learner-centered approach is compatible with the principles of learning already noted: Its focus is on the kind of reasoning required in the absence of specific solutions; on the need to cope with competing alternatives and courses of action; and on the influence of personal constructs or assumptions on how a reality is understood.

The Nature of Reflective Judgment

As the examples previously cited indicate, reflective thinking or judgment is not something that can be taught or even enhanced by way of traditional educational methods–typically, the creation of a bank of knowledge from which the student can draw what ostensibly is needed. Experiential learning is required. The instances previously noted illustrate various types of experiential learning: the Bristol program uses an active, inductive, group-centered approach; Dean and Fleck-Henderson create circumstances in which learners are bound to discover the limits of their respective world views; and Cossom similarly focuses on the influence of personal constructs on real-life situations.

Kitchener (1983) suggests that the educational process may very well founder if students are not actively awakened to the influence of personal constructions of reality. As she observes, reflective thinking may be difficult to achieve for many people whose minds are closed by their beliefs about the nature of their worlds or, as she puts it, by the individual's "logically related network of assumptions about knowledge and reality" (p. 80). If they are not challenged, such a closed system of beliefs will limit the range of questions one might ask about any event; conversely, and in a self-justifying way, the kinds of questions that are asked will determine the answers obtained or, for that matter, desired.[1]

Kitchener and King's (1981) "reflective judgment model," based on extensive studies of students' learning patterns, proves to be enlightening in how it identifies the types of "network of assumptions" that might impede or enhance a learner's development of reflective judgment and thought. In addition, it differentiates the assumptions about reality that support each mode of reasoning and their respective justifications. Thus the model can serve as a useful guide for determining the kind of help and experience the learner may need in order to relinquish certain conventional modes of thinking and problem-solving that get in the way of learning to become a reflective practitioner.

Collapsing the seven stages of the model into three for our purposes, the first and most elementary way of defining reality is a form of knowing that assumes that knowledge exists absolutely. Here the individual is sure that some legitimate authority can provide the answers that are required. This is an unquestioning and secure kind of knowing that searches only for facts, recipes, and instructions. This learner only wants to know "what works" with little room for ambiguity or doubt. Unchallenged, he or she would drift toward a mode of practice "by the book," in strict accord with agency policy or some closed-system model of practice. Passing but beguiling fads or schools of practice might also prove attractive.

The second stage of knowing represents a radical swing to an opposing assumption, a shift from an absolutist to a loosely skeptical position. Here the individual may acknowledge that perhaps there is such a thing as objective truth "out there" but, for various reasons, that truth really can't be known. This learner doubts the possibility of ever gaining rational and dependable knowledge or that any authority can provide the right answer. In this instance, the learner may feel justifiably excused from the need to engage in further inquiry or study. Any knowledge claims are loosely relativistic and idiosyncratic, expressed in such forms as, "I'm just doing my own thing," or "What feels right is what's true for me." In professional practice, this approach may wrongfully be dignified by the label, "eclectic practice" or "intuitive practice."

The third stage most accurately represents what reflective thought and judgment are all about. On this level, the learner can, with a measure of security, abandon the belief that there are ultimate truths and objective realities. But the abandonment of this belief does not justify the abandonment of the pursuit of understanding. Curiosity and critical thinking are, in fact, enhanced. The learner appreciates that reality is known only in subjective terms, as personal constructs about the world and, therefore, always uncertain and problematical. Accordingly, inquiry is seen as an ongoing process of interpretation that must be flexible enough to consider that any observation or judgment must take account of its place in time, context, and history. Although the reflective practitioner may arrive at a plausible impression or solution of a human event, the validity of such conclusions always remains open to new information and observations derived from the helping experience. This level of reasoning gives new meaning to the old social work aphorism, "The effective practitioner is one who can be comfortable with ambiguity." Indisputably, it is this mature level of reflective thinking that we want our students to achieve as they prepare to enter the enigmatic and often obscure terrain of clients' lives.

Implications for Education

This overview of experiential learning and education for reflective judgment recommends the need to rethink our educational philosophy and programs. Research in the field of education supporting the reflective judgment model tells us that we cannot assume that all students of social work share common cognitive styles or ways of defining reality. These cognitive variations raise doubts about the utility of a standard curriculum that prescribes what we believe students ought to know. We cannot anticipate how or even if this knowledge will be processed. While these observations may not apply to most students, it is not uncommon for classroom and field teachers alike to bemoan the tenacity of some students who plead for simplistic "how-to-do" prescriptions while others insist on relying on their own "intuitional" if not anti-intellectual impulses. Instructors often are burdened by their "problem students" who either reject theory in favor of formulas or who see a disciplined preparation for professional practice as meaningless if not a waste of time. And a few more undoubtedly march through their programs doing what is basically required to earn their degree but depart virtually untouched by their exposure to professional education. Integration between field and class, based on the experiential nature of learning, suggests a solution to these barriers to learning.

Field-Class Partnership

As the previous examples of education for reflective practice show, the classroom can and should be used to good advantage for educing and making explicit students' cognitive orientations to reality as a prelude to the development of students' reflective and critical talents. The risk, however, is that reliance on the classroom experience alone can turn out to be merely an intellectual exercise, removed as it is from the more acute exigencies of daily practice.

The real-life emergencies and paradoxes that characterize the field practicum recommend it as the vital center for the development of reflective thinking. Here students are exposed not to cases but to people caught up in a variety of crises and demands. Clients and their problems form only one group; administrators, planners, practitioners, members of other professions, community folk, and various others round out the larger context of learning. Together they shape a particular social and cultural arena at a particular point in time, one that takes its character and complexion from its consensual ideologies, beliefs, and routines.

Thus the learning in the field offers something more penetrating than the analysis of a hypothetical case. Nor is the student limited to a specific problem that may temptingly invite a "right" or "appropriate" method and solution. Instead, the open-endedness and complexity of the protracted human puzzle encountered in the field are more likely to accentuate the need for critical and reflective thought. Not the least, this experience may relieve students' dependence on rigid structures and/or quick-fix answers. As participants and observers, they may come to terms with the idea that uncertainty and ambiguity can indeed be tolerated, and that the expertise they seek is not something to be imposed on the client. Rather, they can be helped to appreciate that expertise is an ethical and sensitive process shared with their clients.

Now this may sound like dropping someone off the end of the dock in a sink-or-swim manner. This is not at all the case. Thoughtful guidance and proper mentorship are needed to establish a structured and secure climate for learning. Before learners can learn to act, they must first learn how to "see" or create some instructive meaning and order for themselves, meanwhile putting their "network of assumptions" to the test. With greater confidence about the validity of their perceptions, the learner can recognize that "what I do" depends on "how I understand" and not on a slick, all-purpose technology or method (Saleebey, 1991).

This proposition hardly diminishes the importance of the classroom and its capacity to provide the intellectual and theoretical component of professional education. To the contrary, reversing the traditional sequence of learning–what Schon (1983) calls "technical rationality" or the application of scientific principles to concrete problems–will foster greater harmony and integration between class and field. Perhaps "reversing" is not the most accurate term since the most desirable arrangement between field and class should involve discourse and exchange. In what might be considered a feedback loop, students and mentors in the field can advise and consult with the curriculum and classroom about the kinds of knowledge and skills required in their particular community of practice. For example, abstract theoretical constructs such as culture, values, ethics, discrimination, and social policy become more lucid, integrative, and relevant when they are linked to real-life dilemmas within specific human communities. This integration can more readily be attained by way of a "bottom up" approach–that is, through the study of the actual human story–rather than a "top down" mode in which abstractions are imposed on and in some way distort that story (Bruner, 1986).

The form and structure that such class-field partnerships might take cannot be prescribed as a universal model. Inevitably form and structure must express a curriculum plan that at least takes account of its culture and community, its social service system, and the particular mission and philosophy of the school.

Some things can be said, however. The field educator or mentor must be accorded equal status with the classroom teacher. In fact, the former's educational responsibilities can be considered even more complex and demanding, considering the goals of education already described. Among them, the ability to plan a coherent educational scheme, to enable learners to transcend the limits of their well-worn ways of knowing and doing, and to exploit the unexpected opportunities for learning that momentarily arise in the field are pretty stiff pedagogical requirements.

Although the choice of the practicum setting may have to depend on the availability (and collaboration) of services and agencies in the community, this should not necessarily dictate its design. Whether the setting of the practicum is a single social agency, a host organization, a teaching center comprising several agencies, or a venue established by the academy that is focused on a particular field of practice (e.g., aging, youth, poverty), a variety of possible learning modes–including the use of the student collectivity–might be explored.

Careful study can reveal other alternatives, including the "feminist alternatives" described by Chernesky (1986), that call for a collegial climate for learning and growth. The potential for integration of knowledge and experience is amplified when the learner is confirmed as the determining link between the "knowing" and "doing" components of the educational program. Inevitably, she or he will need to judge the relevance of each for the other.

LAST WORDS

There is more to this essay than only the proposal for re-formation or the re-construction of one component of social work education–the field practicum. To be sure, any serious changes in field education would disturb and perhaps alter all other aspects of the curriculum. An overriding issue is the tendency of the profession (like any other longstanding institution) to allow itself to be bound by its own constructs. When this occurs, there is a disinterest in history, an indifference to the origins of constructs or creeds that, as my brief historical jaunt shows, may have been useful only for their own era or, for that matter, merely accidents of history. In what we inherit we may discover wisdom; among these lovely pearls, however, we are just as likely to find some outworn relics.

NOTE

1. The author has previously developed these ideas and their relevance for social work practice within a cognitive and social learning framework in the following: *Social Learning and Change: A Cognitive Approach to the Human Services* (Columbia: University of South Carolina Press, 1981); *Creative Change: A Cognitive Humanistic Approach to Social Work Practice* (New York: Routledge, 1984; and A cognitive-humanistic/social learning perspective on social group work practice. *Social Work with Groups* 11(1/2) 1988, 9-32.

REFERENCES

Altany, C. (1992). Power in the midst of powerlessness: The contributions of Sophonisba P. Breckenridge to social work during the formative years of the profession. Unpublished doctoral dissertation. Case Western Reserve University.

Bellah, R. N., Madsen, R., Sullivan, W. S., Swidler, A., & Tipton, S. M. (1991). *The Good Society*. New York: Knopf.

Ben-David, J., & Collins, R. (1966). Social factors in the origins of a new science: The case of psychology. *American Sociological Review, 31*, 451-465.

Bernstein, R. J. (1966). *John Dewey*. New York: Washington Square Press.

Bruner, J. (1986). *Actual minds, possible worlds*. Cambridge: Harvard University Press.

Bruno, F. (1948). *Trends in social work*. New York: Columbia University Press.

Burgess, H., & Jackson, S. (1990). Enquiry and action learning: A new approach to social work education. *Social Work Education* (British), *9*, 3-19.

Chernesky, R. H. (1986). A new model of supervision. In N. VanDenBergh & L. B. Cooper (Eds.), *Feminist visions for social work*, pp. 128-148. Silver Spring, MD: National Association of Social Workers.

Cossom, J. (1991). Teaching from cases: Education for critical thinking. *Journal of Teaching in Social Work, 5*, 139-155.

Dean, R., & Fleck-Henderson, A. (1990). Teaching clinical theory and practice through a constructivist lens. Paper presented at Annual Program Meeting of Council on Social Work Education, New Orleans.

Dewey, J. (1938). *Experience and education*. New York: Collier.

Gergen, K. J. (1985). The social constructionist movement in modern psychology. *American Psychologist, 40*, 266-275.

Gitterman, A., & Miller, I. (1991) Should salaries be contingent on outcomes achieved with client? No. In E. Gambrill & R. Pruger (Eds.), *Controversial issues in social work*. Boston: Allyn & Bacon.

Heisenberg, W. (1958). *Physics and philosophy*. New York: Harper & Brothers.

Kitchener, K. S. (1983). Educational goals and reflective thinking, *The Educational Forum, 48*, 75-96.

Kitchener, K. S., & King, P. M. (1981). Reflective judgment: Concepts of justification and their relationship to age and education. *Journal of Applied Developmental Psychology, 2*, 89-116.

Saleebey, D. (1991). Technological fix: Altering the consciousness of the social work profession. *Journal of Sociology and Social Welfare, 18*, 51-68.

Schon, D. A. (1983). *The reflective practitioner*. New York: Basic Books.

Siporin, M. (1975). *Introduction to social work practice*. New York: Macmillan.

Webster's Third New International Dictionary (1971). Springfield, MA: G. & C. Merriam.

The Student as Consumer

Joan Hardcastle

SUMMARY. In this article, a recent social work graduate reports on her experience as a student in a social work practice course informed by constructivist and social constructionist theory. Based on a weekly journal, the student takes the reader on a journey through a class in which students were invited to share responsibility for the learning process. An isomorphic process in which students experienced the classroom as clients might experience the social worker in practice is described.

INTRODUCTION

Practice from a constructivist/social constructionist perspective can illuminate those values that form the core of the profession of social work. There is increased interest in schools of social work in teaching practice from this theoretical approach and in evaluating the effectiveness of such instruction. This paper describes my experience as an M.S.W. student at the University of Georgia in learning social work practice from a theory base of constructionism. In this article, I will describe portions of both the content and process of one course, Family Treatment and Family Dynamics,[1] in which a constructionist epistemology provided a framework for learning.[2]

Joan Hardcastle, MSW, is employed in a public mental health center in Gainesville, GA. The author would like to thank Dr. Paul Gallant of the University of Georgia for his support and encouragement in the preparation of this article.

[Haworth co-indexing entry note]: "The Student as Consumer," Hardcastle, Joan. Co-published simultaneously in *Journal of Teaching in Social Work* (The Haworth Press, Inc.) Vol. 8, No. 1/2, 1993, pp. 183-196; and: *Revisioning Social Work Education: A Social Constructionist Approach* (ed: Joan Laird) The Haworth Press, Inc., 1993, pp. 183-196. Multiple copies of this article/chapter may be purchased from The Haworth Document Delivery Center [1-800-3-HAWORTH; 9:00 a.m. - 5:00 p.m. (EST)].

This learning experience was one I can best refer to in terms used by Michael White and David Epston (1990)–"unusual"– by which I mean both significant and preferred. What I share here stands as an interpretation of my own experience in a classroom of 26 students. I used a journal, which I entitled "The Reflecting Student: Dialogues about Dialogues," as my witness of the weekly process and as a text which would endure the passing of time and the blurring of memory. Portions of that journal will be shared as I describe the process of this class experience. It is an experience that I am interested in sharing with others who may be curious about such learning. Further, the writing of this narrative provides me with an external audience and contributes to the endurance of my new academic story.

In order to help others better understand the meaning of this experience for me, I will briefly state those prior ideas and restraints which across time had become part of my story and, therefore, which I brought with me to this class. From early childhood I was the sort of person who found ways to help others. I would further describe myself a person who complied with the constructs of those institutions with which I came into contact, someone who adapted herself to perform those expectations and requirements necessary to be well regarded. I married young, abandoned career aspirations for family, and did not begin to pursue my social work career in earnest until age 42. I obtained my B.S.W., worked part time in a psychiatric hospital for one year, and then began working on my M.S.W. at the University of Georgia. Throughout both my undergraduate and graduate classes, I was a serious and dedicated student. Socially and culturally I had learned well about authority and power. I understood what Michel Foucault refers to as "the gaze" and being subjected to "normalizing judgements" (discussed in White & Epston, 1990). In fact, I learned very well how to listen to each professor, how to adopt their style, and how to successfully give back to them their own ideas, theories, and approaches. Participating in class meant knowing the "right answer," and only when I was relatively certain in my response did I venture to express my ideas during class discussions. Although I earned excellent grades, the classroom certainly was not a space in which I felt creative.

COURSE CONTENT

Seminar in Family Dynamics and Treatment, SW 843/944, was offered as a 6-hour advanced social work seminar for 26 students. It is a required course in clinical specialization, one in which family therapy theories and practices compatible with an ecological model are studied in relation to social work practice with individuals, couples, and families presenting with a variety of life's difficulties. The professor adapted and integrated a constructionist perspective in framing this course.

Materials drawn upon included 6 texts, 29 journal articles, and several videotapes. In addition, on two separate occasions, guest clinicians came to share new ideas and present materials on post-modern social work practice with families. Attendance at a one day marriage and family seminar was another learning option. Although these learning tools and resources may sound quite usual, all of them were offered in a unique way. This can best be described by my speaking to the process and key themes of the course.

CLASS STRUCTURE

The structure provided by the professor for this class was indeed quite different from any I had experienced in my educational travels. I am using the idea of structure to include the syllabus, evaluation, texts and other materials, assignments, and the daily agenda. One key difference I noticed in the structure in this constructionist approach was in the degree of flexibility and emphasis on student responsibility, along with an openness to student ideas for learning.

The syllabus provides an example of this flexibility in structure. During the second class meeting, the syllabus was offered as a draft proposal only. Each student was asked to participate in making additions, critiques, or changes to suit their learning needs. This process was one of co-creating both content and expectations of the course. We were accepting responsibility for our learning, with the freedom to select our own best avenues.

One traditional academic aspect of a syllabus is to address the means for grading each student. This approach had in the past contributed to a focus on the grade rather than the learning process. For this class, the evaluation of learning was based on a contract. Each student was asked to write up a learning contract, including their desired grade, around which each "expert student" determined what learning experiences would work best for them. Along with these choices, the student described ways for demonstrating her or his individual learning. With the idea of the evaluation contracted for, I felt a freedom and shift of focus to my own learning process.

For me and a number of my fellow students, this kind of freedom in the academic world was a welcome change. For many others it was anxiety producing. There were complaints and requests from those students who were uncomfortable with such an unusual occurrence. It would be several weeks before the traditional academic story, one in which the professor acts as authority and power figure, would be replaced with one in which the professor occupies the roles of collaborator and facilitator.

A second feature which contributed to the open context for learning was the weekly class format. Each class began with a discussion of the day's agenda. Through open discussion, students made requests for types of learning for that day, describing any unmet needs. This again provided a kind of learning in which the student takes responsibility for defining his or her own learning needs. Requests included options such as role plays, supervision on specific cases, consultations, and videotapes. The entire class became part of the negotiation on such choices. As we proceeded, the professor frequently inquired about the class's satisfaction with the process. Again, there was considerable leeway to make changes in the agenda to meet the needs of the students.

As mentioned, the texts and materials offered as resources for our learning included 6 books and 29 articles. The ways in which they would be utilized would depend on each student's learning contract and desire. Each week several articles were offered by the professor. The students were asked to read and critique one of these articles. At first glance, this appears to be a traditional type of assignment. However, there were variations in how students chose to participate in this assignment. Negotiations took place between students and professor to better adapt assignments for each individual. There was a suggested structure for these critiques, which included five questions to be answered. These questions asked the students to reflect on the article and to share their own ideas and impressions. The nature of the questions again reflects a constructionist philosophical base:

1. What points, if any, in this material did you like, agree with, find interesting or helpful? Take note of any key concepts.
2. What points, if any, did you not like, disagree with, or find not helpful?
3. What ideas or concepts in this material require clarification in the classroom?
4. What question do you have from reading this material that you think would be good for class discussion? Come up with one.
5. What ideas, if any, did you find personally meaningful, i.e., ideas that might have an impact on how you think about your way of practicing with clients or ideas that you might consider incorporating into your personal style of working with families?

This critique, approximately three pages in length, was turned in to the professor each week. Some weeks we discussed the articles as well as any feelings or questions they elicited; other weeks we did not. The articles stimulated my thinking and offered creative practice examples. I found these articles to be resources and examples of constructionist theory and practice, and fuel for our classroom dialogues and exercises. In general, all of the texts, articles, and materials felt like resources and options available for me to use in my own best fashion. All of these structures–the syllabus, texts and other reading materials, contracts and grades, assignments, and class agendas–contributed to the process of learning social work practice from a constructionist perspective. I will share my experience of this learning process by describing some of the key themes I noticed.

Opening a Space

Beginnings can be of utmost importance in many arenas. The initial class session began with the unusual. First, the physical setting of the classroom took on a certain importance. We were asked to move all of the tables and chairs into a large circle. This circular type arrangement spoke to an underlying notion that we were a group of people joined together with some common interest. Gone were the notions of a front or back of the classroom, and everyone was equally visible. After this was accomplished, the traditional academic process of passing out a syllabus, class requirements, and assignments did not occur. Instead, we began with our first "conversation" as we practiced working with a family problem; we became, for the first time, a "reflecting team" (Andersen, 1991). The emphasis, we were told, was to have conversations, and to share as many ideas or possibilities as we could create. We were divided into groups or teams, with each team having an opportunity to have a conversation while the others listened, an exercise which afforded each class member a chance to participate. This was my first taste of this form of an adult learning model, and I experienced the value and power that can be realized from different or alternative versions of a problem. We would repeat this reflecting team approach in a variety of combinations many more times to come. Our circle had been formed, and in the words of one student, "a thinking space" was provided. The atmosphere was one of an open space in which creativity was encouraged and fostered.

The reflecting team format was unique in and of itself. However, the special ingredient present for me was the collaborative, non-expert stance central to practice models being generated from a constructionist perspective. Our open space was a place in which no one "right way" to do things or no one correct interpretation was sought. I felt a new freedom to hear ideas from others and to create new ideas myself. Our instructor was not the all-knowing expert, but rather a facilitator expressing respect for students and a curiosity about the meaning of each student's experience. The freedom to say whatever we thought, with no threat of being judged correct and with no grade at stake, opened the class to an enormous amount of participation. I was astounded by the numbers of ideas, possibilities, and interventions which were offered. I felt excited at allowing my mind to create ideas with no worry about "the right answer"! At times this new academic story seemed a bit too much unusual and we would look to the professor for an expert answer. We were, after all, accustomed to our old restraints and sought what we were accustomed to–the reperformance of the old story. Dr. Gallant consistently reminded us of our strengths, maintaining a bi-directional dialogue to create this "assisted learning." It occurred to me at this time that this was exactly the atmosphere we were seeking to create for our clients. I was just beginning to experience this isomorphic process.

Authority and Power

The structures of many of the social systems of our culture are ripe with technologies of power. Such structures shape individual thought and behavior, creating systems in which some are subjugated and scrutinized (White, 1991). Instructors and supervisors can provide quite a different experience for students by teaching practice from a non-expert stance. In place of presenting as the authority and/or power figure, the instructor models what it can mean to be a co-author of possibilities. For this class, many of the structures which inherently reinforce a relationship of great power differential were abandoned. On several occasions the instructor spoke to the use of power and authority and solicited responses from the students about his own uses of power. It became apparent that he intended to minimize existing power and authority inequalities however and whenever possible.

Collaborating

Like the clinician in emerging constructionist clinical models, the instructor maintains a stance of curiosity and quest for understanding rather than one in which he or she purports to hold particular "truths" or sets of privileged ideas. Students then are invited to offer their own questions, intuitions, and perspectives about clients and their problems. Students' strengths become the focus, as their own life experience and meanings are incorporated into the learning process, on one level, and their clinical work, on another. The assumption that we as students were the experts in our own lives, capable, resourceful, with our own particular strengths, served to create a firsthand experience of the very message essential between client and clinician. The classroom became a model of a therapeutic environment where safety, acceptance, respect, and empowerment flourished.

The classroom setting provided weekly opportunities for the principles of constructionism to be modeled. The posture of the professor during a variety of learning exercises reinforced the non-expert/collaborator relationship. One student requested a supervision type exercise around a difficult case from his practicum. Prior to beginning this exercise, the class agreed to divide up into reflecting teams, each with a specific focus. In this fashion, we all were participants in this supervisory process. After the student and professor had their conversation about the case, each team also had an opportunity to respond to the conversation. Throughout the conversation between the student and professor, I noticed a consistent emphasis on the strengths of both the client and student. After this conversation, some reflecting teams offered ideas about the case itself, others on the supervisor's role, and still others on the entire interaction. Each group was given time to add ideas and responses without interruption. Not only did this exercise encourage all students to participate, but it also provided an alternative form to the usual cross-conversing style of communication. This process reinforced for me the idea that there can be many valid perceptions rather than one "right answer."

The idea of "right answer" is worthy of more attention in this narrative, not only because it was a concept I had experienced as restraining and oppressive in the past, but also because it seemed to frequent this classroom experience as well. I believe Michael White (1991) refers to this idea as using the language of "restraints of redundancy" because we, as students, are restrained from forming new distinctions around learning when "right answer" dominates our conversations. One of my journal entries gives evidence to this experience.

During a consultation exercise in one class session, our conversation took a turn. I noticed that the reflecting team format had been abandoned. Students were presenting ideas only to find others disagreeing with them and offering their own ideas as more correct. A debate ensued about what was "right" and views became more fixed. The atmosphere changed into one in which new information was neither allowed nor promoted. No longer were we engaged in a reflexive interaction. The flow of the conversation was random, and we were into our old ways of consulting–advice giving, expert stances, and judgements. The feeling for me was that of a storm wherein ideas were not being exchanged; rather a debate was taking place. Either/or stances were taken, with students arguing that particular pictures were right or that certain distinctions were more important. Factions and coalitions formed within the classroom, as we became what Tom Andersen (1991) calls a "standstill" system, one with no movement toward alternative ideas. These stormy experiences were not comfortable for me. Rather than collaborating or co-creating new ideas, we fell into a more traditional adversarial pattern. I became acutely aware of the differences in the learning context.

Strength versus Pathology

Practice from a constructionist perspective emphasizes client strength rather than pathology. We learned, through the materials we were exposed to in this class, the language of externalizing problems, of focusing on client strengths, energy, and insights rather than labeling and diagnosing (Goldstein, 1990). These ideas were embraced by many students early on in the course; nevertheless, old habits were difficult to shed. What became obvious was our previous training in pathology seeking and the propensity to think in those terms when listening to client stories. Students would ask for discussion around a variety of client problems, doubting that certain problems could be dealt with effectively from a strengths perspective. A number of different descriptions in which cases were approached from a constructionist perspective dispelled doubt after doubt. Our readings, our guest speakers, and our class discussions provided many creative new ideas for having conversations which supported this approach.

On several occasions our student conversations would reveal our own discomfort with so much uncertainty. As stated so well in an article by Karl Tomm (1989), "a complication of reflexive questioning is that it can foster disorganization, uncertainty, and confusion" (p. 12). If we, as students, abandoned the labeling and diagnosing approach, we would also leave behind some structures of security for ourselves. No wonder that many students in this class questioned the feasibility of a strengths approach. At first it may have been too unusual, with too many choices and uncertainties and, after all, we had worked very hard to become good diagnosticians.

Students as Consultants

The constructivist/social constructionist principle of the client as consultant was also modeled effectively in this class. As students, we were asked to participate in a research project. While participation was completely voluntary and anonymous, we were asked to contribute to the evaluation of teaching skills. We had experienced this sort of layering of interactions through the use of peer reflecting teams. Through participation in this research, we were being asked to give feedback to the professor, just as the constructionist clinician includes the client in a reflexive process about the therapeutic process. There is a sense of changing places in these interactions, as the client/student is afforded the position of consultant. That client/student then is providing the therapist or professor with an alternative view, another meaning system. This layering of ideas and exchanges contributes to the conversation and mutual understanding. For me, this interaction so obviously expressed respect–a core social work value.

I took the opportunity to further this consultant perspective through an exercise with my own journal. After each class period I would write my own dialogue about the classroom, as much as possible using the language and ideas of constructionism. I understood from this assignment how each experience was mine alone, and frequently would be reminded of that as other students expressed their unique experience of the prior week's exercise. At the suggestion of Dr. Gallant, I chose to provide each student with a copy of this journal prior to the quarter's end. The request was made that each person use the weekly critique questions in order to respond to my journal. It was agreed upon by the class that I would be allowed to read their responses for my own experience of their experiences. I was reminded by their contributions that we do not have direct knowledge of the world nor even an objective description of reality. What I had was my own experience of the class and that was of utmost importance for me, just as each of my peers had her or his own interpretations and meanings.

A Reflecting Team at Work

One particular reflecting team exercise stood out as an important contribution in my learning process. As a class, we agreed to a project involving an actual client of one student. The student had obtained the permission of this client to discuss anonymously the client's current difficulties. This conversation about the client's difficulties, along with the role play of the reflecting team participants and the student observers, was videotaped for the client. This videotape, which indeed was our feedback to the client, was reviewed by the client and student/therapist during a subsequent appointment. The client reported a sense of empowerment from the experience of listening to the group's conversation of her situation, in which evidence of her perseverance and other positive qualities were brought forth and given a voice. My journal entry about this event speaks of the intensity and energy with which the student participants worked. It also reveals my own feelings of being so humanly connected and deeply touched. After being part of this reflecting team, I understood on a different level the potential and power of this strengths approach. Sincerity and respect were reflected in the content and tone of that videotape. The student was later able to bring back the next layer, reflections of our reflections from her client. This videotape and subsequent reflections stood as evidence to our developing constructivist practice skills. Everyone agreed they found this experience extremely helpful.

The Old Academic Story

There was a process and movement during this 10-week class which I later learned is predictable. As I spoke of earlier, the course was not without storms. We would embrace the principles of constructionism and experience class periods of exciting and different interactions. We also, on several occasions, would experience "hiccups" (White & Epston, 1990). During these times I would notice a return to the performing of our old academic story. Students would request that the professor be more directive and ask for his expert knowledge. The old habit of subjugating ourselves to academic authorities would seduce us into reverting to old ways of being students. These invitations were consistently rejected by Dr. Gallant, and his language around these attempts would remind us of our own power and strength. In place of answers or directives he would use a type of reflexive questioning (Tomm, 1987). In response to this approach, students began once again attending to the their own truths and experienced meanings.

The New Academic Story

At the conclusion of this 10-week course I was aware it had been a meaningful and important part of my social work education. I began my practicum experience at a community mental health center and found I was able to bring this experience into my practice. One of my first clients became the subject of my exit exam. Within that piece of work I was able to relate the telling of her story and our collaborative work together. That narrative reflected my own style of opening up conversations and listening for the meaning of that client's life experience. I learned that the constructionism stance was not one which simply appealed to me, but also was one which I felt comfortable practicing.

In this new story the professor does not proclaim to be the expert in others' lives. He is merely interested in structuring teaching practices which, like therapy, create a context for re-authoring of lives. Several class exercises ended with our own applause. That was indeed both significant and preferred.

Being a participant in this class was a significant event for me. I believe it is a kind of marker which I will look back on as a milestone. This class experience served as a reconstruction of my academic story, opening a space for the possibility of new responses from me.

CONCLUSIONS

From my first introduction to the profession of social work, I heard about the principles of non-judgmental attitude, self-determination, empowerment, respect, and appreciation for diversity.

These were the very ideas which drew me to social work as a profession and made the profession unique for me. As I pursued my formal education, however, I found my practice courses teaching models in ways which did not demonstrate those beliefs. Many times during my academic process I was subjected to a scrutinizing gaze by those in positions of power and authority. I began by believing I had some good instincts and a way of being with people and learned to doubt my own abilities and internal resources. In many ways the social work education process contributed to my learning that others were the experts from whom I needed to learn as many "right answers" as possible. This could equip me in turn to subjugate my clients, pathologize and judge them, and submit them to the same gaze I had experienced–all under the guise of "treatment."

I believe that people cannot give what they have never experienced or received in some way. If we do not offer students an opportunity to experience learning and growth in a safe and open space, how can we expect them to have those practice skills with their clients. The course I have described gave me that opportunity. In the environment of that classroom we students had the chance to experience the ideas of joint discovery and mutual exploration. Our own stories were being told and retold in a new way that served to effect a change in me on a deeper level. I experienced first hand the listening for meaning of others and exploring those meanings to bring about understanding. With the removal of many instruments of power which had in the past contributed to oppressive and reductionistic learning, I was offered a new freedom. Each class session was a conversation, many dialogues, and certainly a model for the ways in which I wanted to be with people. It was strength strengthening, a deconstruction of the old and reconstructing of the new story. I learned about my own power, my own okayness and uniqueness, my special talents and gifts, and my own reality. I was better able to tune in to my own feelings and intuitions, and I learned to listen with a new openness to both external and internal thoughts and ideas. In the words of one of my classmates: "This was a singular learning experience."

My own narrative describes the ways in which it was singular for me. Language feels inadequate here, but I simply say–this was a powerful and meaningful way to learn.

NOTES

1. The course syllabus and reading list can be obtained by contacting Paul Gallant, PhD, School of Social work, Tucker Hall, University of Georgia, Athens, GA 30602.

2. While there are some important epistemological differences between the ideas expressed in "constructivism" and "social constructionism," the term "constructionism" will be used in this article to refer to clinical ideas generated from both philosophical frameworks.

REFERENCES

Andersen, T. (Ed.) (1991). *The reflecting team: Dialogues and dialogues about the dialogues.* New York: Norton.

Goldstein, H. (1990). Strength or pathology: Ethical and rhetorical contrasts in approaches to practice. *Families in Society: The Journal of Contemporary Human Services, 71,* 267-275.

Tomm, K. (1989). Externalizing the problem and internalizing personal agency. *Journal of Strategic and Systemic Therapies, 8*(1), 54-59.

Tomm, K. (1988). Interventive interviewing: Part III. Intending to ask circular, strategic, or reflexive questions? *Family Process, 27,* 1-15.

Tomm, K. (1987). Interventive interviewing: Part II. Reflexive questioning as a means to enable self healing. *Family Process, 26,* 167-183.

White, M. (1991). Deconstruction and therapy. *Dulwich Center Newsletter,* No. 3, 21-39.

White, M., & Epston, D. (1990). *Narrative means to therapeutic ends.* New York: Norton.

Notes on Interpreting the Human Condition: A "Constructed" HBSE Curriculum

Dennis Saleebey

SUMMARY. The objective of this paper is to challenge the assumptions of the usual approaches to the Human Behavior in the Social Environment (HBSE) curriculum, and to forward the beginning of another approach that affords itself a more critical stance toward understanding elements of our daily world and various theoretical construals of them. The basis of the critique is both constructivist and "postmodern" (see below) in that we live in a world that is hardly imagined by more conventional content. This is a work underway, however, not a work complete.

INTRODUCTION

... an image is not cumulative, and the late stages of life are not the finest and fullest presentations of one's self.

(Hillman & Ventura, 1992, p. 64)

With these words, James Hillman cautions against uncritical belief in the predictive finery of most developmental theories. Rather than rote passages through various physical, cultural, and social

---

Dennis Saleebey, DSW, is Professor and Chair of the PhD program in social welfare at the School of Social Welfare, Twente Hall, University of Kansas, Lawrence, KS 66045.

[Haworth co-indexing entry note]: "Notes on Interpreting the Human Condition: A "Constructed" HBSE Curriculum," Saleebey, Dennis. Co-published simultaneously in *Journal of Teaching in Social Work* (The Haworth Press, Inc.) Vol. 8, No. 1/2, 1993, pp. 197-217; and: *Revisioning Social Work Education: A Social Constructionist Approach* (ed: Joan Laird) The Haworth Press, Inc., 1993, pp. 197-217. Multiple copies of this article/chapter may be purchased from The Haworth Document Delivery Center [1-800-3-HAWORTH; 9:00 a.m. - 5:00 p.m. (EST)].

197

portals driven by general epigenetic ground plan, the more interesting thing about human beings is that we are continually negotiating the intersection of context, contingency, and conceptualization. We do this, more or less successfully, with the inventiveness of the novelist, the transforming eye of the painter, the cozy mutuality of the conspirator, and the circumspection of the critic.

I begin with some guiding assumptions. Any curriculum is, at some level of understanding, shaped by metaphor. For example, the ecological perspective, general systems theory, Freudian theory, and theories of stress and adaptation are, whatever else they are, symbolic and narrative devices for organizing the swarming confusion that is human behavior. In Isaiah Berlin's (1976) words, metaphor is

> neither mere embellishment, nor a repository of secret wisdom, nor the creation of a world parallel to the real world, nor an addiction to, or distortion of reality . . . it is the natural, inevitably transient, but at the time of its birth or growth, the only possible way of perceiving, interpreting, explaining that is open to . . . that particular time and place. . . . (p. 104)

Western social science (among other sciences) has long had a fear of metaphor that has been expressed primarily through the prominence of the "myth of objectivity" (Spence, 1987, p. 3). Without metaphor, however, we are doomed to lame description and superficial numerizing. Another assumption of this paper is that, while there are "many ways of knowing" (Hartman, 1990), the social work profession has not sampled deeply from all of those wells of knowledge. Our "theories" are seriously bereft of story, narrative, myth, and knowledge shaped by the tools of qualitative research, historiography, phenomenological analysis, and ethnographic analysis, for example. What often is most absent from our theoretical appreciations are depictions and accounts of the life-worlds of consumers.

Finally, the postmodern condition (Lyotard, 1989) does require of us some perspectives that implicitly challenge the idea that there is a singular truth to be mined in understanding human nature and the human condition. More will be said about this later.

What follows is a brief critique of the current convention in HBSE, a discussion of the central idea of an HBSE curriculum founded upon constructivist and postmodern ideas, and an outline of the curriculum, with some specific examples of content and exercises. The essential reason I ask you to take this journey is to help in developing a curriculum that reflects the richness and variety of life and that can be transported from classroom to context without embarrassment.

THE TRADITIONAL APPROACH TO HBSE

If there has been one element in social work education that has labored under the burdens of lore and tradition it is the Human Behavior in Social Environment (HBSE) sequence. From the accounts and anecdotes I have gathered–with a few exceptions–it appears that HBSE curricula are dominated by the theories (and associated assumptions) of individual development, most often theories of stage-ordered development. This perspective carries with it certain presumptions and imagery.

- The most important events in life are early ones and frequently what happened to the individual earlier "causes" what happens to him or her later. Here, as Hillman (1992) points out, history is not story but cause.
- The central focus of interest (in both theory and practice) has been the individual (although more now is available about family development which seems somewhat less burdened by the idea of personal history as cause). As many have pointed out, the focus on the individual is more an expression of the preoccupation of the culture with individualism than it is an expression of a studied and evolved intellectual preference (Gergen, 1991; Hillman & Ventura, 1992; Lasch, 1984; Sampson, 1983). Such an exclusive focus is risky for a profession that claims for itself a person/environment orientation (Morrell, 1987). While our gaze is directed to the individual, it specifically falls on the individuals' feelings, thoughts, and relationships. Rarely does our eye seem to be caught by the individual as political, economic, and social actor. We assume

cognition and sometimes ignore conation and citizenship (Hillman & Ventura, 1992). At most, we regard the individual as adapting to particular environmental conditions (Germain, 1991).

* Another enduring appreciation of the current developmental approach in HBSE is the idea, associated with all of the above, that personality development is continuous and follows a trajectory that can be plotted, even predicted (if we had enough data).

Given these ideas and assumptions, and the view of some critics that they do not reflect accurately the nature of human experiences (Bruner, 1986; Gergen, 1991; Goldstein, 1990), perhaps it is time to offer another approach for consideration. The constructivist approach offers a number of intriguing possibilities that will be explored–with great humility–in this paper.

THE CONSTRUCTIVIST APPROACH

Lewis Lapham (1990), commenting on the veracity of contemporary journalists writes:

> We are all engaged in the same enterprise, all of us caught up in the making of analogies and metaphors, all of us seeking evocations and representations of what we can recognize as appropriately human. Stories move from truths to facts, not the other way around, and tellers of tales endeavor to convey the essence of a thing. Journalists have less in common with diplomats and sooth-sayers than they do with vagabond poets. (pp. 6-7)

The same could be said, not just of ordinary folk, but of theorists and practitioners of all colors and stripes. Our stories (read: our truths) illuminate the world for us in very particularistic ways.

Robert Coles (1989), who has gathered the stories of children in all imaginable circumstances over the past 35 years, recalls that as a psychiatric resident he had two supervisors, one who was adamant about maintaining the appropriate psychiatric linguistic, symbolic, and categorical conventions in diagnosis and treatment, and another who seemed much more interested in the stories of the people who came to him. The latter encouraged Coles to attend to these chronicles.

[Dr. Ludwig] . . . urged us to let the story itself be our discovery. He urged me to be a good listener in the special way story requires: note the manner of presentation; the development of plot, character; the addition of new dramatic sequences; the emphasis accorded to one figure or another in the recital; and the degree of enthusiasm, of coherence, the narrator gives to his or her account. (pp. 22-23)

The fascination with story is not simply that it provides a vivid picture of the self in context, in history and in development. Stories also tie us to the larger world. Michelle Rosaldo (1984) argues that the self "grows not from 'inner' essence relatively independent of the social world, but from experience in a world of meanings, images, and social bonds, in which all people are inevitably involved" (p. 139). These meanings and images are typically transported on the vehicle of story and narrative (Bruner, 1990).

The Centrality of Meaning

If the *real* world is for any one person or for any one culture a construction that is more compelling, then the sentiments expressed above may stand as an assertion of the constructivist slant on Human Behavior in the Social Environment. The constructivist approach encourages us to attend to the stories, metaphors, and myths by which people and peoples explain themselves and their worlds. Beneath this assumption is the most fundamental one: It is the very character of human nature that we must define our condition, our world, our experience. Few stimuli come at us pristine and raw; we always construe and interpret them. Human beings are inveterate meaning-makers. We are not built into the world instinctually. Rather, we must make sense of and control our world symbolically (Becker, 1973; Bruner, 1990; Rosaldo, 1989). Our place in the world is only assured to the extent that we are sure of our meaning. Likewise, the symbolic control and narrowing of the fabulous (and terrifying) array of stimuli that comprise the world of experience is essential to existence with some degree of equanimity and poise. Luckily for us, we only rarely have to construct meaning on our own, unsupported by others. Culture is at hand to deliver to us, through its many devices, the material of meaning–pictures, icons, language, stories, tropes, rituals, myths–so that we may ground ourselves and our life projects in some shared and resonant understanding (Bruner, 1990; Rosaldo, 1989). In one sense, culture is an epical narrative(s) about origins, purpose, destiny, and future; about difficulties and possibilities; about surmounting and becoming. Cultures are songs of not only what has been and is, but also what might be–the subjunctive (Bruner, 1990).

Meaning also protects us against allusions and intimations of our mortality and of our real situation in the world and cosmos (Becker, 1973). At the cultural level, the essentiality of these illusions (meanings) can be seen when they turn deadly, as one culture confronts another about the truth of a particular matter (Becker, 1973; Lifton, 1979).

Without meaning we cannot survive as individuals, cultures, and species. But individuals rarely create meaning on their own (there may be exceptions to this–the work of the "genius," perhaps). Usually meaning forms in league with others, as we have said, through the instrumentalities of culture. Bruner (1990) draws attention to the obvious truth that psychologists historically have missed:

> The symbolic systems that individuals used in constructing meaning were systems that were already in place, already "there," deeply entrenched in culture and language. They constituted a very special kind of communal tool kit whose tools, once used, made the user a reflection of the community. (p. 11)

Meaning, then, is a product of transaction, colloquy, dialogue, negotiation and, very importantly, social and institutional power (Foucault, 1980). No knowledge (or meaning system) is ontologically privileged and knowledge that seems true in one world may not even exist or may be thought to be blatantly false in another (Goodman, 1978).

Belief and personal identity are closely intertwined (from a constructivist point of view the identity *is* a system of beliefs and meaning about the self). People may take or surrender life to conserve personal identities. Typically, this is done in the guise of political, social, and religious beliefs. Inspiring leaders, admen and ad-women, politicians, charlatans of every stripe often evoke a response in us because they are able to connect a belief, a value, a symbol to our identity and make such a connection seem fateful for our survival and the security of our group, family, or community.

The interpersonal vehicles for the transport of meaning are often story, narrative, and myth (Laird, 1989). These typically come in two forms–the canonical and the exceptional (Bruner, 1990). The canonical story celebrates, if not prescribes, the imperatives and norms of culture and society. It instructs, chastens, and cautions individuals from the vantage point of the requisites and taboos of cultural life. Other kinds of stories, however, do not celebrate the rhetoric of the expected but rather make an accounting of that which is unexpected, novel, and anomalous. Much of the storytelling we do in the helping professions is an effort to convert the exceptional circumstance or situation into the coin of the canonical.

"Truth," today, "is in trouble" (Gergen, 1991, p. 81). If we have in the world a multiplicity of voices and if we have within ourselves a similar multiplicity of selves [because of the "saturation" of the self with continuing, brief, intense experience, incredibly cacophonous bits of information (Gergen, 1991)], then how are we to assess the validity or truth of the matter; how can we ever assume an objective standard by which to understand the nature of things, including the human condition and experience? If this is the "postmodern" condition, how can we ever take a stand, theoretical or conceptual, on human behavior within the social environment? If we cannot really separate the "real" world from the perceived world, what can we possibly teach our students about the "facts" of human nature?

CONSTRUCTING HUMAN BEHAVIOR

This is not a fully developed curriculum to be presented for your examination and critique. Rather, it is a patchwork of assumptions, themes, ideas, beliefs, and process guiding the gradual development of a human behavior course governed by a postmodernist, interpretive frame of mind–or should I say minds? Before discussing some of the principles that drive this curriculum and some examples that illuminate it, let me lay out the content of the course and how content is selected.

Course Outline

The first third of the course is spent examining, in significant detail, what I propose as the essence of the human condition–the need to make or find meaning. We search for how human beings manage to do this; how they are abetted and stultified by culture and institution in the process; what happens when meaning is subverted or becomes fugitive; and how individuals and groups develop conviction about their meaning system. We also spend some time in examining modern American culture (as well as some subcultures) as a font of meaning for individuals and groups. It is important to examine the actual content of culture and social institutions and not treat them merely as abstracts as in, say, an ecological approach (Lasch, 1989).

The second third of the course undertakes the examination of other kinds of meaning, namely some of the "theories" which inform social work practice. These are taken, among other things, to be metaphors which may or may not be enlightening or helpful. We may look at Freudian theory, cognitive theories, biological theories, and, more directly appropriate to social work, ecological (biopsychosocial) and strengths approaches. Obviously, these can only be highlighted but the message is clear: These are interpretations and can best be understood not as "truths" about the human condition but ways that may or may not promote understanding and help secure the values and commitments of the profession.

The last third of the course focuses upon the transformations and transitions, both expected and unexpected, of family life. However, rather than emphasizing the durability of these transitions, we approach them with a sense of their variety and evanescence through time and culture. We argue, without conclusion, the immutability or even the necessity of any particular "stage" of family development or passage. The idea is, too, that these stages, with some acknowledgement of biological realities, are social constructions that have political, economic, social, and ethnic meaning. For every teenager in a middle-class suburb who brings certain things to the family which require their response, we imagine a similar teenager in Pratt,

Kansas who brings to the family a very different set of challenges and opportunities.

Given the aleatory nature of such a curriculum, how are decisions made about content? Acknowledging those unspoken and unrealized elements in such a choice, there are some standards. Gergen's (1982) criteria for generative theory serve well here. Does the content help cast doubt on some elements of conventional wisdom? Does the knowledge suggest viable alternatives for understanding and action? These generative theories, as Goldstein (1990) says, are typically "more pliable, inductive, open-ended" (p. 39) and lend themselves more easily to transformation into practice. Obviously a critical attitude is inherent in these choices. In addition, the knowledge selected ought to forward, certainly not undermine, the values of the social work profession. Normative theories often do not and are inherently conservative (in terms of conserving established, dominative modes of thought and action, as well as realms of power and influence). Likewise, normative theories are not always translatable into professional appreciations and helping because they do not reflect the lifeworlds of those whom they would explain. Finally, students are urged to come to learn the "folk psychology" (Bruner, 1990) of those they deign to help.

Guiding Principles

Any curriculum flows from a watertable of values, and commitments. It is important to be as clear about these as possible; clarity and recognition here is, in fact, an interpretive imperative.

Theories as perspectives, not truths. As has been argued, to make sense of the world is to proceed from a perspective, a system of meaning. We do not discover the external world, we invent and reinvent it symbolically. We create "communities of interpretation," like-minded individuals who share the same appreciations, conventions, language, and interpretive devices that we do (Gergen, 1991). But we are not immune to the larger forces of institution, accident, nature, and history so that our meanings continually change and/or are commingled with those from other communities. Thus it is with social and psychological theory. Donald

Spence (1987), writing of psychoanalytic theory as metaphor and of the attendant dangers of mistaking metaphor for truth, says this:

> . . . to take the Freudian system for granted–to deaden the metaphor and rule out other approaches–is to reduce our options to only one and mistakenly transform metaphor into pseudo-science. To use it in this way is to diminish the poetry of Freud's original inspiration and, in the long run, to miss the spirit of the whole adventure. (p. 8)

So theories, in a sense, are texts, narratives composed of metaphor and other interpretive devices. Like all stories they are built out of intentions and expectations, accountings and surmises, but they have a special role, too. They must be, in the end, "interpretations of interpretations" (Bruner, 1987, p. XIII).

Power is as important as persuasiveness in the rise and fall of theories. The long history of exclusion of the views and sensibilities of most of humankind has led to a recent explosion of writings from those historically denied voice in the fields of academe. It is not so long ago that

> a few privileged men defined themselves as constituting man kind/humankind . . . [and] at the same time they removed women and nonprivileged men within their culture and other cultures from 'mankind,' they justified the exclusion on the grounds that the excluded were by nature and culture 'lesser' people. . . . (Minnich, 1990, p. 38)

The reign of any knowledge is always a political phenomenon.

(Foucault, 1980)

In teaching students, then, about theories of human behavior, it is as important to talk about the origins of the theories you propose–to discuss their sociocultural, political, relational, and negotiated roots–as it is to talk about their basic principles. To reach for their metaphoric and symbolic dimensions is likewise important. A telling example of such an approach to theory for students is the story of Freud's abandonment of seduction and incest as realities and the conversion of them into fantasies of wish fulfillment in hysterical women (Masson, 1984). Of course, this story is contested by loyalists who have other stories to tell, but nevertheless it is a compelling narrative. Students are intrigued to imagine the factors that may have led Freud to change his mind and so the course of modern psychotherapy. Freudian revisionism and the recent explosion in the culture of tales of incest and abuse are, in effect, intertwined. Some students readily come to a conclusion that, for much of its history, psychotherapy has put the veil of silence over the experiences of women who have been abused in order to preserve one of the canonical tales of the psychotherapeutic enterprise.

Another useful exercise for students is to have them consider a piece of knowledge about human behavior that they are confident enough to share with someone else as a "truth" about the way we are. The same is done later with American culture. The students are also asked to think about how they came to "know" that particular idea about the human condition. You can imagine the heterogeneous display and the conflicts that spontaneously erupt (there are many agreements as well) over various depictions of human behavior. "Human beings are basically evil (good)." "People are more selfish (selfless) than we assume." "People are basically dependent (independent)." "People are guided principally by emotion (reason)." And so it goes. I have taken some liberties in representing these ideas to show more directly the typical tensions that unfold in this kind of discussion, but the fact is that, before we go very far, the class inevitably begins a process of negotiating which of these statements we can take as true. It is when we begin to talk about the possible sources of their knowledge that the idea of interpretive and narrative communities and the politics of knowledge-building become more real. Many students admit not to having "discovered" this knowledge but, instead, having received it. It also becomes apparent that any of these seeming dichotomies could legitimately describe any individual, depending on social and historical placement and the vagaries of the moment. The same exercise about American culture often has the effect of making more pronounced the recognition of the source of much knowledge as folk wisdom, often of the "dominant" culture, more than, say, social science.

Multiplicity not singularity. It has been a staple of social science for some time that there are big (and thus singular) truths about human nature, truths that transcend culture and epoch. These truths can be discovered and, someday perhaps, may achieve the status of "laws" of human behavior. The postmodern and interpretive view is that we are stuck with a plurality of voices, within our culture and within our heads (Gergen, 1991). But instead of lamenting multiplicity, we should try to understand it and to assess what it means for our world and ourselves. It need not throw us into a tizzy, or an orgy of handwringing. In fact, in the field of social work, the idea of multiplicity is an affirmation of certain professional values–including the uniqueness of individuals and cultures. Including multiple perspectives requires us to be open, to be tolerant, and to be willing to engage in dialogue and colloquy about the meaning of given events.

In the HBSE class, the pluralistic approach can be demonstrated in several ways. One of these has been successful over the past few semesters. It is to take a widely known, recent event and to account for it (explain it). Recently, in a midwestern city, a young woman attempted to murder her father. Her defense–constructed by a lawyer–was that she was suffering from multiple personality disorder and one of her "alters" was the culprit. Such a defense, of course, if successful, puts her in the hands of the psychiatric community and not the correctional one. We chose to look at this through the normative psychiatric lens (represented by DSM-III-R) and through a constructivist one. In brief, the former might affirm that she had been sexually abused as a child and the development of multiple selves was a massive psychological defense designed to keep the horror of remembrance at bay as well as to fuel the need for revenge. The latter assumes that multiple personalities are the rule, not the exception, and that this woman's experience is not so far from the reality of many selves that occupy our psyche on a day-to-day basis. Thus, the question of her sanity becomes less germane than the meaning of her act. The point of the exercise is not to decide what is true, but what the consequences of each view are, and which, from the stand point of helping the individual (or society) might be most beneficial.

A powerful example which brings together the principles discussed above is the forwarding of a "disease" conception of the human condition. Students are adept at looking at any number of human phenomena through this lens and with the language of the victim and pathogen. Then we examine the same phenomena (the most recent example we used was the adult children of alcoholics) using a different lexicon and frame: the "challenge" model (Wolin & Wolin, 1992), the strengths perspective (Saleebey, 1992), and the resilience orientation (Rhodes & Brown, 1991). Rather than dwelling on how these children, now adults, have been victimized and have developed their own impressive array of disorders, we look at how so many have endured, survived, even thrived. We examine what children learned as they struggled with the unpredictability and occasional cruelty of their parents; we look at the impressive data that suggests that 70 to 80% of these children as adults have not fallen into alcoholic ways; we contemplate (and there are always students who can give real testimony to this) what sorts of strengths, talents, aspirations and sources of pride these individuals have; and we discuss what the "damage" model (Wolin & Wolin, 1992) has done to the pride of these individuals as well as to the ways in which professionals understand and treat them. The excitement (and skepticism) of students as we ponder the meaning of this alternative view is palpable. I must agree, too, with the Wolins (who say it about therapy but I think it may apply to education) that "pride drives the engine of change; shame jams the gears" (p. 5). But the larger lesson here is that our interpretations and the data they illuminate or foster make a significant difference in how we understand and how we go about helping.

Individuals as social phenomena. As Edward Sampson (1983), among others (e.g., Lasch, 1984), has pointed out, we are a culture that dotes on the idea of the individual as autonomous being, navigating the self purposefully through a sea of other individuals and institutions. The power of this idea is such is that it virtually pervades every realm of social theory and social thought. (Developmental theory, discussed below, is one prominent example.) In a postmodern world the self is a relational phenomenon, whether understood as an effect of the cumulation of one's relationships, the remnants of relationships and other selves in one's head, actual face-to-face connections, or the effects of immersion in any one of a number of larger, more symbolic (American culture), and smaller institutional (the school system) social contexts (Gergen, 1991, pp. 239-245).

No one is autonomous. Ideas, beliefs, images, dreams, intentions, actions are a collective and relational work. As I sit trying to write this essay, many voices, imagined and unknown, clear and real (known), speak to me and end up, sometimes, on paper. If I write another day, I may have another chorus of voices (selves) to which I respond, reshaping ideas and propositions.

The fact that the self is only a self in a network of relationships, real and imagined, past and present, is not lost on students when asked to talk about, in differing circumstances, with different people, at different times, how they feel, think, and act differently. Examples are readily mined. Evidently, no one pulls the trigger or writes the song alone. The consequences of such a view of the self, however, are not as clear, and remain to be more fully elucidated. But certainly, if it is the case in a postmodern understanding that we are multiple selves, contextually derived, it does call into question many of the presumptions of standard conceptual lore that have defined the HBSE sequence. But it also calls more clearly to mind some basic social work appreciations, especially respect for the multiplicity of ways of being, and for the importance and reality of different voices in our heads and in our community. Likewise, it confirms the centrality of the notion of interdependence, often expressed as person-in-environment.

Language and intersubjectivity. Language and its devices are the carriers of meaning. The constructivist position is that language is not necessarily the vehicle of truth or objectivity, nor is it necessarily an accurate reflection of the inner state of the speaker. But what it clearly is, is the coin by which we negotiate and mediate our everyday encounters; by which we attempt to make known our subjective state and our "realities" as they collide with those of others. What is important here, then, is to try and come to some tentative and satisfactory accounting of how people discharge their "truth claims" and/or revise them when confronted with more compelling (or more oppressive) ones. As the self is relational, so, then, is the negotiated reality of the interactional moment (Gergen, 1991).

For students, the nearest examples that express or exemplify these ideas occur in the agency or in the academy. In the latter instance, we talk about, as honestly as we can, the claims, in the academy, of the subjectivities, the language, the perspectives of "competing" groups–women, Hispanics, African-Americans and Asian-Americans, for instance. What have been students' experiences of these competitive voices? How do they resolve competing claims? How might they create an environment in which truth is not the goal but the co-existence and melding (and "unmelding") of different lexicons? Agencies, on the other hand, often represent a serious clash between the language and knowledge of client groups and that of the agency or the institutional canon. How is such a clash experienced by all parties? How could it be resolved? How do they experience it?

If social workers come to understand that, to wend their way in the contemporary world, they must be tolerant and seek, as far as possible, the integration of different languages and constructions, then the kinds of practice in which they engage, the policies of agencies, the preferred theories that drive professional behavior might all look quite different. As stated previously, the relationship of power and knowledge (Foucault, 1980; Weick, 1983) has been evident for some time. Fears that constructivism leads to some sort of limp and fatal relativism may be more an expression of the fear of the waning superiority and dominance of a particular language or discourse style than it is fear of the rise of a multiplicity of voices demanding to be heard and taken into account. The message here, and students can be given opportunities to experience this, is that dialogue and dialectic tension may be the avenue to social and personal truths, rather than method-driven discovery.

Inevitably, and rightfully so, students ask, "Well, what are we to 'believe' if there is no truth, only perspective?" Beyond the outcomes of negotiating multiple viewpoints, again Gergen's (1982) ideas about generative theory are useful, since it is meant, first and foremost, to "serve intelligibility in an ever-shifting sea of ambiguous events" (p. 165). But beyond securing an intelligible world (or set of experiences), generative theory challenges the canons of convention and culture, raising questions about contemporary life. At the same time, it generates other possible, more useful or morally pertinent, alternatives to the conventional wisdom. Since it stimulates doubt about rigidified and lingering constructions of the world, it is obligated, too, to forward alternatives of construction, action, and investment.

Any theory serves values or implies them. The same is true with a generative theory except that it does so purposefully and it does so contrarily–that is to say, it may fortify fugitive, disenfranchised, or even unconsidered values.

Students are asked to consider more generative theories in the light of their capacity to generate both doubt and possibility. The "challenge" model discussed earlier is such an example. We also consider the fact that in an interpretive world we are all, potentially, generative "theorists."

THE TEST CASE–HUMAN DEVELOPMENT

If any body of theory and research exemplifies the staying power and influence of more conventional scientific thought, it is that which seeks to understand and explain the course of human development. In a constructivist orientation to the curriculum what are we to do with this hardy staple of HBSE? While much of this, as with that which has preceded it, has to be worked out, here are some basics of an interpretive appreciation.

The Assumptions

As with any body of theory, lore, or received wisdom, it is useful to look at the assumptions buried within. In the case of developmental theory, we have already reviewed some in the very first part of this essay. To reiterate the essential ones: Development passes through predictable, universal stages which must follow one upon the other, more or less successfully, epigenetically; the trajectory of self development is toward increasing complexity, mastery, and maturity; the most important events in individual lives are early ones.

The Evidence

The evidence about the universality, even applicability, of stage-ordered development theories is mixed, at best. The weight of whatever evidence exists, however, suggests that the course of much of the development is aleatory (Gergen, 1982). The fact that we are embedded socially and historically in a particular configuration of environments makes statements about stages of development across time or culture risky and somewhat suspect. The predilection of stage-ordered theorizing to assign to children and youth a more stringent and inexorable course of development than adults also seems grounded in preference more than evidence. The following quotes exemplify some of the concerns about current developmental theory.

- "... growth is more individualistic than was thought and it is difficult to find general patterns" (Brim & Kagan, 1980, p. 13).
- "We are ... incomplete or unfinished animals who complete or finish ourselves through culture" (Geertz, 1973, p. 44).
- "For any individual, the life course seems fundamentally open-ended ... Development is *aleatory* or chance-dependent" (Gergen, 1982, p. 53).

There is a crisis in stage-ordered developmental theory and it comes in several guises. Some research tends to show that constructions of childhood, for example, change over time and between cultures (Aries, 1962). The search for continuity in personal development has likewise been elusive (Baltes & Reese, 1984). Finally, personal and cultural constructions–folk and local knowledge–have a profound influence on how children are regarded and, thus, how they develop (Gergen, Gloger-Tippelt, & Berkowitz, 1990). The message here seems to be that, "universal" neuro-physiological patterns and genetic constraints aside, much of development is a fact of symbolic construction and situational chance (Bruner, 1986).

The Alternative–Aleatory and Constructed Development

Who people are, at any given time, is as much a function of the sociopolitical, relational, historical context in which they live as it is some constitutional, genetic, or early developmental programming. Likewise, who people seem to be at any moment in their individual biographies is also an effect of accident, luck, and contingency. Possibilities and limits may be set by as yet unspecified but suspected congeries of genes and constitution, although there is still considerable controversy over the role of genetic predisposition (Gould, 1977; Lewontin, Rose, & Kamin, 1984). It does seem supportable to say that there are capacities and structures which unfold on a more or less expectable schedule, but those capacities and essences that seem to mark our particular humanity are constantly subject to the evanescence of context and contingency.

In class, we can take any example from students' personal lives or professional work and see if we can understand the effects of these chances and constructions. A recent example: A student encounters in her field placement an African American female, age 21, with 5 children, living in public housing. The woman is clearly under stress but, as nearly as the student can tell, is doing a remarkable job of caring for her children. The student's comment is that at that age (which she was three years ago) she thinks she would have difficulty raising even one child and not alone. Normative developmental theory would, under whatever conceptual guise, probably agree with the student's assessment of her own capacity as being more nearly the norm and would predict multiple problems for this young woman. But other factors clearly come into play:

- In the client's (let's call her Barbara) world, so-called adolescence is foreshortened because of the economy and the multiple hardships that poverty imposes on families. One can look at that closure of adolescence as a developmental liability or as a capacity imposed, in part, by context, circumstance, and expectation.
- In Barbara's world, many other females help her take care of the children, and give her relief, instruction, and support.
- A social worker has been helpful over the years in getting various social resources Barbara needs to raise her children.
- The relational network in which Barbara is ensconced has never made it a point that things should be otherwise. The message to Barbara is that this is your situation and you will do the best you can. That is to say, friends' constructions of the situation at this point are more useful to Barbara than some others might be, including those of some professionals.
- The church, specifically Barbara's faith and the faith of those around her, has been important in maintaining her steadfastness.
- She has not been threatened nor had her apartment overrun by drug dealers (a critical event in the life of many young women in this public housing complex).

- Barbara is in robust good health, it appears; a combination, perhaps of good genes, good hygiene, good humor, and "good" constructions.
- In her mind, Barbara has something very definite to "live for"–her kids.

The assessment, the outcome, and the developmental picture would all be very different if there were a different combination of the contingent, the contextual, and the constructed. The presumed categories and stages of development that appear in texts and as part of conventional wisdom and child-rearing practices may be, beyond luck, a matter of continuing social negotiation and striving within a culture (Gergen, Gloger-Tippelt, & Berkowitz, 1990).

CONCLUSION

Clearly, this is a curriculum in the making. Standing alone, not in league with attempts in other sequences to author a constructivist approach, it may make little sense. But its inspiration is the rise of, to use a puzzling and misused word, the postmodern understanding. The old "totalizing discourses" (Gergen, 1991, p. 245) of most curricula may be in jeopardy (although the current "political correctness" brouhaha suggests they won't die easily). The idea of the multiplicity of voices and cultures struggling to make sense of their world and to make those worlds subjunctively promising brings a kind of excitement to the job of trying to make sense, however provisionally, of individual and collective behavior. In the classroom, as the constructivist approach has slowly emerged, there seems to be more excitement and a sense of relevance about the matters that we address. That's no "test," but for my class, today, it's OK.

REFERENCES

Aries, P. (1962). *Centuries of childhood.* New York: Vintage.
Baltes, P.B., & Reese, H.W. (1984). The life span perspective in developmental psychology. In M.H. Bornstein & M.E. Lamb (Eds.), *Developmental psychology: An advanced textbook.* Hillsdale, NJ: Lawrence Erlbaum.

Becker, E. (1973). *The denial of death.* New York: Free Press.

Berlin, I. (1976). *Vico and Herder: Two studies in the history of ideas.* New York: Viking.

Brim, O.G., Jr., & Kagan, J. (1980). Constancy and change: A view of the issues. In O.G. Brim, Jr., & J. Kagan (Eds.), *Constancy and change in human development.* Cambridge, MA: Harvard University Press.

Bruner, J. (1986). *Actual minds, possible worlds.* Cambridge, MA: Harvard University Press.

Bruner, J. (1987). Foreword. In D. Spence, *The Freudian metaphor.* New York: Norton.

Coles, R. (1989). *The call of stories: Teaching and the moral imagination.* Boston: Houghton Mifflin.

Foucault, M. (1989). *Power/knowledge: Selected interviews and writings, 1972-1977.* New York: Pantheon.

Geertz, C. (1983). *Local knowledge: Further essays in interpretive anthropology.* New York: Basic Books.

Gergen, K.J. (1982). *Toward transformation in social knowledge.* New York: Springer-Verlag.

Gergen, K.J. (1991). *The saturated self: Dilemmas of identity in modern life.* New York: Basic Books.

Gergen, K.J., Gloger-Tippelt, G., & Berkowitz, B. (1990). The cultural construction of the developing child. In G.R. Semin & K.J. Gergen (Eds.), *Everyday understanding: Social and scientific implications.* Newbury Park, CA: Sage.

Germain, C.B. (1991). *Human behavior in the social environment.* New York: Columbia University Press.

Goldstein, H. (1990). The knowledge base of social work practice: Theory, wisdom, analogue, or art? *Families in Society, 71,* 32-43.

Goodman, N. (1978). *Ways of worldmaking.* Hassock, Sussex: Harvester Press.

Gould, S.J. (1977). *Ever since Darwin.* New York: Norton.

Hartman, A. (1990). Many ways of knowing. *Social Work, 35,* 3-4.

Hillman, J., & Ventura, M. (1992). *We've had a hundred years of psychotherapy and the world's getting worse.* San Francisco, CA: Harper.

Laird, J. (1989). Women and stories: Restorying women's self-constructions. In M. McGoldrick, C. Anderson, & F. Walsh (Eds.), *Women in families: A framework for family therapy,* pp. 427-450. New York: Norton.

Lapham, L. (1990). *Imperial masquerade.* New York: Grove Widenfeld.

Lasch, C. (1984). *The minimal self: Psychic survival in troubled times.* New York: Norton.

Lewontin, R.C., Rose, S., & Kamin, L.J. (1989). *Not in our genes.* New York: Pantheon.

Lifton, R.J. (1979). *The broken connection: On death and the continuity of life.* New York: Simon and Schuster.

Lyotard, J-F. (1989). *The postmodern condition.* Minneapolis: University of Minnesota Press.

Masson, J.M. (1984). *The assault on truth: Freud's suppression of the seduction theory.* New York: Farrar, Straus, and Giroux.

Minnich, E.K. (1990). *Transforming knowledge.* Philadelphia: Temple University Press.

Morrell, C. (1987). Cause *is* function: Toward a feminist model of integration for social work. *Social Service Review, 61,* 144-155.

Rhodes, W.A., & Brown, W.K. (Eds.). (1991). *Why some children succeed despite the odds.* New York: Praeger.

Rosaldo, M.Z. (1984). Toward an anthropology of self and feeling. In R.A. Schweder & R.A. LeVine (Eds.). *Culture theory: Essays on mind, self, and education.* Cambridge: Cambridge University Press.

Rosaldo, R. (1989). *Culture and truth: The remaking of social analysis.* Boston: Beacon Press.

Saleebey, D. (1992) (Ed.). *The strengths perspective in social work practice.* New York: Longman.

Sampson, E.E. (1983). *Justice and the critique of pure psychology.* New York: Plenum.

Spence, D.P. (1987). *The Freudian metaphor: Toward paradigm change in psychoanalysis.* New York: Norton.

Weick, A. (1983). Issues in overturning a medical model of social work practice. *Social Work, 28,* 467-474.

Wolin, S., & Wolin, S. (1992). The challenge model: How children can rise above diversity. *Family Dynamics of Addiction Quarterly, 2,* 1-9.

A Constructivist Approach to "Human Behavior and the Social Environment I"

Ann Fleck-Henderson

SUMMARY. This paper describes a two-semester foundation course in Human Behavior and the Social Environment, taught from a constructivist perspective. Three levels of constructive activity, related to different intellectual traditions, are identified: the individual, the interactional, and the social-cultural. Questions addressed include: (How) can developmental theories and systemic/cybernetic theories be taught from this perspective? An analogy is drawn between the epistemological demands this course makes of students and the epistemological position of the field.

INTRODUCTION

This paper describes a foundation course in the Human Behavior and Social Environment sequence, designed and taught from a constructivist perspective. "Constructivist," like many terms in social work, is amorphous enough to warrant the question, "In what

Ann Fleck-Henderson, MSW, is Associate Professor at the Simmons College School of Social Work, 51 Commonwealth Avenue, Boston, MA 02116. The author would like to acknowledge the central role of Sophie Freud in developing the course described in this paper. Deanna Brooks, Kathleen Reardon, Johnnie Hamilton-Mason and Stefan Krug have taught in it and participated in its evolution.

[Haworth co-indexing entry note]: "A Constructivist Approach to "Human Behavior and the Social Environment I," Fleck-Henderson, Ann. Co-published simultaneously in *Journal of Teaching in Social Work* (The Haworth Press, Inc.) Vol. 8, No. 1/2, 1993, pp. 219-238; and: *Revisioning Social Work Education: A Social Constructionist Approach* (ed: Joan Laird) The Haworth Press, Inc., 1993, pp. 219-238. Multiple copies of this article/chapter may be purchased from The Haworth Document Delivery Center [1-800-3-HAWORTH; 9:00 a.m. - 5:00 p.m. (EST)].

sense?" I will describe in what sense the perspective is constructivist and then describe the course itself in some detail. The following questions, with which we who have been teaching the course have grappled, will be discussed: How can developmental theories be taught from this perspective? How can systemic theories be taught from this perspective? What theories and what teaching methods are most consistent with this perspective? How do we respond to students who ask "Where is the truth?" and, finally, how might we, as a field, understand our own epistemological position?

Two contexts are important influences on the content of this course: the school in which it is offered and the profession as represented by its accrediting body, the Council on Social Work Education. Simmons College School of Social Work is located in Boston, Massachusetts, and its master's degree program has a single concentration in direct practice. Students are being trained for a professional community which has a strong psychoanalytic tradition that continues to inform professional discourse. "Human Behavior and the Social Environment I" is a two-semester foundation course required of all students in the first year and is accountable to the Council on Social Work Education's guidelines.

CONSTRUCTIVISM

Constructivism, which is the way of thinking we are most concerned with here, has many meanings. These meanings have varied throughout this volume, and it is necessary to locate myself among them. My own background has been in cognitive developmental psychology, humanistic psychology, and symbolic interactionism—traditions which are fundamentally constructivist.

Constructivism is no news in cognitive psychology. It has been clear for a long time that perception is an interactive phenomenon; that expectancies, response sets, schemas, all cognitive structures variably described, shape perception. It is also no news in developmental psychology. The work of Jean Piaget, and a rich tradition of writing and research following from him, rests on the observation that people differ in the ways they construct their experience, that there are regularities to these differences associated in early life with age and later with a logically necessary sequence of capabilities. Symbolic interactionism is a branch of social psychology in which there is profound interest in the ways in which experience is symbolically organized socially. Its focus is on meanings, as is the focus of cognitive developmental theory, but its attention is on the ways meaning is negotiated and communicated socially, in face-to-face interaction, more than on the mental structures shaping meaning. To these traditions I have added the social constructionist perspective. This tradition, drawing on social psychology (Gergen, 1973), sociology of knowledge (Berger & Luckmann, 1967), and anthropology (Geertz, 1973) draws our attention to the ways in which all theories and meanings are not only cognitively, but culturally, shaped. It invites us to see the meanings we and our clients make as not so much an individual matter but a social-historical-political one. It relativizes any particular theory (such as Piaget's) and asks: What cultural agenda does that theory express and serve? Cognitive developmental psychology, symbolic interactionism, and social constructionism attend to cognitive, interactive, and social/cultural meanings respectively.

A COURSE OVERVIEW

In this course students learn the languages of a variety of theories of personality and systems, and they consider research findings on a variety of topics. These theories and topics are the most explicit content of the syllabus. The theories selected are, largely, those that constitute the discourse of our profession locally. The topics, also, are selected for their relevance to practice. The teaching and learning of these theories, however, is not the central purpose of this course. The underlying principles or ways of thinking are, most fundamentally, what we hope the students will learn. Theories and research findings become obsolete quickly. While the student, practicing in a particular place, time, and community of discourse, must know them, she or he must also, and more importantly, know how to reflect on them, evaluate them, and build from them.

What are the core ways of thinking which provide the coherence for this course? They are constructivist, transactional, and developmental. To think as a constructivist means to attend to how the client is organizing her or his experience and how you, as the clinician, are organizing your experience of the client. To think as a transactionalist means to attend to the mutual shaping of experience by the client and the context, to the in-between, to the ways in which meaning is being negotiated between you and the client, between you and the context. To think as a developmentalist means to attend to processes of change and growth, to be conscious of the developmental agendas of your clients and the developmental agendas of your theories. Each of these core ways of thinking is operative on two levels: as a principle of human behavior theory in relation to clients; and as a reflective principle in relation to the students themselves.

While the course has a fairly consistent constructivist perspective, which this paper is intended to elucidate, the first semester is clearly developmental and the second semester clearly transactional. The first semester includes introductions to: culture and diversity, symbolic interactionist thinking, psychoanalytically-based theories, and Piagetian theories in relation to child and adolescent development. The second semester extends these theoretical approaches to adult development and adds the frameworks of systemic/cybernetic theories, family development models, structural models, and constructivist approaches to family treatment. These are related to topics in adult life (work, sex, parenting), aging, particular stressors (chronic illness, divorce), death and grief.

How, you may wonder, does one achieve any coherence in such an assortment? Partly, the instructors provide coherence by reiterating the basic themes of constructivism, developmentalism, and transactionalism. Partly, coherence resides in the consistent presentation of theories as tools or lenses and consistent attention to the students' (evolving) capacities to use them thoughtfully. The students themselves are the fundamental sources of coherence as they integrate, in their own way, the material of the course with their own experiences and with the implicit and explicit theories they bring to the course (Fleck-Henderson, 1989). Often, this sense of coherence or integration comes only at the end of the first term, after a period of review in preparation for the exam. For most students, the exam-preparation experience involves finding (creating) a way to hold, organize, and synthesize the term's work and "make it their own."

The course begins with the idea of meaning-making, of human

beings as active organizers and construers of experience. Examples of cultural and developmental differences in the way any particular event or "fact" is understood, as well as students' own differing (re)constructions of a shared event or data, demonstrate the fundamental idea that reality is not a given. This is a baseline of all constructivist approaches: that reality is mediated, is always reality-as-known, is not independent of the knower.

In keeping with the cognitive developmental tradition and with insights from anthropology and ethnography, much of the content of the first semester concerns regularities in cultural and developmental meaning-systems. Given that all human beings are meaning-makers, we can find some consistencies and regularities in the forms meaning takes, in the ways reality is experienced. Some of these relate to developmental stages, some to particular cultures and contexts. For instance, the thinking and feeling of four-year-olds, generally, has some common features; likewise the thinking and feeling of Cambodian refugees in Boston. We have clinical and research data about, for instance, how five-year-olds commonly understand friendship or how Irish-Americans understand marital obligations. As a social worker one needs an appreciation of the client's ways of constructing the situation, some sense of the categories and capacities, the schemas and structures the client brings to the encounter. From a social constructionist point of view, we acknowledge that our conceptualizing of these regularities inevitably itself expresses a cultural and linguistic community. For some students, however, this second level of reflection may be unassimilable early in the year. To appreciate that reality is relative to a personal perspective is already a big step. The important learning for the students is that their clients' realities or assumptive worlds may be quite different from their own and that there are some initial orienting maps (theories, metaphors, pictures) of that unknown territory with which they can be familiar. Student papers observing and/or interviewing people of different life-phases and cultures, as well as shared personal experience in class are vehicles for this learning.

At the same time, students need to develop a perspective on their own constructive activity, on their implicit and explicit theories and on their culturally and personally shaped assumptions and values. While this sort of self-reflection and self-awareness was intrinsic to professional education and practice well before social constructionism as such became influential, the social constructionist position adds a dimension. The implicit assumptions, norms, values, and theories which students bring to their practice are seen as not only personal, but importantly cultural, a product of one's social position. Any references to "normal," "healthy," "well-adjusted" or their opposites are explored for the normative system from which they arise. Explicit formal theories are presented as historically and culturally situated, necessarily value-laden tools.

Students are asked to master the terms of these theories, demonstrate their ability to use them in relation to clinical data and, at the same time, be able to stand back from them intellectually, reflecting on their assumptions and values. The attention is always dual: learning about cultures (out there) and about one's own internalized culture; learning about formal theories and about one's own theories-in-use; applying developmental theories to observations of and conversations with children and being able to reflect on the values and assumptions implicit in those theories. Clearly, this is a tall order. For some students it raises the question: Where is the truth?

(HOW) CAN A CONSTRUCTIVIST TEACH DEVELOPMENTAL THEORIES?

This course is heavily informed by theories which are in some sense developmental: psychodynamic, Eriksonian, interpersonal, cognitive developmental, attachment, family life-cycle. Once we are aware that all such theories are culturally and historically situated, how can we continue to teach them? To discuss this I would like to draw a distinction between developmental theories, on the one hand, and normative models, on the other. Developmental theories imply change in the direction of increasing adequacy. Something is becoming more complex or mature, and there is some dynamic of development implicit in the theory. Child development is seen as the evolution of the child's ability to hold and coordinate increasingly complex experiencing–cognitively, socially, and affectively. Normative models, on the other hand, are descriptions of the typical, regular, or normal in the statistical sense, and sometimes the idealized developmental journey of a people. They are accounts of the usual course over time and are more or less explicitly about particular historical and cultural situations.

This course takes a developmental perspective in the sense that it focuses on processes of change and growth as a central principle. We make the assumption that there is an inherent tendency toward growth (Weick, 1983), although the particular forms may vary. We present a model of personal growth derived from two dominant traditions in the field, and we accept that there are some universals in development in childhood. When we get to adolescence and adulthood, we rely more on normative models.

The two major developmental traditions on which we rely are psychoanalytic developmental psychology and cognitive developmental psychology. In both cases the focal unit is the individual in transaction with her or his immediate environment. In each theory something internal to the individual is seen as becoming more complex. In psychoanalytic theory it is the sense of self, ego, and defenses. In cognitive developmental theory it is scientific reasoning, cognitive structures, ways of knowing. While we think of these two traditions as quite different and as about either affect or cognition, they are, in their most modern forms (e.g., Kegan, 1982; Noam, 1988; Stern, 1985), surprisingly similar in many respects. If we ask of each of them "What is developing," the answer would be "Internal structures," conceived of as cognitive schemas (Noam, 1988), or working models (Bowlby, 1988), or representations of interactions generalized (Stern, 1985). These structures[1] are, of course, inferences made by observers about individual capacities to hold increasingly complex information and stimuli, to be increasingly reflective (cognitively) and increasingly mediated (affectively and behaviorally). If we ask "How is this occurring?" again the answers would be similar: The individual's inner world grows by taking in prior lived (inter)actions and experiencing. Piagetian theory uses the metaphor of assimilation, accommodation, and equilibration, while psychodynamic theory uses the metaphor of internalization and integration. Both imply that different lived experience results in different internal structures. What we are teaching here is a model for the processes of development. While we also require familiarity with particular descriptions of stages within these theories, the basic processes are the central component.

The model of development derived from psychodynamic and cognitive developmental theories has strengths and weaknesses. As Gergen (1980, p. 51) has pointed out, these theories are sufficiently abstract that they are untestable and unfalsifiable. (It is worth noting that some of the normative descriptions from both traditions have been "disproved," and the theories live happily on.) They are also sufficiently abstract and elastic that they can include a great range of experiences (Gergen, 1980). That is part of both their resilience and their weakness. Both psychodynamic theory in its more narrative forms (Fingarette, 1983; Klein, 1967; Spence, 1982) and cognitive developmental theories focus on the person's own meaning-making processes, are growth-oriented, and are organic more than mechanistic. They also have similar significant weaknesses. Because they focus attention on internal processes of growth and because they locate meaning in the individual, they disattend to contextual factors. In addition, their very generality and abstraction leads to their being, at times, vacuous, empty jargon, the particular meanings of which are unknowable.

We use stage theories to teach child development. While Germain (1987) has argued against the utility of these theories, given the diversity and lack of uniformity of human experience, her arguments seem to us most applicable to adult development. True developmental theories, as we are defining them, are not rigidly tied to ages, but are sequential and do assume some regularity in the sequencing of particular developments. These regularities seem to exist in child development cross-culturally if we describe them in sufficiently general terms and limit our attention to areas that are tied to biological-neurological maturation and to the features of the environment that are arguably universal (Ross, 1988). For instance, babies start moving in the rhythms of their local language community at a few weeks of age; response smiles appear at a few months; attachment behaviors and evidence of particular objects of attachment in the first year; beginnings of language in the second year; evidence of internal representation or evoked memory in the second year; ability to delay impulses, follow rules, have a sense of right and wrong, tell coherent stories and learn the culture's stories from about the ages of five to seven. The learning of cultural and gender roles and norms in the school-age prepubertal years may be universal, though the content of those rules and norms of course is not. The older the child, the less secure the generalizations. Culture plays an increasingly larger role, as does the child's own self-governing process.

Even if there are universals in child development, the way we conceptualize them is culturally informed. Kagan (1984) points out that cultures often conceptualize infants as lacking whatever the value is in the culture. Thus, American infants are seen as undifferentiated, and development is about becoming autonomous and individuated; while Japanese infants are seen as autonomous, and development is about becoming relational and connected. Developmental theories inevitably embody values, and we teach students to recognize those values. For instance, every developmental theory focuses on particular dimensions of experience. Piaget is about cognition, but he is not about all cognition so much as about scientific reasoning. Kohlberg is about moral judgment, but he is not really about all moral judgment so much as about constructions of justice. Sullivan is about the development of the self-system, but he is mostly about the development of immediate interpersonal relationships. These dimensions reflect values. We might have a cognitive developmental theory that focused on development of the ability to communicate with spirits, or the development of extra-sensory perception, but we do not because these are not valued dimensions in our cultural world. Values are also implicit in the end-point (highest or final stage) of the scheme.

So, we teach these stage theories partly because they are part of the professional language and lore; partly because they are powerful ways of conceptualizing human development. We present them as value-laden, historically rooted, and personally shaped constructions themselves; constructions which assist students in organizing and retaining some aspects of the complexity of human development. Necessarily, they simplify that complexity; that is much of their value. Students, as they become more seasoned, seem to outgrow them. Perhaps there is a stage theory stage (Perry, personal communication). Part of what we hope they learn is to discern the implicit values and relevant contexts for any theory and to be selective in its use.

When it comes to adult development, we abandon the effort to think in terms of universal developmental sequences (Germain, 1987; Ross, 1988; Weick, 1983). With age, social-contextual influences are broader, biomaturational changes more idiosyncratic, and development more self-directed (Ross, 1988, pp. 130-134). Regularities in adolescence and adulthood are largely socio-culturally constituted. Thus, in considering adult development and family development, we rely on normative models, such as that of Carter and McGoldrick (1989), and on theories which are not developmental. Some kind of normative model is implicit in every culture. Unlike developmental theories, normative models are in a sense "folk psychology" (Bruner, 1990). Lay people can describe them. They constitute accounts of cultures' developmental journeys, the seasons of life within a particular culture. Each of us lives with some notions of the normative or prescribed developmental pathways of our culture. We notice them most, probably, when we violate them, when we are "off-time." Without being able to describe normative models for every client group, we can alert our students to the usefulness of exploring them, of listening for the implicit norms for adulthood of their clients.

While psychodynamic and cognitive developmental theories form the base of the first semester's learning about child development, they are complemented by two theoretical traditions which are more truly transactional: symbolic interactionism (Greene & Ephross, 1991) and Harry Stack Sullivan's (1953) interpersonal psychiatry. The second semester is grounded in systemic theories applied particularly to the family, but also to other larger systems. The second semester's theory base is, therefore, more adequatedly transactional, less clearly developmental, and at some points problematically constructivist.

(HOW) CAN A CONSTRUCTIVIST TEACH SYSTEMIC/CYBERNETIC THEORIES?

The theory base of the second semester rests largely on systemic-cybernetic theories developed in relation to families. Again, the choice of theories is powerfully influenced by the dominant theoretical orientations of the local clinical world. Derived from general systems theory and from Gregory Bateson's (1972) work on ecology, a number of "schools" have evolved in conceptualizing and treating families. The language of systems theory is very abstract, intended to be applicable to any living or not living system. For us it offers a way of conceptualizing a group (family, work-group) as one organism, as intrinsically interrelated, as the focus of attention. The students become familiar with the language of boundaries, feedback loops, subsystems, circular causality. For many students it is a radical switch to locate meaning in the collective, to see individual behavior as a product of the social situation. Structural and strategic theories add further ways of conceptualizing a social group in terms of information exchange, hierarchies, alliances, and the function of symptoms or problems in the system.

These theories are congruent with a constructivist perspective insofar as they acknowledge the non-neutral position of the observer or therapist and in their clear recognition of the mutuality or co-creation of meanings. However, in some fundamental ways they are not congruent with a cognitive constructivist perspective. First of all, it is impossible to focus on the subjective meaning-making process of the individual and on the family or other group as a system simultaneously. Once the focus is switched to the group, it is no longer a matter of listening to another's subjectivity. When the client is a group, the client's construction of experience must refer to how the group organizes experience. This could involve their world-view, shared beliefs, values, rituals, and stories. The systemic/cybernetic theories, including structural and strategic therapies, focus on behavior and formal properties of families and seem to disregard or even discount family members' "stories" (e.g., Haley, 1976; Minuchin, 1974). The highly directive and sometimes authoritarian stance of some of the earlier family therapists of these schools is seen as of historical interest, just as are the techniques of psychoanalysis. Recently, constructivist approaches to the family have directed attention back to the meanings, stories, narratives, and rituals of a family (e.g., Imber-Black, 1989; Laird, 1989; Sluzki, 1992; White & Epston, 1990). Attention in this recent theoretical tradition seems to be exclusively on what is "languaged," a radical shift from some of the earlier theories.

We teach these various approaches partly for the tools they can provide the student in organizing information about a family or other group. General systems theory and ecological theory are useful beginnings because they provide an abstract template that highlights interrelatedness. The family is not simply environment for its members, but an organism itself in a larger environment. That larger environment–extended family or community–can in turn be seen as an organism in its own environment. In each case, the questions of goodness of fit, of support and stress, can be addressed as they were for individuals. Structural approaches (Minuchin, 1974; Umbarger, 1983) create static portraits of a group and provide ways to conceptualize closeness-distance, hierarchies, alliances, and boundaries. Strategic approaches (e.g., Haley, 1976) invite attention to the consequences of any particular problem or symptom in a system, to the ways it may be self-maintaining. Systemic and cybernetic approaches (e.g., Freud, 1988) attend to patterned relationships, how behaviors cohere. Historical approaches (e.g., Carter & McGoldrick, 1989) draw attention to intergenerational patterns. These approaches provide useful tools for the student's construction of a story about the family. Recent constructivist and narrative approaches to family therapy direct attention to the family's own stories. The stories the students discern and create may be shared with the clients in a tentative way, becoming part of that system's (client-student) shared understanding.

THE SEARCH FOR THEORIES
WHICH ARE CONSTRUCTIVIST AND TRANSACTIONAL

Modern psychodynamic theories and attachment theory are transactional in the sense that they see personality arising out of interactions, rather than out of channelled drives or conditioning. Cognitive developmental theory is transactional in that the environment shapes the mind as much as vice versa. However, both of these traditions put power and meaning primarily in the individual. Systemic/cybernetic theories are profoundly transactional, but have to be carefully reconciled with a constructivist approach. The theoretical traditions which seem to me most philosophically compatible with a constructivist social work approach are, unfortunately, not dominant traditions in our field. These are symbolic interactionism (see Ephross & Greene, 1991 for a summary) and Harry Stack Sullivan's interpersonal psychiatry (e.g., Sullivan, 1953).

Symbolic interactionism has its roots in the work of a group of sociologists mostly at the University of Chicago in the early decades of this century. It is concerned centrally with the ways situations are defined and the ways relationships and meanings are negotiated. It is consistently transactional and constructivist. It is, as it has evolved, not at all developmental. The work of Goffman (1959, 1963), for instance, systematically disattends to personal history and inner meanings, major omissions for a clinical profession. However, George Herbert Mead (Strauss, 1956), a major figure in this tradition, did have a developmental theory, based in the evolution of role-taking ability, and completely congruent with cognitive developmental theories.

Because this course must help students become conversant in the theories they will use in practice settings, symbolic interactionism is not, at this time, dominant in the course. We do present it in three of the early weeks of the course. Students read Goffman's (1963) work on stigma and an introduction to symbolic interactionism (Ephross & Greene, 1991) from a social work text. Kohlberg's (1984) debt to Mead is emphasized, his stages presented as evolutions in role-taking ability. The hope is that when we move to the "inner space" ([Loewenstein] Freud, 1979) bias of both psychodynamic and cognitive developmental theories, this initial awareness of the negotiated nature of meaning will persist.

Sullivan's (1953) work is the only developmental theory we study that is arguably "sociocentric" (Sampson, 1985), that is, a theory in which personal meaning is seen as centered in connectedness. Sullivan had an early sense of the ways in which individuals are constituted by their relationships, and changes in those relationships have the power to change personality. At the same time, Sullivan was attentive to his clients' stories, had a clearly developmental perspective, and saw himself therapeutically as a "participant observer" (Havens, 1983), a kind of commentator on the client's experience. However, this tradition is present in the course in a very small way. Sullivan's own writings are quite "dated," and he has been uniformly neglected in social work literature.

THE SEARCH FOR METHODS
WHICH ARE CONSTRUCTIVIST AND TRANSACTIONAL

The medium is part of the message. How this course is taught is as important as what is taught. An enduring and consistent attention to each student's construction of the material and a truly transactional process will, hopefully, support student development. Some of the exercises we use have been described earlier (Dean & Fleck-Henderson, 1992). For instance, in the first class, students are given a two-page case summary and asked to comment on what seem to them the important aspects. The class discussion is designed both to introduce the variety of theoretical premises underlying their comments and to increase each student's awareness of his or her theoretical premises. We stress that none of them comes to this class a "blank slate," but rather that each of them has highly developed, more or less conscious theories of human behavior which must be brought into dialogue with the new material they find in the course. In the second class this year we adapted an exercise on cultural awareness (Nakanishi & Rittner, 1992) which involved students' naming their own cultural membership(s) and, in discussion with each other, identifying cultural elements of their assumptive worlds. Their first paper is an exercise which extends this introspective process and invites them to illustrate how their cultural learnings shape their experience and might shape their clinical perceptions and responses. The co-constructed nature of the classroom situation is frequently stressed, e.g., that each of us is making different sense out of any particular common information such as might be contained in a case or in a presentation, or that the instructor's behavior is shaped by theirs. They are assigned four papers which require observations or interviews and then some analysis. Attention is directed to the ways their presence and behavior shapes the stories they observe and hear. They are reminded of Sullivan's admonition that one can say nothing about the client, only about the client with me.

While it is important to learn something about the history of a client or a situation, it is also important to remember that any particular history is a current construction and also a product of the teller's present self and situation. They are continuously asked to be self-reflective, in class and in written work, to locate their own position and perspective, to attend to the ways their understanding is shaped by culture, personal history, agency mission. If, from the instructor's perspective, a student misunderstands material, the instructor takes the time to sit with the student to try to understand the logic of the misunderstanding, how it is sensible to the student, how the student is making sense. Thus the gap between what the instructor believes she is teaching and what the student is learning can hopefully be bridged: bridged because effort has to come, and change may come, from both sides. If a student makes unwarranted inferences or truth claims, the student's reasoning process must be engaged.

WHERE IS THE TRUTH?

I want to return now to an issue raised early in the paper, the student for whom this constructivist approach is troubling. At the bottom of a quite competent paper discussing observations of a toddler from the perspective of a number of theories, a student wrote: "I think I can use these theories, but when do we find out which one is true?" I asked the class who among them was troubled by this question, and a few, maybe one fifth of the class, were. In the discussion that followed the students who were not troubled by the question talked about how they evaluated theories if none was "true": How congruent is the theory with the client's world view? How consistent is the theory with my values? How well does the theory seem to account for or fit the clinical situation? How much evidence is there that the theory has been useful in similar situations? There is, of course, an epistemological divide between these students and their worried fellows. In the terms of some cognitive developmental theories (Belenky et al., 1986; Perry, 1970), this course demands contextual thinking. There are, however, students for whom contextual thought, in which there are multiple perspectives and justifiable ways of committing oneself to a particular perspective for a particular task, is an unmanageable stretch. The ability to make that stretch comes slowly, and, for some students, it will not come during the course. While it may not be a criterion for passing the course, it is an educational goal.

I would like to elaborate on this educational goal and on the developmental theory that I use in relation to it. This is intended to serve two purposes: to illustrate a constructivist's use of developmental theory (the kind of use we hope our students learn); and to provide a scheme for thinking about the epistemological evolution in our field that constructivism represents.

Perry's (1970) theory (or scheme) of intellectual development in young adulthood (from which other schemes such as Belenky et al.'s [1986] and Kitchener's [1986] are largely derived) posits evolving epistemological positions. First, in childhood, comes dualistic thought, in which knowledge is seen to consist of right and wrong answers and external authority is presumed to be the source of these answers. As the student perceives that authorities sometimes disagree, multiplistic thought evolves. In this position, the student sees that in some areas there are no clear right and wrong answers. Different questions or problems may require different kinds of solutions. Authority now becomes the source for methods of reasoning. Belenky and her colleagues call this procedural knowledge because of its emphasis on going through the right procedures. (Note there is a new dualism of right and wrong procedures.) Multiplism can evolve in more than one way, but a common next position is some form of rampant relativism: any opinion is equally good as long as it is sincerely held; as long as no one is clear on the answers, it does not matter what you think. This may contain a loss of faith in authority, or the student may be caught in the paradox that authority is telling her or him to think independently. Contextual thinking or contextual relativism consists of the insight that truth is relative to context and accompanies the awareness that authority does not have the answers either, that one has to think independently not because *they* say so, but because that is the nature of knowledge. This awareness also carries the responsibility of making some commitment to "the truth as I see it." Commitments are necessarily tentative, because the truth is never absolute. Every opinion is not equally valid; one has to test it against some criteria for evaluating truth in a particular context. This is one way of interpreting what the untroubled students described above were doing and trying to demonstrate to their (more multiplistic or relativistic) colleagues.

This scheme is itself, of course, a particular historical and cultural product. It implicitly values multiple perspective taking, independence of authority, and rational criteria for justifying commitments. It assumes a pluralistic world, that is, more than one world-view. It is, in fact, pluralism that demands the more complex epistemologies. It also assumes that any knowledge or truth is relative to context and time, that we must make wholehearted commitments in the absence of certainty. The scheme, generated at a college counseling center, embodies the value agenda of a liberal education. It seems to me justifiable to claim this also as a value agenda for student social workers. Their ability to see multiple perspectives, to see any particular knowledge or truth as relative to context, and to be able, nonetheless, to take positions and justify them, is intrinsic to their effectiveness as professionals in a pluralistic culture.

This scheme is also useful as a kind of analogue to the epistemological journey in social work. The era of dualism, of right and wrong answers, is long gone. Perhaps there was, until fairly recently, a kind of multiplism: many theories with champions arguing for their generic rightness and considerable uncertainty about how to find our way among these theories. Social constructionism in some ways invites rampant relativism or the loss of faith in any theory. If they are all relative, biased, particular to context, maybe we have to throw up our hands; maybe anything goes. This interpretation of constructivism is mentioned by many writers as a risk (Efran, Lukens, & Lukens, 1988; Nichols & Schwartz, 1991). Contextual thinking demands commitment, thoughtful commitment with some form of justifiable and explicit rationale. That is where we are now, I think, and that is what this course is trying to teach.

OTHER FORMS THE COURSE MIGHT TAKE

I have occasionally had a fantasy about the ultimate constructivist approach to teaching this course: to teach it completely inductively. We might begin with a case or a videotaped interview in response to which each student would write her understanding of the presented situation. From those documents we would collectively elicit, with each student in turn responding to questions from her classmates and instructor, the underlying theories and assumptions. In that discussion, and from listening to others' formulations, students should begin to question and elaborate their understandings.

Based on the theories they begin to articulate, they would be directed to relevant literature and bring that back into the class discussion. Case materials would be carefully selected, and the instructor would be responsible for bringing in over time the body of knowledge that constitutes a more traditional syllabus. However, the process would be learner-driven to a much greater extent.

Social work has been troubled by the variety of theoretical allegiances we encompass. We seem able to come together only on theories at the most abstract level, as in general systems theory, ecologically-based theories such as Germain and Gitterman's (1980) life model and (possibly), a developmental model such as that outlined early in this paper. It is important that we share and teach these very abstract models. However, they are not sufficient: students need more specific, testable, operationalizable theories as well. Each of our programs will and must teach some theories that social work, as a whole, does not embrace. The particular theories and topics covered in this course could change radically without changing the underlying principles or core agenda. In another part of the country or at another time, we might focus on behaviorism (behaviorism in its more mature social learning form which allows for mental mediation) or information-processing, or organizational development. The particular content is relative to context. From this constructivist's point of view, that's O.K.

NOTE

1. The term "structure" may be problematic to some constructivist thinkers. Obviously, "structure" and "constructivism" have the same root (Latin for heap together or pile up). "Structure" can be used to describe any static representation of a system; thus, social structure, structural differences in power, personality structure, and so on. It seems to me unnecessary (and very difficult) to limit ourselves to process conceptions and to rule out structural conceptions.

REFERENCES

Bateson, G. (1972). *Steps to an ecology of mind.* New York: Random House.
Belenky, M.F., Clinchy, B.M., Goldberger, N.R., & Tarule, J.M. (1986). *Women's ways of knowing.* New York: Basic Books.
Berger, P., & Luckmann, T. (1967). *The social construction of reality.* New York: Anchor.

Bowlby, J. (1988). Developmental psychiatry comes of age. *American Journal of Psychiatry, 145*, (1), 1-10.

Bruner, J. (1990). *Acts of meaning.* Cambridge, MA: Harvard University Press.

Carter, B., & McGoldrick, M. (1989). *The changing family life cycle.* Needham, MA: Allyn & Bacon.

Dean, R., & Fleck-Henderson, A. (1992). Teaching clinical theory and practice through a constructivist lens. *Journal of Teaching in Social Work, 6*(1), 3-20.

Efran, J.S., Lukens, R.J., & Lukens, M.D. (1988). Constructivism: What's in it for you? *The Family Therapy Networker*, Sept/Oct, 27-31.

Ephross, P., & Greene, R. (1991). Symbolic interactionism. In R. Greene & P. Ephross (Eds.), *Human behavior and social work practice*, pp. 203-225. New York: Aldine.

Fleck-Henderson, A. (1989). Personality theory and social work practice. *Clinical Social Work Journal, 17*, 128-137.

Fingarette, H. (1963). *The self in transition.* New York: Basic Books.

(Loewenstein) Freud, S. (1979). Inner and outer space in social casework. *Social Casework, 60*, 19-29.

Freud, S. (1988). Cybernetic epistemology. In R. Dorfman (Ed.), *Paradigms of clinical social work*, pp. 356-387. New York: Brunner/Mazel.

Geertz, C. (1973). *The interpretation of cultures.* New York: Basic Books.

Gergen, K. (1980). The emerging crisis in life span developmental theory. In P. Baltes & O. Brim (Eds.), *Life span development and behavior, Vol. 3*, pp. 31-59. New York: Academic Press.

Gergen, K. (1973). Social psychology as history. *Journal of Personality and Social Psychology, 26*, 309-320.

Germain, C. (1987). Human development in contemporary environments. *Social Service Review, 61*, 565-580.

Germain, C., & Gitterman, A. (1980). *The life model of social work practice.* New York: Columbia University Press.

Goffman, E. (1959). *The presentation of self in everday life.* New York: Doubleday.

Goffman, E. (1963). *Stigma.* Englewood Cliffs, NJ: Prentice-Hall.

Haley, J. (1976). *Problem-solving therapy.* San Francisco: Jossey Bass.

Havens, L. (1983). *Participant observation.* New York: Jason Aronson.

Imber-Black, E. (1989). Rituals of stabilization and change in women's lives. In M. McGoldrick, C. Anderson, & F. Walsh (Eds.), *Women in families: A framework for family therapy.* New York: Norton.

Kagan, J. (1984). *The nature of the child.* New York: Basic Books.

Kegan, R. (1982). *The evolving self.* Cambridge: Harvard University Press.

Kitchener, K.S. (1986). The reflective judgement model: Characteristics, evidence, measurement. In R.A. Mines & K.S. Kitchener (Eds.), *Adult cognitive development: Methods and models.* New York: Praeger.

Klein, G. (1967). *Psychoanalytic theory.* New York: International Universities Press.

Kohlberg, L. (Ed.) (1984). *The psychology of moral development.* Vol. 2. New York: Harper and Row.

Laird, J. (1989). Women and stories: Restorying women's self-constructions. In M. McGoldrick, C. Anderson, & F. Walsh (Eds.), *Women in families: A framework for family therapy,* pp. 427-450.

Minuchin, S. (1974). *Families and family therapy.* Cambridge, MA: Harvard University Press.

Nakanishi, M., & Rittner, B. (1992). The inclusionary cultural model. *Journal of Social Work Education, 28,* 27-35.

Nichols, M., & Schwartz, R. (1991). *Family therapy: Concepts and methods.* Boston: Allyn and Bacon.

Noam, G. (1988). A constructivist approach to developmental psychopathology. In E.D. Nannis & P.A. Cohen (Eds.), *Developmental psychopathology and its treatment,* pp. 91-121. San Francisco: Jossey-Bass.

Perry, W. G. (1970). *Intellectual and ethical development in the college years: A scheme.* New York: Holt, Rinehart & Winston.

Perry, W.G. (1976). Personal communication.

Ross, A.T. (1988). Early development in life span perspective. In P. Baltes, D. Featherman, & R. Lerner (Eds.), *Life span development and behavior.* Vol. 9. Hillsdale, NJ: Erlbaum.

Sampson, D.E. (1985). The decentralization of identity: Toward a revised concept of personal and social order. *American Psychologist, 40,* (11), 1203-1211.

Sluzki, C. (1992). Transformations: A blueprint for narrative changes in therapy. *Family Process, 31,* 217-230.

Spence, D. P. (1982). *Narrative truth and historical truth.* New York: Norton.

Stern, D. (1985). *The interpersonal world of the infant.* New York: Basic Books.

Strauss, M. (1956). *The social psychology of George Herbert Mead.* Chicago: University of Chicago Press.

Sullivan, H.S. (1953). *The interpersonal theory of psychiatry.* New York: Norton.

Umbarger, C. (1983). *Structural family therapy.* New York: Grune & Stratton.

Weick, A. (1983). A growth task model of human development. *Social Casework, 64*(3), 131-137.

White, M. & Epston, D. (1990). *Narrative means to therapeutic ends.* New York: Norton.

A Human Rights Approach
to Social Work Research and Evaluation

Stanley L. Witkin

SUMMARY. Although the advancement of human rights and research are considered important aims for social work, they are viewed as relatively independent activities. This paper presents an argument for the integration of human rights and social work research and proposes some ways this objective might be accomplished. Suggestions for teaching a human rights approach to research are also described.

Traditionally, human rights and social research have been viewed as relatively independent. Human rights are derived from beliefs about morality, values, and human nature; research, on the other hand, is concerned with documenting what is, the extant universe. Even when research is directed toward human rights issues as, for example, in a survey of human rights abuses, the distinctiveness of each domain is preserved: The "objective" lens of research is focused on the "subjective" terrain of human rights.

The profession of social work is strongly committed to the promotion and protection of social justice and human rights (Centre for Human Rights, 1992) as well as the development of social work

Stanley L. Witkin, PhD, is Professor and Chairperson, Department of Social Work, University of Vermont, Burlington, VT 05405. An earlier version of this paper was presented at the *26th International Congress of Schools of Social Work,* Washington, DC, July, 1992. The author would like to thank Susan Roche for her helpful comments.

[Haworth co-indexing entry note]: "A Human Rights Approach to Social Work Research and Evaluation," Witkin, Stanley L. Co-published simultaneously in *Journal of Teaching in Social Work* (The Haworth Press, Inc.) Vol. 8, No. 1/2, 1993, pp. 239-253; and: *Revisioning Social Work Education: A Social Constructionist Approach* (ed: Joan Laird) The Haworth Press, Inc., 1993, pp. 239-253. Multiple copies of this article/chapter may be purchased from The Haworth Document Delivery Center [1-800-3-HAWORTH; 9:00 a.m. - 5:00 p.m. (EST)].

research (Task Force on Social Work Research, 1991). Consistent with the above view, these activities are perceived as separate; the former concerned with social work's "moral mission" (Siporin, 1991), the latter with its empirical foundation. Thus, while human rights and research may inform each other, they remain within separate spheres of activity. In contrast, the aims of this paper are: (1) To provide a rationale for the integration of human rights and social work research; and (2) to show how this integration could occur. Suggestions for teaching a human rights approach to research will also be described.

The possibility and desirability of a human rights approach to social work research stems from at least two interrelated developments: the demise of foundationalism and the consequent specter of relativism, and the growth and influence of interpretive and critical social science. These developments have led to the formulation of alternative criteria for the assessment of knowledge claims (e.g., Witkin & Gottschalk, 1988); to increased understanding of how social research generates categories of understanding and prescriptions for ways of acting (Gergen, 1986; Gottschalk & Witkin, 1988, 1991; Witkin, 1989a); and to the generation of approaches to inquiry that are responsive to the needs of social work practice and consistent with the mission and values of the profession (Tyson, 1992; Witkin, 1989b).

A promising framework that has emerged from these developments is critical constructionism. Critical constructionism incorporates the constructionist interest in the historical and social determinants of knowledge, while emphasizing the political, moral, and practice implications of theory and research (Gergen, 1986; Sampson, 1989; Witkin, in press). By providing an alternative ontological and epistemological understanding of social life, critical constructionism encourages alternative forms of inquiry and theory development (Gergen, 1985; Gergen & Davis, 1985).

THE DEMISE OF FOUNDATIONALISM
AND THE SEARCH FOR MEANING

Foundationalism (or justificationism) is the doctrine, at least in its empiricist version, that knowledge rests on the brute facts of experience (Trigg, 1985). This foundation provides the ultimate justification for knowledge claims and is assumed "as the starting point for empirical knowledge" (Weimer, 1979, p. 21). Over the last several decades, the basis for foundationalism has eroded to the point where it is no longer considered tenable as an arbiter of truth claims. In particular, the theses of factual relativity and the theory-ladenness of observations have undermined the belief that experience can provide an absolute foundation for knowledge (Hanson, 1958; Weimer, 1979). A troubling consequence has been the specter of relativism in which no reason for warranting a knowledge claim is seen as superior to any other (cf. Feyerabend, 1976). This has led to extensive debate about how knowledge claims are and should be assessed (e.g., Kuhn, 1970; Morawski, 1986; Laudan, 1977). The attempt to find a rational (scientific, valid) way of distinguishing knowledge claims has led, in the social sciences and social work, to consideration of nontraditional criteria such as utility, emancipation, empowerment, dialogue, and social justice (Smith, 1990; Witkin & Gottschalk, 1988). The search for non-foundationalist epistemologies encouraged new ways of looking at theory and research. Philosophers such as Wittgenstein (1963), Dilthey (1976), and Gadamer (1975) as well as social scientists like Winch (1958), Berger and Luckmann (1966), and Garfinkel (1967) laid the groundwork for interpretive and critical alternatives to conventional inquiry. Within social work, the reverberations of these developments have been felt in challenges to traditional research and its relevance to social work practice (e.g., Davis, 1987; Heineman, 1981; Heineman Pieper, 1989; Witkin, 1991). Although diverse in their style of inquiry, these "alternative" approaches have led to heightened awareness of the historical, cultural, and political nature of social theories and methods of inquiry. In particular, the recognition that empirical social research is inextricably tied to values, morality, and dominant social arrangements, facilitated the development of approaches to inquiry that acknowledge these connections.

THE SELF-FULFILLING NATURE
OF SOCIAL RESEARCH

All researchers work within multiple, interrelated contexts. Research is affected in various ways by the "macro" context of history and culture, the "mezzo" context of academic institutions and scientific communities, and the "micro" context of personal beliefs and values. For example, Western ideas about individualism and marriage may provide unquestioned presuppositions from which research questions are generated and results interpreted. Similarly, requirements for academic tenure or the need for grant funding may increase the value of certain types of research methods or encourage questions consistent with the prevailing political philosophy. Finally, an individual's unique life experiences may provide incentive to pursue certain areas of inquiry or influence her/his interpretation of existing theory (see Riley, 1988 for examples of how such influences affected the work of various sociologists). The interaction of these contexts eventuate in the studies that fill journals and books. From this perspective, social research informs as much about the ideas and beliefs of researchers and the ideology of social institutions as it does about the objects of inquiry.

Context influences not only research implementation, but observation and description. Trigg (1985) notes that, "instead of facts being discovered in the world, our descriptions are governed as much by our interests and purposes as by what is there" (p. 9). For example, descriptions of mental health and mental illness are not pure linguistic representations of empirical reality, but reflect ideological beliefs, values, institutional relationships, and cultural mores (cf. Albee, 1986). Similarly, when women whose male partners are alcoholics are described as "co-dependent," this is an evaluation (and implicitly, a prescription), not a description. Thus, social research is as much a statement of what should be as it is a description of what is (Bellah, 1983; Howard, 1985).

Truth claims are always pursued within a context of taken-for-granted assumptions, for example, that people are responsible for their own misfortunes, that children "entice" their abusers, that blacks are violence prone, or that people with mental handicaps cannot learn. Often, these assumptions reflect societal stereotypes or beliefs that are based on various institutional arrangements. For instance, blaming poor people for their own plight deflects attention away from broader social issues and how these issues might contribute to poverty. Assumptions such as these are not easily discovered by the research process and often remain implicit, unchallenged, and even "confirmed" by research data. In the Western world, women, people of color, people with disabilities, lesbians and gays have often been the "victims" of such research (e.g., Gould, 1981; Kitzinger, 1987; Peterson, 1987).

Theories and generalizations in the social sciences are not neutral, but inevitably favor certain social arrangements, views of human nature, and forms of social life over others. Additionally, the language, concepts, and explanations provided by the social sciences play an important role in how people view themselves and others and in the reproduction of social life. In this sense, social research is a value-based, culturally-situated process in which knowledge claims are inherently political.

Once the social and dialectical nature of research is realized, its veil of neutrality parts to reveal researchers actively involved in constructing the social reality that they discover. Like practitioners and policy analysts, researchers both reflect and shape the social landscape. "As language users with a high degree of visibility in the culture, sociobehavioral scientists are positioned to have enormous influence on the dominant theories of society and thus on its social patterns and institutions" (Gergen, 1986, p. 153). From a constructionist perspective, not only is this involvement inevitable, but it is a legitimate, even desirable, aspect of social inquiry.

NORMATIVE SOCIAL RESEARCH

This conceptualization of social science has led to a redefinition of the role of researchers and new goals for research. Once researchers can embrace, rather than try to eliminate, the normative aspects of their inquiry and its influence on understanding they are free to engage openly in the dialogue surrounding the important social issues facing humanity. Researchers can move beyond what is to what should be, from a focus on means to one of ends, and from analyses of knowledge claims limited to traditional epistemological criteria to ones that incorporate alternative moral criteria as well. Value choices become more explicit. As Witkin and Gottschalk (1988) stated,

> rather than focusing on poverty and its disabilities, social work researchers might concern themselves with the social destruc-

tiveness of inordinate wealth. They might investigate the implicit violence in contemporary concepts of power and the institutional legitimation of selfishness within political and economic theories. (p. 219)

In the best tradition of social work, researchers can challenge the status quo and generate liberating alternatives. They can ". . . work for the transformation of social orders which inhibit the realization of basic human needs and thus obstruct development, toward alternative orders whose institutions, values, and dynamics would be conducive to the full development and self-actualization of every human being" (Gil, nd., p. 7). Research thus becomes a form of social action and practice. And, like practice, it is not confined to a narrow set of methods, but encompasses a range of approaches to inquiry and analysis. The broad social work goals of social justice and human betterment are now as accessible to researchers as to practitioners.

Given the above interpretation, social work research must address two issues: how to warrant knowledge claims, and how to generate "knowledge in the service of action" (Argyris, Putnam, & Smith, 1987, p. 78). If such knowledge is to be guided by values consistent with the ideology and mission of social work, then it must begin with fundamental human rights.

FUNDAMENTAL HUMAN RIGHTS

Human rights are those rights persons are entitled to simply by virtue of being human beings. Fundamental human rights are those rights which are primary, that supersede all others. They are required of all persons in order to fulfill their basic humanness and, therefore, "essential to life worthy of a human being" (Donnelly, 1985, p. 9). Following Gewirth (1978), two fundamental human rights are claimed: the right to freedom and the right to well-being.

The right to freedom entails the right of individuals to act as they wish without interference from others, including the State. The only limitation on such action is that it "does not threaten or violate other persons' rights to freedom (by coercing them) or to well-being (by harming them)" (Gewirth, 1982, p. 17). Kent (1986) sees the right to freedom as including the protection of freedoms that are guaranteed by the State from the interference of other citizens. For instance, one's freedom to seek employment or attend school should be protected from the interference of others.

The right to well-being consists of the "various abilities and conditions" necessary for "successful action" (Gewirth, 1982, p. 139). Although the determination of well-being involves a value judgment, it is a special kind of value judgement that is "so consistent and so predictable that we can treat it as fixed, as if it were an objective part of nature" (Veatch, 1986, p. 137). By this definition, well-being would include the right to basic necessities such as food, shelter, medical care and education. It would exclude claims such as the right to eat caviar or own a Mercedes.

Rights imply duties, that is, calling something a "right" means that a person has a legitimate, forceful claim on others to comply with that right (Donnelly, 1985). In this way, rights have an instrumental function in social life. Moreover, the obligations associated with human rights are not limited to individuals, but extend to governments and social institutions. Thus, there exists an interactive relationship among human rights and society. The recognition of basic human rights shapes society, which in turn creates the conditions within which human rights can be realized (Donnelly, 1985). Therefore, human rights can be seen as a social practice that provides the foundation for a just society. For social work researchers and practitioners, working on behalf of human rights is central to the mission of their profession.

HUMAN RIGHTS AND SOCIAL WORK RESEARCH

Theory and research can influence how social workers understand human rights, particularly in terms of their application to clients. Conceptualizations of persons or of behavior may serve to obstruct or foster human rights. For example, psychiatry and psychology have a long history of characterizing marginalized persons in ways that legitimate their social control. These include the confinement of such people in institutions, the construction of various "diseases" unique to a particular group (ranging from "drapetomania," manifested by the penchant of slaves to escape from the plantations, to more contemporary diagnoses of hyperkinesis in children), and the support of the status quo through the depoliticization of potential social issues (Kitzinger, 1987). Research which assumes the reality of such conceptualizations and then "documents" their characteristics (e.g., the personality traits of hyperkinetic children) may further legitimate human rights restrictions.

To the extent that conventional research, such as surveys and outcome studies, isolates (decontextualizes) its subject matter and maintains researchers' hegemony over knowledge, its ability to address such human rights issues is restricted. In contrast, constructionist approaches that view putative knowledge claims as historical, cultural, and political expressions and that articulate the voices of research participants may be more sensitive and responsive to human rights issues. Research *about* human rights, although important, retains the separateness of each area. A human rights approach to research, on the other hand *integrates* human rights principles and goals with research practices. There are at least three ways of doing this: (1) by adopting the protection and advancement of fundamental human rights as explicit research goals; (2) by using the protection and advancement of fundamental human rights as evaluative criteria; and (3) by conducting research that respects and fosters the human rights of the participants. These suggestions are not independent and may all be found in a single study.

The Protection and Advancement of Human Rights as Research Goals

This recommendation is a variant on the action research and critical research approaches that seek social change, empowerment, and emancipation as research goals. For example, Argyris, Putnam, and Smith (1987) state that "social science should have an important role in generating liberating alternatives. This objective cannot be accomplished without challenging the status quo" (p. xi). Feminist scholars have been particularly articulate in this regard advocating, for instance, that research should enhance the status of women and the quality of their lives (i.e., contribute to their freedom and well-being) (Gilligan, 1982; Vaughter, 1976).

Human rights are transparent when they are freely exercised and protected. Claims for human rights usually indicate a belief that such rights are not being honored or are being interfered with. Additionally, individuals who are disadvantaged may be said to have special claims on human rights, that is, they obligate others who are more well off to provide the resources necessary for them to achieve a comparable level of well-being. Thus, human rights-based research is change oriented, seeking to empower people to claim their rights, to disempower rights violators, and to bolster mechanisms for protecting rights. Two interrelated approaches to this type of human rights-based research of particular relevance for social work are transformative criticism and generative theorizing. Briefly stated, transformative criticism involves the conceptual critique of the underlying assumptions of theory or research. The discourse generated by such critique leads to a modification of these assumptions (Longino, 1990). Generative theory challenges taken-for-granted assumptions and putative understandings of social life, and proposes alternative conceptualizations as guides for action (Gergen, 1978).

Both of these processes are illustrated in an analysis of the concept of Least Restrictive Environment (LRE) as it is applied to the education of children with disabilities (Witkin & Fox, 1992). The concept of LRE gained prominence in 1978 as part of Public Law 94-142, The Education for All Handicapped Children Act. It was intended to ensure that the rights of students with disabilities to a public education were not unduly restricted and that to the maximum extent appropriate these students would be educated with their non-disabled peers.

Our critique of the LRE concept and its implementation argued that within schools LRE was treated more like an educational objective than a human rights protection. For example, in the development of the legally required "individualized educational plans" (IEP) for students with disabilities, the assessment of whether an environment was "least restrictive" was typically not done until *after* instructional objectives for the student had been formulated. But since the development of these objectives was based on the existing (physical and organizational) environment of the school, the assessment of the LRE presumed that environment. For instance, segregated (self-contained) classes might be viewed as least restrictive simply because the school provided no other alternatives for students with disabilities. In this situation the LRE becomes the "LREE," the least restrictive *existing* environment" (Witkin & Fox, 1992, p. 327).

Based on this analysis, an alternative conceptualization called the most enabling environment (MEE) was proposed. The MEE was based on the notions of fundamental human rights as *minimal* guaranties for all students regardless of disabling conditions or individual learning goals and on the interpretation of social justice as equality of outcomes. The aims of this alternative conceptualization were to sensitize educators to human rights issues regarding students with disabilities, provide new ways of addressing the educational needs of these students, and be a catalyst for school restructuring. The transformational critique made it possible to set aside the implicit assumptions about the LRE, while the MEE offered an alternative way of conceptualizing rights protections, thereby forming the basis for the development of new practices.

The Protection and Advancement of Human Rights as Evaluative Criteria

The recognition that knowledge claims reflect neither an independent reality nor invariant observational transcriptions but rather social practices, encourages consideration of alternative criteria in evaluation and research. For example, Witkin and Gottschalk (1988) proposed that theories in social work be assessed relative to four criteria: the degree to which a theory explicates its historical, cultural, and political context; the degree to which a theory recognizes people as active agents; the degree to which a theory is generated from the actual life world of the people it addresses; and the degree to which a theory promotes social justice. This broadened perspective elevates the warranting power of social and moral criteria. For social work practitioners and researchers, fundamental human rights are the cornerstone of these criteria. Theories or research directives that thwarted or subverted the realization of fundamental human rights would be negated *on these grounds*. Those that showed promise of enhancing the fulfillment of human rights would be encouraged and favored, at least on this criterion. (Of course, this does not mean that theory or research is immune from criticism on other grounds.) For instance, explaining social disadvantage as the result of psychological deficits would be less favored than explanations identifying social and political inequalities.

Respecting the Human Rights of the Research Participants

Traditional research practices have been criticized for their treatment of research participants. These criticisms, however, usually emphasize ethical abuses in the implementation of conventional research, for instance, the use of deception or lack of confidentiality (Gilchrist & Schinke, 1988). Less often identified are the human rights issues involved in treating people as objects or ignoring or distorting their own "voices." There is a basic inconsistency between advocating for human rights and engaging in research practices that deny such rights to the participants. If research practices are to model what we preach, then the researcher-subject dichotomy of conventional inquiry must be eliminated and replaced with a form of inquiry in which all involved are co-participants. This would mean that the subject-participants have a voice in every aspect of the process. A recent project of one of my graduate students (Palmer, 1992) illustrates this point.

This project grew out of a request by a local mental health agency to develop an evaluation system for their services to people with severe and persistent mental illness. In responding to this request, we focused on how to meaningfully include the intended service recipients in the evaluation process. Our aim was to find out from the clients themselves what it was important to know about the agency. Rather than assume that we knew the best way to go about this task, we decided to ask them directly. Thus, the project started with the following statement and question to the clients: "The [mental health] agency wants me to help them develop a way of evaluating services. How should I go about doing this?" This request precipitated a dialogue that took place over a series of meetings and was both revealing and valuable. In fact, the process of exploring *how* to conduct an evaluation itself became an important source of evaluative information. For example, clients' fears about the possible repercussions of providing negative information and their lack of awareness of agency services and policies were important data about the quality of services. Participation in this process was empowering to the clients. Treating them as collaborators from the very beginning of the project, listening to their views, and respecting their suggestions, was rights-confirming.

TEACHING SOCIAL WORK RESEARCH

A critical constructionist approach to teaching social work research stands in contrast to the approach currently taught in most social work programs and endorsed by the Council on Social Work Education curriculum policy statement. Rather than a focus on methods, critical constructionism emphasizes language and theoretical knowledge, critical thinking, historical and cultural sensitivity, and the moral and value implications of inquiry (Witkin, 1990). For the critical constructionist, understanding research as a social practice emergent from, and embedded within, a social, historical and political context is as important an educational objective as knowledge of specific methods. Developing the analytical skills to assess the moral and social implications of these practices is as important as knowing how to perform statistical analyses. The objective of research is not some objective truth, but like all social work practice, an improvement in the human condition. In its most basic sense, this means the furtherance and protection of fundamental human rights.

Teaching an integrated human rights research approach is challenging both to instructors and students. For many students, such an approach runs counter to prior instruction and current beliefs about research. Thus, it is critical that a human rights approach be reinforced throughout the curriculum. As a common denominator of research and practice, human rights can help break down the perceived boundary between these two social practices. Research is practice (and practice research) not because both are "problem solving processes," but because they are disciplined, reflective, value-based, social practices that attempt to further social work goals.

The power of social research lies in its ability to create and control conceptual categories and generate new forms of understanding. As Hess (1990) asks: "Who would deny that the power to name is the power to differentiate, to decide what is to be included and excluded from our discourse, and hence our imaginations" (p. 83).

Constructionists, feminists, critical theorists, and others sensitive to the social dimensions and political ramifications of science and research have attempted to integrate this power into their approach to inquiry. When this power is guided by a vision of human rights it can be a potent force for betterment of all people.

REFERENCES

Albee, G. S. (1986). Toward a just society. *American Psychologist, 41*, 891-898.

Argyris, C., Putnam, R., & Smith, D. M. (1987). *Action science.* San Francisco: Jossey-Bass.

Bellah, R. N. (1983). The ethical aims of inquiry. In Hann, R. Bellah, Rabinow, & Sullivan (Eds.), *Social sciences as moral inquiry.* New York: Columbia University Press.

Berger, P.L., & Luckmann, T. (1966). *The social construction of reality.* Garden City, NY: Doubleday.

Centre for Human Rights (1992). *Teaching and learning about human rights: A manual for schools of social work and the social work profession.* New York: United Nations.

Davis, L. V. (1987). Views of wife abuse: Does the research method make the difference? *Affilia, 2*, 53-66.

Dilthey, W. (1976) [1883-]. *Selected writings.* Trans. and ed. H. P. Rickman. Cambridge: Cambridge University Press.

Donnelly, J. (1985). *The concept of human rights.* NY: St. Martin's Press.

Feyerabend, P. K. (1976). *Against method.* New York: Humanities Press.

Gadamer, H. G. (1975). *Truth and method.* New York: Seabury Press.

Garfinkel, H. (1967). *Studies in ethnomethodology.* Englewood Cliffs, NJ: Prentice Hall.

Gergen, K. J. (1978). Toward generative theory. *Journal of Personality and Social Psychology, 36*, 1344-1360.

Gergen, K. J. (1985). Social psychology and the phoenix of unreality. In S. Koch, & D.E. Leary (Eds.) *A century of psychology as science* (pp. 528-557). New York: McGraw-Hill.

Gergen, K. J. (1986). Correspondence versus autonomy in the language of understanding human action. In D. W. Fiske & R. A. Shweder (Eds.), *Metatheory in social science*, pp. 136-162. Chicago: University of Chicago Press.

Gergen, K. J., & Davis, K. E. (Eds.) (1985). *The social construction of the person.* New York: Springer Verlag.

Gewirth, A. (1982). *Human rights: Essays on justification and applications.* Chicago: University of Chicago Press.

Gewirth, A. (1978). *Reason and morality.* Chicago: University of Chicago Press.

Gil, D.G. (nd). Social sciences, human survival, development and liberation. Brandeis University, Center on Social Change Practice and Theory, Waltham, MA.

Gilchrist, L. D., & Schinke, S. P. (1988). Research ethics. In R. M. Grinnell, Jr.

(Ed.), *Social work research and evaluation*, 3rd ed. (pp. 65-79). Itasca, IL: F. E. Peacock Publishers.

Gilligan, C. (1982). *In a different voice: Psychological development and women's development*. Cambridge: Harvard University Press.

Gottschalk, S., & Witkin, S.L. (1988). Ideology, social justice, and social work research. *Journal of International & Comparative Social Welfare, 4* (1), 1-11.

Gottschalk, S., & S. L. Witkin (1991). Rationality in social work: A critical reexamination. *Journal of Sociology & Social Welfare, 18,* 121-136.

Gould, S. J. (1981). *The mismeasure of man*. New York: Norton.

Hanson, N. (1958). *Patterns of discovery: An inquiry into the conceptual foundations of science*. Cambridge, England: Cambridge University Press.

Heineman, M. (1981). The obsolete scientific imperative in social work research. *Social Service Review, 55,* 371-397.

Heineman Pieper, M. (1989). The heuristic paradigm: A unifying and comprehensive approach to social work research. *Smith College Studies in Social Work, 60,* 8-34.

Hess, B.B. (1990). Beyond dichotomy: Drawing distinctions and embracing differences. *Sociological Forum, 5,* 75-93.

Howard, G. S. (1985). The role of values in the science of psychology. *American Psychologist, 40,* 255-265.

Kent, E. A. (1986). Taking human rights seriously. In M. Tamny & K.D. Irani (Eds.), *Rationality in thought and action* (pp. 31-47). New York: Greenwood Press.

Kitzinger, C. (1987). *The social construction of lesbianism*. Newbury Park, CA: Sage.

Kuhn, T. S. (1970). *The structure of scientific revolutions*, 2nd rev. edn. Chicago: University of Chicago Press.

Laudan, L. (1977). *Progress and its problems: Toward a theory of scientific growth*. Berkeley, CA: University of California Press.

Longino, H. E. (1990). *Science as social knowledge*. Princeton, NJ: Princeton University Press.

Morawski, J. G. (1986). Contextual discipline: The unmaking and remaking of sociality. In R. L. Rosnow, & M. Georgoudi (Eds.), *Contextualism and understanding in behavioral science* (p. 51). New York: Praeger.

Palmer, III, H. (1992). The inclusion of mental health clients in program evaluation activities: A case study. Unpublished paper. Department of Social Work, University of Vermont.

Peterson, V. S. (1987). Re-constructing the "individual" in human rights. Paper presentation at the *National Women's Studies Association Conference*, Atlanta, GA.

Riley, M.W. (1988). *Sociological lives*. Newbury Park, CA: Sage.

Sampson, E. E. (1989). The deconstruction of the self. In J. Shotter, & K.J. Gergen (Eds.), *Texts of identity* (pp. 1-19). Newbury Park, CA: Sage.

Siporin, M. (1991). Strengthening the moral mission of social work. In N.

Reid, & P. Popple (Eds.), *The moral purpose of social work.* Chicago: Nelson-Hall.

Smith, J. K. (1990). Alternative research paradigms and the problem of criteria. In E. G. Guba (Ed.), *The paradigm dialog,* pp. 167-187. Newbury Park, CA: Sage.

Task Force on Social Work Research (1991). *Building social work knowledge for effective services and policies: A plan for research development.* Austin, TX: Author.

Trigg, R. (1985). *Understanding social science.* Oxford, United Kingdom: Basil Blackwell.

Tyson, K. (1992). A new approach to relevant scientific research for practitioners: The heuristic paradigm. *Social Work, 37,* 541-556.

Vaughter, R. (1976). Psychology: Review essay. *Signs: Journal of Women in Culture and Society, 2,* 120-146.

Veatch, R. M. (1986). *The foundations of justice.* New York: Oxford University Press.

Weimer, W. (1979). *Notes on the methodology of scientific research.* Hillsdale, NJ: Lawrence Erlbaum Associates.

Winch, P. (1958). *The idea of a social science and its relation to philosophy.* New York: Humanities Press.

Witkin, S. L. (1989a). Scientific ideology and women: Implications for marital research and therapy. *Journal of Family Psychology, 2,* 430-446.

Witkin, S. L. (1989b). Toward a scientific social work. *Journal of Social Service Research, 12* (3/4), 83-98.

Witkin, S. L. (1990). The implications of social constructionism for social work education. *Journal of Teaching in Social Work, 4* (2), 37-48.

Witkin, S. L. (1991). Empirical clinical practice: A critical analysis. *Social Work, 36* (2), 158-163.

Witkin, S. L. (in press). Family social work: A critical constructionist perspective. *Journal of Family Social Work.*

Witkin, S. L., & Fox, L. (1992). Beyond the least restrictive environment. In R. Villa, J. Thousand, W. Stainback, & S. Stainback (Eds.), *Restructuring for caring and effective education: An administrative guide to creating heterogeneous schools,* (pp. 325-224). Baltimore: Paul H. Brooks Publishing Co.

Witkin, S. L., & Gottschalk, S. (1988). Alternative criteria for theory evaluation. *Social Service Review, 62,* 211-224.

Wittgenstein, L. (1963). *Philosophical investigations.* Trans. G. Anscombe. NY: Macmillan.

Building Knowledge
from the Study of Cases:
A Reflective Model
for Practitioner Self-Evaluation

Kathleen Hannigan Millstein

SUMMARY. This paper offers a teaching and learning model for building practice knowledge through intensive case study and practitioner self-evaluation. This reflective model addresses the challenges of systematizing case study and of using multiple research methodologies within a social constructionist perspective. Examples of research projects conducted by second year master's social work students who participated in a seminar based on this model are discussed.

INTENSIVE STUDY OF CASES IN SOCIAL WORK

Intensive study of cases has been the cornerstone of knowledge building for social work practice since the beginning of the profession. While we have maintained our commitment to building

Kathleen Hannigan Millstein, DSW, is Assistant Professor of Social Work, Simmons College School of Social Work, 51 Commonwealth Avenue, Boston, MA 02116. The author gratefully acknowledges the invaluable contributions of: her colleagues in the Philosophical Issues Study Group in co-constructing the ideas represented in this course; Drs. Helen Reinherz and Abbie Frost in reading earlier drafts of the paper; and Don Lepley in patiently preparing the manuscript.

[Haworth co-indexing entry note]: "Building Knowledge from the Study of Cases: A Reflective Model for Practitioner Self-Evaluation," Millstein, Kathleen Hannigan. Co-published simultaneously in *Journal of Teaching in Social Work* (The Haworth Press, Inc.) Vol. 8, No. 1/2, 1993, pp. 255-279; and: *Revisioning Social Work Education: A Social Constructionist Approach* (ed: Joan Laird) The Haworth Press, Inc., 1993, pp. 255-279. Multiple copies of this article/chapter may be purchased from The Haworth Document Delivery Center [1-800-3-HAWORTH; 9:00 a.m. - 5:00 p.m. (EST)].

knowledge from case materials, how we have systematized this study has changed over the years. These changes are a function of the epistemologies and values which guide inquiry at specific points in history.

In the last 15 years the intensive study of cases has been framed within the context of the empirically based clinical practice model (Siegel, 1984) and single subject research designs. With single subject designs we actively returned to our knowledge building roots in the study of individual cases, using methodologies defined within the dominant scientific paradigm. More recently, the concept of single subject research has come under attack. It is caught in the paradigm battles between empirically based practice proponents and the critics of this logical positivist meta-theory (Heinemann, 1981; Ivanoff, Blythe, & Briar, 1987; Kagle, 1982; Witkin, 1991). It is further challenged by disappointing research findings on the extent to which practitioners trained in single system evaluation implement these evaluation methods after graduation. Follow-up studies (Cheatham, 1987; Gingerich, 1984; Richey, Blythe, & Berlin, 1987; Welch, 1983) have found that most social work practitioners find it difficult to incorporate the methodology.

Many of us in social work education are busily meeting Council on Social Work Education requirements for integration of content on single system practice evaluation into the master's level curriculum. Some of us have observed that making this experience meaningful requires the creative use of a range of methodologies and, while students may not carry the formal designs into practice, they do value the experience of looking at a single case systematically over time. Some graduates report that they apply specific techniques (Gingerich, 1984; Millstein, Regan, & Reinherz, 1990; Richey et al., 1987). Others even feel that it is the most important *clinical* experience in their masters program (Millstein et al., 1990), a special opportunity for intensive case study. The skills learned seemed to enhance graduates' abilities to reflect on practice and to ask practice questions that are based on experiential and abstract knowledge.

Efforts have been made to modify single subject designs by placing less emphasis on experimental designs and more on exploratory and descriptive designs (Alter & Evens, 1990; Dean & Reinherz, 1986; Gingerich, 1990; Nelsen, 1981). Alter and Evens proposed two categories of designs, qualitative and quantitative, and made a distinction between inductive and deductive research questions in the self-assessment process. Yet, in all of these efforts, the practitioner-researcher's participant-observer role in conducting naturalistic research is not addressed. The attention remains focused on methodology and procedures employed by an "unembodied scientist" (Reinharz, 1984). Valuable practice knowledge is lost. What is neglected are the ways that the practitioner is making meaning of the interaction with the client both in the "experience near" of the practice action and in observations of the practice actions through the research process.

Feedback from graduates and practice experience in teaching single subject designs suggest a refocusing of energy from decreasing barriers to and creating modifications of single subject designs to creating a new model for practitioner evaluation of their own work. This reflective model of practitioner self-evaluation would continue the profession's commitment to build practice knowledge from individual case study, but would expand methodologically and conceptually beyond single subject designs. It would encourage practitioners to examine professional activity and the knowledge reflected in that activity against empirically-based theory as well as against their practice wisdom and tacit knowledge, using a range of methodologies which are syntonic with these goals.

A reflective model (Schon, 1983) for practitioner self-evaluation extends beyond the empirical model. It opens up the options for a definition of practice and evaluation in which both are seen as attempts "to learn more; to be surprised; to find out what one does not already expect, predict or hypothesize" (Mahrer, 1988, p. 697). There is no one textbook case which guides practice and there is no one set of designs which can be used to evaluate all cases. There must be room for use of a range of methodologies, including but not restricted to single subject designs. Understanding the uniqueness of each case comes through dialogue, recognition of the limits of knowledge, and a continuous process of practitioner exploration of both his or her practice and research actions and the contextually constructed ways of making meaning of these actions.

The purposes of this paper are to offer a reflective model for

practitioner self-evaluation using the perspective of social constructionism and to present examples of studies conducted by masters
students using this model. These students participated in a year-long
seminar in practice evaluation. Part of the second-year research
curriculum in the masters degree program at Simmons College
School of Social Work, the seminar was one of ten research options.
It provided each student with both didactic learning about methods
of practice evaluation on single cases and an opportunity to apply
these methodologies to an actual case carried in the field.

Guiding Assumptions

Several assumptions are critical to this model:

1. *There are many ways of knowing and many types of knowers.*
Knowledge for practice comes from many sources (tradition, experience, intuition, science). As Hartman (1990) phrases it: "There
are many truths and many ways of knowing. Each discovery contributes to our knowledge and each way of knowing deepens our
understanding and adds another dimension to our view of the
world" (p. 14). Just as there are many ways of knowing, there are
many kinds of knowers; some may need distance and scientific
objectivity and some may not. What makes sense to one practitioner
as a methodology appropriate to a practice research question may
not make sense to another practitioner with a similar question.

We each make meaning of our work differently. Each way of
knowing is based on certain assumptions about knowledge (epistemology), about the nature of being (ontology), and about values.
Understanding current debates about the relevance of various research methods and engaging in practice evaluation involves articulating these assumptions, appreciating the advantages and disadvantages of different ways of knowing, and learning how and in what
ways each of us as practitioners use and create knowledge which
informs our practice acts.

2. *Social construction theory offers a perspective for understanding practice knowledge.* Exclusive focus on scientific ways of
knowing with their emphasis on empiricism, theory, and deduction
may not result in knowledge which adequately represents the complexity of practice actions (Scott, 1990; Witkin, 1991). As Goldstein (1990) stated, "Social work practice is an ever changing and

complex blend of theory, analogue, wisdom and art" (p. 41). A broader conception of knowledge is needed to understand knowledge-based practice; a conception of knowledge which includes contexts, interactions, perspectives, and meanings.

Social construction theory offers such a perspective for understanding knowledge for social work practice (Witkin, 1990; Witkin & Gottschalk, 1988). Social construction theory sees knowledge building as a social phenomenon, "an evolving set of meanings that emerge unendingly from interactions between people" (Hoffman, 1990, p. 3). Within this perspective the practitioner-researcher becomes a participant-observer facilitating the therapeutic conversation. Schon (1983) refers to the knowledge created in this process as "knowledge in action." By observing and reflecting on practice acts, the practitioner has engaged in a continuous process of inquiry in action, inductively evaluating and creating new knowledge.

This process of observation changes the observed as well as the observer and challenges the idea of practitioner objectivity in the therapeutic endeavor (Dean, 1989; Papell & Skolnick, 1992). Every professional encounter has its own uniqueness. "Art, intuition, creativity and practice wisdom" (Papell & Skolnick, 1992, p. 20) become valued components of professional functioning. A direct, linear relationship between knowledge and action then comes under scrutiny as we question whether what we say we do and what we do, "theory in practice," may not be the same (Fleck-Henderson, 1989).[1]

3. *Practitioner self-evaluation is a reflective process.* The reflective process which begins in the "experience near" continues throughout the research process for practitioner-researchers engaged in "inquiry on action" (Schon, 1983). They are continuing to build practice knowledge as they engage in creating meanings for their actions in conversation with themselves, colleagues, and research theories and methodologies. "The roots of both science and practice are to be found in the everyday processes and achievements of human beings who seek to manage (techne) their world and to orient their action (praxis) in relation to others in that world" (Kondrat, 1992, p. 243).

The professional encounter for practitioners engaged in self-evaluation includes the research process. Competent practice requires "acceptance of the idea that at every stage, the uniqueness of the individual social worker and that of the individual client shape the process of helping" (Pray, 1991, p. 83). The term "N of 1" as applied to single subject designs then becomes an impossibility. "If N refers to people, then there are always at least two" (Haworth, 1984, p. 354). In practice evaluation within this model, the social worker attempts to look *at* the lens at the same time he/she is looking *through* it, performing and reflecting on that performance during the course of a practice situation (Scott, 1990). In addition, the practitioner-researcher views the research process itself as context dependent, evolving and focused on understanding multiple perspectives. The role of the "human knower" is critical as every step in the research process yields personal understanding and knowledge (Reinharz, 1992).

4. *It is important to generate practice knowledge from systematic reflection on cases.* Building knowledge inductively through purposeful observation and reflection on cases with attention to contexts, interaction, multiple perspectives, and multiple meanings is characteristic of a reflective model. This process must be systematic. Systematic assessment is a process which is not restricted to one methodology. What specific methods are selected are less an issue than the developmental process in posing a practice question, selecting and evaluating research methods and their assumptions, and assessing if the method selected makes sense for the practitioner. Practitioner self-evaluation can take the form of what Gingerich (1990) calls single subject evaluation, using more quasi experimental or exploratory single subject designs to determine "if a desired outcome for a single client or client system has been achieved" (p. 14). It can also take the form of a more broadly defined self-assessment in which more qualitative research methods are used to help practitioners reflect on the intuitive types of questions they have about their own work. These studies can have as their unit of analysis not only a client and the nature and progress of therapeutic work, but also the practitioner; how he or she reflects on a clinical case. Critical to the use of any of these methods is the practitioner's attention to his or her responses to its application, to the research experience, and to the fit between the method and his or her evolving practice theory. These all become part of the research process.

A FRAMEWORK FOR TEACHING AND LEARNING SYSTEMATIC CASE STUDY

Participating in self-evaluation within the context of these assumptions is not easy for practitioners, researchers, or graduate students. It requires openness, an ability to take risks, exposure to a range of methodologies that extend beyond those learned in a traditional single-subject design course, and an ability to tolerate the uncertainties inherent in building practice knowledge. The challenge for teacher and student can be divided into five major areas:

1. Creation of an atmosphere for individual and group reflection.
2. Encouragement to think clearly and engage in critical interchange and "thick description" of the research process.
3. Identification of the ethical issues inherent to the reflective process.
4. Development of a question to guide the inquiry.
5. Permission to use qualitative and/or quantitative methods to answer the question.

Each of these is discussed in some detail.

Creation of an Atmosphere for Individual and Group Reflection

Individual and group reflection on cases happens in a learning environment in which everyone involved can feel as free as possible to think out loud, to articulate and expand their latent knowledge. Belenky, Clinchy, Goldberger, and Tarule (1986) discuss connected learning and connected classes in which the teacher serves as midwife, facilitating the expression of ideas and questions. Small classes and seminar format are critical for this process. Metatheoretical debates can then be addressed beginning in the first class. Students engage in the debates and are encouraged to develop a position on the kinds of knowledge for practice most reflective of the ways they make meaning of their work. In addition to this focus in class discussions, students are asked to keep a "Dilemma Log." This log offers them the opportunity to record their responses to readings, to the class, and to the steps in the research process: What makes sense to you about what you are doing, thinking, hearing? What doesn't? This vehicle not only provides a way for them to think about how they think, but also to address the sources of disquiet and excitement about the ideas they are learning and the methods they are applying. Ethical as well as value concerns surface through the log.

Encouragement to Think Clearly and Engage in Critical Interchange and "Thick Description" of the Research Process

In all forms of research it is important to establish the "validity" of the process and findings. In practitioner self-assessment concepts such as internal and external validity, reliability and objectivity, which are used to evaluate hypothetico-deductive methodologies, are not applicable since they derive from a concept of empirical reality which assumes a distance between the object of the research and the researcher (Marshall & Rosman, 1989).

"Validity" in the reflective model refers instead to "how the researcher negotiates his or her own claim to an understanding" of an event "with a wider community outside the research situation: for example, the 'scientific community' or the 'community of scholars'" (Salner, 1986, p. 125). Valid knowledge claims emerge from communication and negotiation of conflicting interpretations. Mishler (1990) refers to this as a process of "validation."

Research results are interpreted as part "of an ongoing scholarly debate or 'conversation,' in which reality is socially constructed" (Salner, 1986, p. 125). As Ricoeur (1971/1979) stated,

> To show that an interpretation is more probable in light of what is known is something other than showing that a conclusion is true. In this sense validation is not verification. Validation is an argumentative discipline compared to juridical procedures of legal interpretation. (p. 90)

"Validation" in the reflective model is achieved through "accurate, honest reconstruction" and dialogue (Rodwell, 1990). The reflective model assumes that knowledge is value laden and engages in surfacing these values and assumptions for examination. As Fee (1983) suggests, this process involves

The concept of creating knowledge through a constant interaction with nature, the willingness to consider all assumptions and methods as open to question and the expectation that ideas will be subjected to the most unfettered critical evaluation. (p. 16)

Basic to this process is "thick description" (Geertz, 1983) of both the practice act and the research process itself. Students are required, through their dilemma logs and/or through memos kept throughout the research process, to document their research activities in detail. This documentation is integral to the research and open to examination and discussion. They are encouraged to create an account of the research process which can "invite, compel, stimulate or delight the audience" (Gergen, 1985, p. 272).

Clear thinking and critical interchange among colleagues using "thick description" as a foundation for the dialogue are then central to "validation" of the study findings. In the master's class this level of collegial interaction is encouraged both within class discussion and by assigning each participant an editing partner. The editing partner's role is to read all drafts of the research work-in-progress, to articulate what he or she feels is being communicated and to reflect that understanding and questions back to a partner. "I understand you to mean this in your text." "Is that what you meant?" The partners offer yet another reflection on how the students are making sense of their work and their worlds. They challenge and enrich interpretation, moving their colleagues toward defensible knowledge claims.

Identification of the Ethical Issues Inherent to the Reflective Process

There are many differences between traditional research and practitioners' research on their own clinical cases. The most fundamental difference is the nature of the relationship between the investigator and the subject, between clinician and client. In traditional science it is assumed that there is a distance between researcher and subject. Theoretically, this separation permits an objectivity and minimizes any potential effects on subject and/or researcher. However, when the clinician is the researcher and the client is the subject as in practice research, there are no clear lines and objectivity. Many questions arise for students and practitioners. For example:

- In clinical situations, in which the power differential is what Chenitz and Swanson (1986) call "official," *can* informed consent be freely given by a client?
- Can the practitioner-researcher and the client-subject be more equal partners in reflecting on their work together? Can the client be the co-researcher? *Some* clients can join the process, but what about those who can't? Do we not use their case materials? If we don't, are we violating the experiences of the clients we are excluding from these knowledge-building activities?
- In presenting case materials, how do we balance the requirements of confidentiality and the desirability of "thick description" (Davis, 1991)? The more we falsify details on a case to protect confidentiality, the more we impose our own interpretation on the data and the less it stands for the integrity of the client experience.
- Is the case study the clinician-researcher's own to disseminate? Should the client agree with what we say or write (Clifft, 1986; Stoller, 1988)?

These questions must be raised in class discussion prior to beginning the case study and during the entire research process through to dissemination of findings. Students debate the questions both in the abstract and as they are directly reflected in their individual projects.

Development of a Question to Guide the Inquiry

Practitioners have many questions about their cases and practice. Unfortunately they often feel that there is a wide gap between these clinical questions and "real" research (Strauss & Hafez, 1981). Researchers, in turn, have often supported the perceived gap by not listening to the clinical questions. It is in this perceived gap that much potential knowledge is lost. It is critical in the process of practitioner self-evaluation that the social worker develops a clinical question which he or she cares about and believes is relevant. Careful formulation of this question is integral to the reflective endeavor. What do you want to know? Why do you think you want to know it? What in your life/in your case generated this curiosity? What does the question say about where you are in your professional journey and where you want to go? It is assumed that questions will evolve and become refined.

The following excerpts from a student's Dilemma Log illustrate this critical thinking, self-reflective process (Cook, 1992).

Entry One

... Before I came to Simmons, I was engaged in writing and painting and parenting. I had come to rely on what I labeled as the creative process to do my work and increase my competence. When I enrolled at Simmons, I assumed I would be required to switch to what Schon refers to as a technical/rational way of looking at things. I was willing to do that because I wanted to become a professional. I believed that the two were mutually exclusive. . . .

I was terrified of first year Research. Surely I would be found out as less than committed to the technical/rational model and I might fail to meet the requirements of the course. What convinced me to enter the swamp was a diagram of the research process handed out in class. I remembered that I was a visual learner. I saw on that paper a picture of the same process I used to get through my stories and my paintings. . . . Strauss & Hafez (1981) speak of the vulnerable question that needs to be tested in conversation with others, but guarded from destruction. The negative reaction of the not-so-brave is not a reason to keep from trying.

I faced the same dilemma in first year Clinical Practice. I couldn't imagine how I was going to keep myself detached in order to assess and treat other people. . . . Finally, I got to Constructivism which taught me the value of conversation in creating meaning and in exploring ethical dilemmas.

... I found myself thinking about what got said, defining my reaction, talking to others, taking a break, changing what I did next time, but especially not backing down. . . . Papell & Skolnick (1992) reassure me that I may label the process "professional" . . . . My fear is that I won't have time to reflect, only to react; I will lose space for my process.

Entry Two

When I began reading I wondered what is my way of knowing. I also wondered how I would evaluate my practice when I was feeling that I didn't have a practice. Moustakas' (1990) contention that a research question begins with a "passionate desire to know, a devotion and commitment to pursue a question that is strongly connected to one's own identity and selfhood" (p. 40) is the direction I would like to take. Even Alter & Evens (1990) suggest that the question have enough substance to be worth the time and effort. Where do my practice passions lie? I am in search of my own question. I thought of the understanding gained in a case conference with the addition of the patient's artwork from her Occupational Therapy group. Perhaps I could think of studying what goes on there. But Ruckdeschel's (1985) second point is that "knowledge is gained most directly by participation and involvement" and OT and even the patients doing it . . . are not within the scope of my practice.

. . . According to Alter & Evens (1990) I possess "divergent knowledge." Apparently I am more comfortable with inductive methods. The deductive method outlined in Chapter 2 meant less to me than some of the other readings. So I have learned something about my way of knowing. Where is the passion in what I am actually doing?

Entry Three

. . . How is my enthusiasm for contructivist theory being translated into practice? . . .

I am enthusiastic about constructivist ideas that include making meaning by telling stories and having conversations. However, I have grown up in a tradition of "scientific" knowledge, the "right" way, and "objective" point of view, cause and effect, and "the" answer. My language expresses my biases and it is not so easy to change my perspective. I would like to discover how much of my new approach is actually reflected in my practice and, where it isn't, how much of that I want to change and how.

Entry Four

. . . I would like to report, especially in light of my fears, misgivings, connections to the past, and wonderings about where I fit in all I'm hearing about research, my excitement and enthusiasm for the process that has begun. I think it resonates with the surprise and the unexpected.

Entry Five

. . . I am an advocate of process. I often feel awash in it and wonder why I muck around in the swamp while others seem to see and articulate more precisely. I have believed I was lacking in a strong grasp of theoretical concepts to verify, without which I was to be condemned to amateur status. With the specific example of Gonzalez' paper (1992) I accepted the idea that what I have been engaged in is an inductive method of understanding and evaluation. The way Giorgi (1985) reaches an abstract grasp of the principles embedded in the story of the chess set, echoed by Charmaz' (1990) description of coding and memoing, is what I have been trying to do in my practice. . . . I think at this point I would want to reread some of these articles and I think I need to pin down my question. In any case I know I'm using the method. I'm reminded of Rex Harrison singing in "My Fair Lady": "She's got it! I think she's got it! By George, I think she's got it!" Have I come to the Rubicon?

Entry Six

The steps in front of me are to do some soul-searching about what I believe I have taken from constructivist theory and made my own and to look at a case to see what is there. I would also like to review Strauss & Corbin (1990) about memoing to make sure that what I am writing down about what I'm doing fits with the research process and is not wasted.

I was relieved in class to discover that the others who presented were in a similar place, that the concerns they mentioned such as fear of not having enough data/not having time
to collect enough data and not being so grounded in theory
were mine as well. . . .

Entry Seven

I have read through my logs. I like to read what I write,
although I'm conscious of its being a point in time and I have
moved beyond wherever I was. I am seeing my process unfold: . . . a search for my own practice; a concern for fitting
into my organization; a couple of forays into questions about
what a family worker does and how to introduce myself to a
patient; and finally a sense of method to reach a question. I
think I have been writing about the context of my work and
hence of my question. I am aware now that I do have a
practice–family work–with process recordings to prove it,
that my method has a name– inductive, and that my work
with categories has captured enough of my imagination to be
willing to focus on continuing with a grounded theory approach.

Entry Eight

I have entitled my question "Constructing Very Brief Treatment: Family Work in an Unlocked Inpatient Psychiatric
Unit." I have chosen a grounded theory study as a way to look
at how I use constructivist theory in my practice. What language do I use to elicit stories from clients? When and under
what circumstances do I elicit those stories? What language do
I use to describe those stories to other team members and in
the charts? . . .

Additional examples of questions in student projects include:
How do I use self-disclosure in my work? When and how am I
empathic when treating clients on a brief short-term inpatient
psychiatric unit? Having one to three sessions, how do I form an

empathic connection? What is my experience of recognizing and using countertransference in brief treatment with clients in a health maintenance organization? These questions suggest what Rodwell (1987) described when discussing the complex problems practitioners face: "It is better to achieve approximate answers to the right questions than exact answers to the wrong questions" (p. 237).

Permission to Use Qualitative and/or Quantitative Methods to Answer the Question

A reflective process respects individual differences in ways of knowing. As a result, selection of a research method is viewed as more complex than a marriage between the research question and the method. Answering research questions generated from practice also demands extending beyond theory verification and deductive methods. The practitioner must be able to choose methods from a broad menu of qualitative and quantitative options. Which method is chosen is a function of the question, the current level of professional knowledge about the study area and, perhaps most importantly, the way or ways of knowing best fitted to the practitioner-researcher's own epistemology of practice. What method makes sense for the clinician's own knowledge-building process? What methods fit best with the clinician's values and assumptions about how and why clients have problems in living and what constitutes behavioral change?

Designs appropriate to practitioner self-evaluation range from what Alter and Evens (1990) and Gambrill and Barth (1980) refer to as descriptive and exploratory single subject designs to qualitative self-assessment (Pray, 1990) to more phenomenological approaches.

Descriptive and exploratory single subject designs. These designs include simple AB designs or B only case studies in which client problems and goals are specified, an intervention to meet these goals is selected, and progress toward these objectives is monitored over time. Operational definitions are developed for each goal and, using content analysis of process recordings or tapes, these dependent measures can be counted for each session or rated using scales or standardized measures. The findings are then graphed and analyzed. These designs are quantitative and on the surface it would seem that they would be antithetical to a reflective model, yet they can be used effectively in the service of reflection and in the spirit of inductive discovery and knowledge building.

For example, Neild (1992), in formulating her project, felt uncomfortable with the idea of employing qualitative methods; they seemed too unstructured and thus she chose to conduct a single-subject design. She was working with a client who had failed to complete the written assignments in his courses in his first year of graduate school. She conceptualized his issues using a psychodynamic model of fear of success related to unresolved Oedipal wishes and began a course of brief insight-oriented psychotherapy. This formulation made sense to her and she began using her process recordings to track the client's depressive comments, self-esteem comments, references to parents, and his school behaviors reported in each session. Within several months, based on her observations, clinical wisdom, and increased understanding of herself, of the theory she was attempting to apply, and of the client, this formulation no longer "fit." She recast the question: How effective is short-term treatment in helping a 22-year-old graduate student accomplish the tasks of young adulthood? Using separation-individuation theory, the developmental tasks were redefined as the abilities to set and achieve academic/career goals and to develop a relationship with a woman. Recognizing that these long-term goals would need to be broken down into intermediate objectives, three goals were set for short-term work: to maintain an empathic relationship with the client, to assist the client in identifying and expressing feelings, and to facilitate the client's ability to identify and express his needs. The process through which this student shifted her formulation was part of her self-reflection as was what the process said to her about her professional development, practice knowledge and uses of theory in her work with this client.

Qualitative methods. These methods directly address the interactive nature of the knowledge-building process. They attempt to describe experience and are concerned with how people, in this case clients and/or clinicians, define events and how they act in relation to their beliefs (Ruckdeschel, 1985). They are based on the assumption that "the reality or meaning of the situation is created by people and leads to actions and the consequences of action" (Chenitz & Swanson, 1986, p. 4).

The qualitative method most frequently selected by students in the seminar has been grounded theory (Glaser & Strauss, 1967). The grounded theory method involves exploration and inspection of the data with the goal of theory development. In contrast, with the traditional single subject designs, theories about the nature and causes of client problems are thought to guide understanding, selection, formulation, and definition of client problems and the choice of interventions. Operational definitions of problems, goals and interventions derive from these theories and the research process proceeds as a way to validate how and in what ways the client has changed relative to criteria drawn from these theories.

In grounded theory, theory is built inductively from the data:

> By starting with the data from the lived experience of the research participants, the researcher can from the beginning attend to how they construct their world. That lived experience shapes the researcher's approach to data collection and analysis. (Charmaz, 1990, p. 1162)

In building practice knowledge this approach can translate well to a focus on the lived experience of client and/or clinician within the therapeutic work; a focus on the individual case.

Grounded theorists begin with a general research question. As data are collected the perceptions of the practitioner/grounded theorist are continually open to correction and modification through interaction with new data. The method contains several essential steps (Giorgi, 1985; Rennie, Phillips, & Quartaro, 1988):

1. Reading through all of the clinical material in an attempt to gain a general sense of the whole. In systematic case study this often means reading the process, transcription, or listening to the tape of a session.

2. Going back to the beginning and reading the description again with the specific aim of identifying meaning units "from within a psychological perspective and with a focus on the phenomenon being observed" (Giorgi, 1985, p. 10). For example, one might

examine the description and ask: When am I being empathic with this client? What is an empathic intervention? What are self-disclosing comments that I make as a therapist? When am I self-disclosing?

3. Examining the meaning units and forming categories to describe the units. Further data from additional sessions or clients are then collected and the categories become more defined and multidimensional until they are saturated, which means that analysis of additional material reveals no new categories.

4. Synthesizing the categories and the analytic process into a consistent statement of the experience being studied. Categories are prioritized, relationships among them explained, and an overarching framework or most central category explaining the categories and relationships is put forth.

As part of these procedures the researcher keeps track of his or her own process in doing the research by keeping a journal or "memoing" each time work is done with the data. These memos have several functions. They help the researcher to obtain insight into tacit, guiding assumptions, encourage thinking beyond single incidents to themes and patterns in the data, and record thoughts about relationships to theory and ideas which can be used later in the analysis.

Grounded theory can be used in building practice knowledge in a number of ways. Examples from masters projects suggest a range of applications. Gonzalez (1992) used grounded theory to build knowledge of empathic skills used in short-term therapeutic relationships. She explored her own use of empathy in her work with clients on an inpatient acute care psychiatric unit in which her involvement was limited to one to three sessions. She was interested in identifying: What do I think I am doing when I am being empathic? What do these behaviors say about my use of self? How do these behaviors relate to the literature on empathy? She began with five process recordings using the procedures described earlier and explored an additional five as her naming units and categories evolved. She examined one process recording at a time for her responses, recording each evidence of an empathic response and labelling or naming the responses.

She eventually arrived at 25 labels or categories, examined relationships among them, and finally derived eight individual categories or conceptual labels: exploring, reflecting, clarifying, validating, supporting, sustaining, interpreting, and bridging. These eight categories were described fully, using examples from the process recordings and staying as close as possible to the actual data. She then returned to the literature on empathy, examining more closely the connections among these eight categories and developing a single core category which she called "exploration" and which she saw as descriptive of her empathic style. This core category reflects the main theme reflected in the data. Finally, she again revisited the literature to identify relationships among the data, the existing theory, and her single core category, concluding that her own "exploring mode, especially during the opening phases of the first or second meeting, demonstrated an empathic style that helped clients express thoughts and feelings."

Calame (1992) combined several qualitative methods, such as therapist self-anchored rating scales and journals and memos which incorporate the researchers feelings and perceptions as part of the analytic process, to reflect on the role of feminist theory in her work with eating disordered female adolescents and its function in guiding her practice actions. She asked three questions: In what ways do my espoused feminist values and understanding of eating disorders appear to me to translate into my interventions? In what ways do my espoused feminist values and understanding of eating disorders appear to me to translate into my continued and evolving formulation of cases? In what ways does my work with clients change or impact my understanding of my feminist values as they relate to theories of treatment for eating disorders?

She collected data from her process recordings and formulations for each session held on three clients and from her personal journal over an eight week period. Calame identified what she felt to be her espoused feminist interventions, such as analysis of gender roles/oppression, directiveness, and empowerment techniques and rated each session on the degree to which these interventions were used. She then identified three feminist themes which she felt would translate into her formulations:

1. explicitly feminist thinking about women's enculturation,
2. formulation of client's situation in terms of conforming to or rejecting societal norms, and
3. feminist thinking reflected in specific goals and treatment plans.

These were also rated for each session. In addition, using a form of grounded theory, she thematically analyzed her process recordings and formulations for reflections of her feminist values. Finally, she maintained a journal in which she recorded her ongoing reflection about how she "viewed the intersection of her feminist construct and her treatment with eating disordered adolescent clients." She analyzed this written narrative thematically, noting shifts in emphasis, tone, and understanding.

Calame's analysis yielded the following findings: First, from her rating of her interventions, she learned that she used fewer explicit feminist interventions and was more directive than she expected. She also rated empowerment techniques as her most frequently used feminist intervention. Second, ratings of her interventions showed similar findings in that explicitly feminist formulations about gender roles were rarely employed, as was specific feminist thinking, while expressions of societal impact on the client were quite frequently reflected. Third, the thematic coding and analysis of interventions and formulations suggested two central categories: cultural interpretations and self-empowerment techniques. Over two-thirds of the interventions identified in the coding as feminist fell into the selfempowerment category, supporting the self-anchored scores indicating that explicit gender analysis of gender roles was only a small part of her practice and that empowerment techniques made up the bulk of her interventions. Finally, the richest data came from the narrative accounts of the shifts in how her understanding of how feminist therapy related to her work and what she identified as feminist. She began to distinguish between directive and active, understanding an active stance "to be one in which client and therapist were both vocal in 'actively and collaboratively co-constructing,' as opposed to a passive client's being pushed and prodded by the designs of a directive therapist." She also recognized "that each client needs different components of what (she) had come to term empowerment interventions and that various levels of overt feminist intervention are useful/appropriate/stimulating in different contexts."

CONCLUSION

In our teaching and in our efforts to examine our work, it is important that we focus on practitioner self-evaluation using multiple methodologies and a reflective model. We must focus not only from the perspective of an illusory "high, hard ground where practitioners can make effective use of research-based theory and technique," such as formal single subject designs, but also from the perspective of the "swampy lowland where situations are often confusing 'messes' incapable of technical solution" (Schon, 1983, pp. 42-43). It is in these "swampy lowlands" that we can gain understanding of practice actions. This challenge involves:

1. Viewing knowledge as a social construction developed through interaction of the observer and the observed. This interaction continues throughout the research process.

2. Examining the values and assumptions underlying our choices of theories, which in turn can help us make sense both of practice and of the research methods we use to observe our practice actions.

3. Exploring the relationships between the theories that we think we are using in practice, that we espouse, and those theories that are reflected in our actual practice activities and formulations (Fleck-Henderson, 1990). Am I doing what I think I am doing? If not, what am I doing?

4. Building an understanding of our own use of knowledge in action from asking clinically relevant questions and using continuous observations of our work to answer these questions. What does my work tell me about how I make meaning of practice? What ways of knowing inform my meaning-making?

5. Beginning to articulate an individual epistemology of practice and the values underlying this epistemology as a step in the journey to formulating practice knowledge.

6. Learning to share these evolving ideas with colleagues in a clear, credible way while embracing the challenge of building social work practice knowledge from the systematic study of cases.

7. Broadening our definition of practice evaluation to include qualitative and quantitative research methods which permit and value reflective self-evaluation of our practice actions.

8. Engaging actively in identifying and struggling with the ethical paradoxes inherent to using our own clinical case material to build practice knowledge.

NOTE

1. Many of these basic ideas are influenced by the interpretive social sciences (Gergen, 1982, 1985; Rabinow & Sullivan, 1979) and are rooted in mainstream theoretical and critical traditions such as the naturalistic (Rodwell, 1987; 1990), qualitative (Ruckdeschel, 1985), ethnographic (Geertz, 1983), hermeneutic (Scott, 1989), heuristic (Moustakas, 1990), symbolic interactionist (Blumer, 1969; Denzin, 1978), phenomenological (Giorgi, 1985), and feminist (Reinharz, 1992).

REFERENCES

Alter, C., & Evens, W. (1990). *Evaluating your practice: A guide to self-assessment.* New York: Springer.

Belenky, M., Clinchy, B., Goldberger, N., & Tarule, J. (1986). *Women's ways of knowing.* New York: Basic Books.

Blumer, H. (1969). *Symbolic interaction: Perspective and method.* Englewood Cliffs, NJ: Prentice-Hall.

Calame, C. (1992). The politics of feminist therapy as a construct: A therapist's self-evaluation of work with young women who have eating disorders. In *Evaluating process and outcome in clinical social work: The challenge of single subject design.* Unpublished masters research report, Simmons College School of Social Work.

Charmaz, K. (1990). 'Discovering' chronic illness: Using grounded theory. *Social Science and Medicine, 30,* 1161-1172.

Cheatham, J. (1987). The empirical evaluation of clinical practice: A survey of four groups of practitioners. *Journal of Social Service Research, 10*(2/3/4), 163-177.

Chenitz, W., & Swanson, J. (1986). *From practice to grounded theory.* New York: Addison-Wesley.

Clifft, M. (1986). Writing about psychiatric patients: Guidelines for disguising case material. *Bulletin of the Menninger Clinic, 50*(6), 511-524.

Cook, J. (1992). Dilemma Log. Unpublished research assignment. Simmons College School of Social Work.

Davis, D. (1991). Rich cases: The ethics of thick description. *Hastings Center Report,* July-August, 12-17.

Dean, R. (1989). Ways of knowing in clinical practice. *Clinical Social Work Journal, 17*(2), 116-127.

Dean, R., & Reinherz, H. (1986). Psychodynamic practice and single system design: The odd couple. *Journal of Social Work Education, 22*(2), 71-81.

Denzin, N. (1978). *The research act: A theoretical introduction to sociological methods* (2nd ed.). New York: McGraw-Hill. New York: Pergamon.

Fee, E. (1983). Women's nature and scientific objectivity. In M. Lowe & R. Hubbard (Eds.), *Women's nature: Rationalizations of inequity* (pp. 9-27). New York: Pergamon.

Fleck-Henderson, A. (1989). Personality theory and clinical social work practice. *Clinical Social Work Journal, 17*(2), 128-137.

Gambrill, E., & Barth, R. (1980). Single-case study designs revisited. *Social Work Research and Abstract, 16*(3), 15-20.

Geertz, C. (1983). Thick description: Toward an interpretive theory of culture. In R. Emerson (Ed.), *Contemporary field research* (pp. 37-59). Prospect Heights, IL: Waverly Press.

Gergen, K. (1982). *Toward transformations in social knowledge.* New York: Springer-Verlag.

Gergen, K. (1985). The social constructionist movement in modern psychology. *American Psychologist, 40*, 255-275.

Gingerich, W. (1984). Generalizing single case evaluation from classroom to practice. *Journal of Education for Social Work, 10*(1), 74-82.

Gingerich, W.J. (1990). Rethinking single-case evaluation. In L. Videka-Sherman & W. Reid (Eds.), *Advances in clinical social work research* (pp. 11-24). Silver Spring, MD: NASW Press.

Giorgi, A. (Ed.) (1985). *Phenomenology and psychological research.* Pittsburgh, PA: Duquesne University Press.

Glaser, B., & Strauss, A. (1967). *The discovery of grounded theory.* Chicago: Aldine.

Goldstein, H. (1990). The knowledge base of social work practice: Theory, wisdom, analogue, or art? *Families in society: The journal of contemporary human services, 70*(1), 32-42.

Gonzalez, M. (1992). Empathy: An examination of its use in short term therapeutic relationships. In *Evaluating process and outcome in clinical social work: The challenge of single subject design.* Unpublished masters research report, Simmons College School of Social Work.

Hartman, A. (1990). Many ways of knowing. *Social Work, 35*(1), 3-4.

Haworth, G. (1984). Social work research, practice, and paradigms. *Social Service Review, 58*, 343-357.

Heineman, M. (1981). The obsolete scientific imperative in social work research. *Social Service Review, 55*, 371-396.

Hoffman, L. (1990). Constructing realities: An art of lenses. *Family Process, 29*(1), 1-12.

Ivanoff, A., Blythe, B., & Briar, S. (1987). The empirical clinical practice debate. *Social Casework, 68*(5), 290-298.

Kagle, J. (1982). Using single-subject measures in direct practice: Systematic documentation or distortion? *Arete, 7*(Spring), 1-9.

Kondrat, M. (1992). Reclaiming the practical: Formal and substantive rationality in social work. *Social Service Review, 66*(2), 238-255.

Mahrer, A. (1988). Discovery oriented psychotherapy research: Rationale, aims, and methods. *American Psychologist*, September, 694-702.

Marshall, C., & Rossman, G. (1989). *Designing qualitative research.* Newbury Park, CA: Sage.

Millstein, K.H., Regan, J., & Reinherz, H. (1990). Can single system methodology be generalized to non-behavioral practice? Paper presented at the 36th Annual Program Meeting of the Council on Social Work Education. Reno, Nevada.

Mishler, E. (1990). Validation in inquiry-guided research: The role of exemplars in narrative studies. *Harvard Educational Review, 60*(4), 415-442.

Moustakas, C. (1990). *Heuristic research: Design, methodology and applications.* Newbury Park, CA: Sage.

Neild, E. (1992). Moving on: Time-limited psychotherapy with a young adult with identity problems. In *Evaluating process and outcome in clinical social work: The challenge of single subject design.* Unpublished masters research report, Simmons College School of Social Work.

Nelsen, J. (1981). Issues in single-subject research for non-behaviorists. *Social Work Research and Abstract, 17*(2), 31-37.

Papell, C., & Skolnick, L. (1992). The reflective practitioner: A contemporary paradigm's relevance for social work education. *Journal of Social Work Education, 28*(1), 18-26.

Pray, J. (1991). Respecting the uniqueness of the individual: Social work practice within a reflective model. *Social Work, 36*(1), 80-85.

Rabinow, P., & Sullivan, W. (1979). *Interpretive social sciences: A second look.* Berkeley: University of California Press.

Reinharz, S. (1992). *Feminist methods in social research.* New York: Oxford University Press.

Reinharz, S. (1984). *On becoming a social scientist.* New Brunswick, NJ: Transaction Books.

Rennie, D., Phillips, J., & Quartaro, G. (1988). Grounded theory: A promising approach to conceptualization in psychology. *Canadian Psychology, 29*(2), 139-150.

Richey, C., Blythe, B., & Berlin, S. (1987). Do social workers evaluate their practice? *Social Work Research and Abstracts, 23*(Summer), 14-20.

Ricoeur, P. (1979). The model of the text: Meaningful action considered as a text. In P. Rabinow & W. Sullivan (Eds.), *Interpretive Social Sciences: A Reader* (pp. 73-101). Berkeley: University of California Press. (Original work published 1971)

Rodwell, M. (1987). Naturalistic inquiry: An alternative model for social work assessment. *Social Service Review, 61*, 231-246.

Rodwell, M. (1990). Naturalistic inquiry: The research link to social work practice? Paper presented at the 36th Annual Program Meeting of the Council on Social Work Education. Reno, NV.

Ruckdeschel, R. (1985). Qualitative research as a perspective. *Social Work Research and Abstracts, 21*(2), 17-21.

Salner, M. (1986). Validity in human science research. *Saybrook Review, 6*(1), 107-130.

Schon, D. (1983). *The reflective practitioner: How professionals think in action.* London: Temple Smith.

Scott, D. (1989). Meaning construction and social work practice. *Social Service Review, 63,* 39-51.

Scott, D. (1990). Practice wisdom: The neglected source of practice research. *Social Work, 35*(6), 364-368.

Siegel, D. (1984). Defining empirically based practice. *Social Work, 29*(4), 325-331.

Smith, P. (1990). Qualitative self-evaluation of direct practice: Implications for social work education. Paper presented at the 36th Annual Program Meeting, Council of Social Work Education, Reno, NV.

Stoller, R. (1988). Patients' responses to their own case reports. *Journal of the American Psychoanalytic Association, 36*(2), 371-392.

Strauss, A., & Corbin, J. (1990). *Basics of qualitative research.* Newbury Park, CA: Sage.

Strauss, J., & Hafez, H. (1981). Clinical questions and "real" research. *American Journal of Psychiatry, 138*(12), 1592-1597.

Welch, J. (1983). Will graduates use single subject designs to evaluate their casework practice? *Journal of Education for Social Work, 19*(2), 42-47.

Witkin, S. (1990). The implications of social constructionism for social work education. *Journal of Teaching in Social Work, 4*(2), 37-48.

Witkin, S., & Gottschalk, S. (1988). Alternative criteria for theory evaluation. *Social Service Review, 62*(2), 211-224.

Witkin, S. (1991). Empirical clinical practice: A critical analysis. *Social Work, 36*(2), 158-163.

Teaching Research:
Beyond the Storybook Image
of Positivist Science

Catherine Kohler Riessman

SUMMARY. Different assumptions about reality and knowing underpin different research methods. Contrasting a phenomenological/interpretivist approach with the assumptions of positivism, I describe teaching about philosophical issues in master's and doctoral courses. At the master's level, exercises in observation introduce students to social constructionist concepts; at the doctoral level the framework emphasizes five levels of re-presentation of experience: attending, telling, transcribing, analyzing, and reading. Greater attention to methodological diversity and contrasting philosophical underpinnings would strengthen research education in social work.

INTRODUCTION

Teaching social constructionist ideas in research courses seems like an oxymoron. Research, we have been taught to believe, un-

Catherine Kohler Riessman, PhD, is Professor of Social Work and Professor of Sociology at Boston University. The author wishes to thank Cheryl Hyde and Bob Thomas for introduction to the class exercises described here, and Stanley Witkin for calling to her attention the ending fish metaphor. A section of the paper is adapted from C.K. Riessman (1993), *Narrative Analysis*, Newbury Park: Sage Publications. Reprinted by permission of Sage Publications, Inc.

[Haworth co-indexing entry note]: "Teaching Research: Beyond the Storybook Image of Positivist Science," Riessman, Catherine Kohler. Co-published simultaneously in *Journal of Teaching in Social Work* (The Haworth Press, Inc.) Vol. 8, No. 1/2, 1993, pp. 281-303; and: *Revisioning Social Work Education: A Social Constructionist Approach* (ed: Joan Laird) The Haworth Press, Inc., 1993, pp. 281-303. Multiple copies of this article/chapter may be purchased from The Haworth Document Delivery Center [1-800-3-HAWORTH; 9:00 a.m. - 5:00 p.m. (EST)].

covers objective knowledge about the world. Recent developments in social and clinical theory, however, challenge a monolithic view (Agger, 1991; Dean, 1993; Dean & Fenby, 1989; Gergen, 1985). It is not possible for an investigator to be neutral, to "merely represent" (as opposed to interpret) the world (Peller, 1987).

The idea of representation, which has captured the imagination of social scientists of diverse disciplines in the last decade (Behar, 1993; Clifford & Marcus, 1986; Van Maanen, 1988) belongs in social work education. Both clinical practitioners and social researchers try to understand individual experience, but neither has direct access, only ambiguous representations of another's experience—talk, text, interaction. Quantitative researchers create numerical scores to stand for experience, whereas qualitative investigators create texts of a variety of sorts. Although there are important differences between the two approaches (Riessman, forthcoming), both face similar questions: How will subjects' responses to questions be re-presented, and interpreted; where does the investigator stand?

Few textbooks in social work engage such "meta" questions. Research is presented as a set of techniques that, if followed, will generate reliable and valid findings. Guided by textbooks, master's students struggle to learn the "correct" vocabulary and objectivity in research. Philosophies of science that undergird research practices are rarely included in the master's curriculum, although they may be at the doctoral level.

This paper describes how I teach about representation (and related issues) in the master's curriculum, and presents the lecture on the topic I give in a doctoral elective. The rationale for including the material, a definition of key terms, and a metaphor introduce my perspective.

METHODS AS MAPS

Beliefs about the nature of social reality and how we are to know it (ontology and epistemology) deeply shape the research methods we choose. The quantitative model dominant in social work research today was derived from the natural sciences, which are based in positivist thinking (see Heineman, 1981; Heineman Pieper, 1985;

Kolakowski, 1993; Phillips, 1987). This explanatory framework assumes a realist ontology, that is, reality consists of a world of objectively defined facts. Put simply, there is a world "out there," separate from us, and we can know it through observable qualities– sensory data that can be isolated, measured, and related causally. The possibility of objectivity is assumed in positivism; the distorting influences of a researcher's personal perspective and subjectivity can be eliminated. Not all approaches to empirical research make such a claim and, ironically, it is increasingly questioned in the natural sciences.

Philosophy is essential because it forces us to locate the assumptions about reality and knowing that underlay the research methods we choose. Methods are like maps, they focus inquiry, lay out paths which, if followed, are supposed to lead to valid knowledge of how the world works. But like maps we consult in everyday life, they contain assumptions about what is important, and consequently make certain features of the terrain visible and obscure others.

When hiking along the coast, I consult a topographical map because it represents the trails, elevation, ridges from which to view the sea. When sailing, I use a nautical chart that represents rocks, soundings, buoys that mark a channel into the harbor. The same coastline could be mapped in yet another way, to represent a world of property lines, taxation districts, and political divisions. Not objective pictures, maps are representations of reality that reflect the interests of the mapmaker, a point of view. Like research methods, they are powerful tools for making statements about the world.

Many question whether the positivist/natural science map is appropriate for human studies. A number of other maps exist to guide inquiry. Each makes distinctive features of the terrain visible that are useful for social work research. Two (often used in combination) contrast with the map of positivism.

Phenomenologists begin with human experience. Rather than locating worldly objects "out there," the map privileges human awareness, since our capacity to know any object depends on awareness. Based in 20th-century development in philosophy (Husserl, 1939/1973; Merleau-Ponty, 1962/1989; Schutz, 1932/1967), psychologists and sociologists are examining consciousness with phenomenological research methods, focusing on subjects' experienced meaning instead of their overt actions or behavior (for a review see Polkinghorne, 1989).

Interpretive social scientists add that our capacity to know any object in the world is rooted in our definitions, so their map privileges language (for example, an informant's definition of her situation). Rabinow and Sullivan (1979/1987) summarize an aspect of the interpretivist position:

> We are fundamentally self-interpreting and self-defining, living always in a cultural environment, inside a 'web of signification we ourselves have spun.' There is no outside, detached standpoint from which we gather and present brute data. When we try to understand the cultural world, we are dealing with interpretations and interpretations of interpretations. (p. 7)

Contemporary social work problems call for diverse maps and modes of investigation. One map is not sufficient for all research problems. Different ones connect us to realities that we could not know without the map.

TEACHING RESEARCH THROUGH OBSERVATION

Teaching master's social work students about the philosophical underpinnings of research methods is not easy. Many do not have undergraduate backgrounds in philosophy, they (like most of us) take the world for granted, they struggle with the relevance of research and abstract intellectual ideas to their daily lives as front line workers. Creative teaching is required to make concepts meaningful. I introduce the ideas through observational exercises in a foundation master's research course; students pursue inquiry in a written assignment involving field work.

In the second week of the course, I present students with a situation from everyday life: You're in line in a supermarket at the checkout counter and notice the person in front of you has left their basket momentarily. It contains a frozen dinner, a generic brand shampoo with conditioner, a six pack of beer, a box of Pampers, a dozen eggs, a bag of potato chips. What kind of person is this? What do they look like? Where do they live? What do they do for a living?

The exercise generates a great deal of class participation and laughter. Many are convinced the person is single, poor and female (from the Pampers), probably overweight (from the beer and potato chips). Some women students use the cheap shampoo and beer to argue it is a man, and men in the class protest the construction. Invariably, an older woman student speculates that grandchildren and their parents are visiting (hence the Pampers, beer, and snacks). Race, class, gender, and age stereotypes surface; students get uncomfortable. Reflecting on the exercise, they realize how difficult it is to step outside one's own social group and "objectively" view the world. The exercise helps students bring assumptions into consciousness, see them challenged, and critically reflect on them.

Another exercise asks students to go to a movie and report back on what they observe. The following week, students comment on how hard it was to keep an observing eye, because they got caught up in the movie. Like investigators, they are part of the world they are trying to study. I ask them to comment on what they did see. Some note actions by audience members (physical touching, trips for popcorn), while others become intrigued with employee behavior (sequences of words repeated over and over). Pushed to explain the differences, students discover that choice of focus involves selection from a stream of consciousness. By attending to certain phenomena and not others, they construct knowledge about social life in movie theaters. Students create alternative versions of what is significant. All are based on "facts," but because they are put together in radically different ways, meaning differs. Students become aware, with my prodding, of how quickly they categorize (psychologically usually) to explain what they see. So much of what they take for granted derives from the social order of professionalism, which they maintain by privileging clinical formulations.

The two exercises, taken together, help students to get in touch with epistemological and political assumptions, begin to identify their own, and question them. The exercises also serve to engage students in a research course they would rather not take. I encourage connections to practice wherever possible; different theoretical maps (paradigms) guide them to notice certain aspects of clients and ignore others. Using maps, social workers compose clients' problems in particular ways.

A written assignment follows upon the class exercises, which asks students to do systematic observation at their field placements or, if not in placement, in a setting where individuals congregate. In a four-page paper they must describe the purpose and method of observation, the "findings," and submit field notes. Some students observe waiting rooms and note the avoidance of contact between clients, or how space is organized (there are physical barriers separating staff and clients). Others observe staff meetings or case conferences, and note gender and professional privilege (certain groups speak more than others, some are "heard" while others making the same points are not acknowledged). Some students write about how difficult it is to assume the position of an outsider. They take certain social and professional practices for granted.

Most students, however, produce traditional research reports, written in the third person, and often summarize data with frequency counts. Philosophical positions, and associated maps for knowing, remain hidden in their papers. I devote a class session to bringing them into view, and begin by asking about the contradiction between the "messy" process of doing research (evident in field notes) and its re-presentation in "tidy" reports. Reality gets constructed through inscribing practices such as these. Drawing from their papers, I introduce the following phenomenological/interpretive concepts for class discussion:

1. *Standpoint.* Where you stand determines what you see. One student observed adolescents leaving school on public transportation; she noted that sitting in the back of the bus, she could observe sub-groups and leadership, which she missed when she sat in the front. I urge students to consider how their class and status position, race, gender, and theoretical persuasion influence what they see. There is no view from nowhere, no way to see the world as it "really" is, separate from ourselves (Ford, 1975; Nagel, 1986).

2. *Interpretation.* Data are theory laden, because understanding is circular. Students bring cultural categories and unacknowledged values to their observations (oversimplified as "bias" in positivism). A student observing in a shelter for homeless women and children wrote that clients were "chronically late" for meetings; she valued clock time whereas homeless women did not. I teach that we cannot help but bring assumptions to research, projections

shaped by our expectations and preconceptions, culture, and traditions, but we can reflect on them, and "deconstruct" the categories we privilege.

3. *Observer and Observed.* There is no way to be an "unobtrusive" observer, because of the inevitable relationship between the knower and the known. A student placed in a nursing home observed residents at religious services and wrote (as an aside) how the rabbi greeted her after the service and inquired about her religion; she seemed not to know the "moves." The research relationship can change informants, the investigator, even the study issue (for an example, see Gregg, forthcoming).

4. *Counting.* Quantifying behavior is synonymous with research in most textbooks. Accordingly, students summarize their observations in neat tables. I press the group to consider why they chose this form of representation for field experiences. We discuss where they learned that research means counting, what frequencies reveal and what they obscure. Numbers are one way to re-present observations, but are ill-suited to many phenomena, especially the study of process (e.g., conversation in a staff meeting, therapy interaction).

5. *Locating Ourselves.* The investigator is present in a study, whether acknowledged or not. I ask the group why most wrote about themselves in the third person ("the researcher"), and we have a conversation about the assumptions of positivist science–an investigator explains from an objective, external viewpoint. A different map values reflexivity–reflection about interpretive practices. I argue that reflexivity strengthens research, as it does clinical practice. Personal biographies, institutional locations, and communities of reference shape the problems we pick, how we go about studying them, what we "notice" in the stream of data. Locating ourselves, instead of pretending we're not there, helps a reader evaluate the situated knowledge we produce. The experience of doing research contrasts with the storybook image of it presented in textbooks and research reports (for a discussion of reflexivity in action, see Hyde, forthcoming).

I make the five points inductively, drawing on examples from students' work in the written assignment and referring back to the class exercises. I use the teaching process–how I am constructing concepts from the "data" (e.g., student papers)–to introduce the grounded theory method in qualitative research (Charmaz, 1983, 1990; Glaser & Strauss, 1967). A subsequent class session is spent on the method.

At the doctoral level, I rely to a greater extent on readings and lectures, because students generally bring a high level of motivation to research courses. But I teach inductively wherever possible because, in my experience, it engages students better than dense, philosophical debates. What follows is part of a lecture I give in a doctoral elective, "Qualitative Analysis of Clinical Data." Students are in their second year of a doctoral program that combines social work and sociology. The course also draws Ph.D. students in clinical psychology and other social science disciplines. The topic on the syllabus is "Issues in Representation," and it is placed in the third week of a 13 week-course, before we examine three qualitative methodologies (grounded theory, narrative analysis, and approaches to therapy discourse). As background for the lecture, I assign Van Maanen (1988) and Geertz (1983). Figure 1 is a handout. By the third week students have begun to know me, so the personal experience I draw on relates to prior conversations about my interest in South Asian society, gender relations, and feminist theory. Although I re-present the class session here as a lecture, in actual practice I present the ideas less formally.

THE PROBLEM OF REPRESENTING EXPERIENCE

It is perhaps a sign of our times that investigators are questioning how we "represent life" in scientific work (Lynch & Woolgar, 1990). Qualitative researchers often seek to depict others' experiences, but act as if representation is not a problem. Feminists, for example, emphasize "giving voice" to previously silenced groups of women by describing the diversity of their experiences (Fonow & Cook, 1991; Gilligan, 1982; Gluck & Patai, 1991; Reinharz, 1992). I share the goal, but am more cautious. We can't "give voice," but we do hear voices that we record and interpret. Representational decisions cannot be avoided; they enter at numerous points in the research process, and qualitative analysts including feminists must confront them.

Investigators do not have direct access to another's experience.

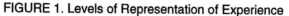

FIGURE 1. Levels of Representation of Experience

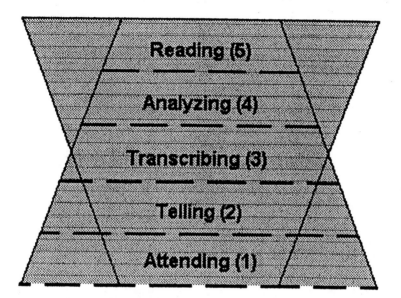

PRIMARY EXPERIENCE

We deal with ambiguous representations of it–talk, text, interaction, interpretation. At the risk of oversimplifying, there are, at a minimum, five levels or kinds of representation in the research process, with porous boundaries between them, depicted in Figure 1. (The danger of my representation, of course, is to make the borders more real than semantic.)

To ground what would otherwise be an abstract lecture, I will make my points a bit unconventionally. I interweave discussion of the figure with a narrative about an experience on a recent trip to South India.

I went to India to make arrangements for field work I am beginning there on the meaning and management of infertility. For a respite from seemingly endless train rides to meet potential collaborators and locate an appropriate setting for the research, I went to stay for a few days at a tropical resort in Kerala. Early one morning, I took a walk from my hotel, along a deserted beach.

If we adopt the starting point of phenomenology and the lived world of immediate everyday experience, the world of this inhabited beach is " 'already there' before reflection begins—as an inalienable presence" (Merleau-Ponty, 1962/1989, p. vii). Walking at dawn I encounter it at a prelinguistic realm of experience—images, plays of colors and lights, noises, fleeting sensations—in the stream of consciousness. I am one with the world and make no distinction at this point between my bodily perceptions and the objects I am conscious of that comprise the beach. Like all social actors, I experience this world from the "natural attitude," taking it for granted, not thinking about and analyzing it (Husserl, 1939/1973; Schutz, 1932/1967).

Attending to Experience

Then I attend to and make discrete certain features in the stream of consciousness—re-flecting, re-membering, re-collecting them into observations. I scan the beach (metaphorically speaking) and isolate certain images, which are known in a given language community by certain words—sunlight, sand, waves, fishing. On this particular occasion, the sound of fishermen chanting is the "object" I attend to, not the smell of the surf, or the feel of the water—yesterday's images. I stop and watch. Men pull in giant nets, their synchronous movements aided by the rhythmic chant among them. The men in patterned lungis eventually sell the fish to women in brightly colored saris who, placing on their heads pails filled with fish, leave for market. By attending, I make certain phenomena meaningful, the first level of representation in Figure 1.

There is choice in what I notice, a selection from the totality of the unreflected upon, the primary experience. The truth of hearing and vision predominate over evidences of touch and smell, for example. The gendered nature of fishing work also strikes me, because of theoretical interests and values. I actively construct reality in new ways at this first level of representation, to myself, by thinking.

Telling About Experience

Next comes the telling, the performance of a personal narrative. I come back to the U.S. from India and subsequently relate to friends at dinner the experience of the walk–coming upon the fishermen, their chant, the women, my marvel. I re-present the events, already ordered to some degree, to these listeners in conversation, with all the opportunities and constraints the form of discourse entails. Although the walk happened many weeks before in another land, I relate it as one inside the experience, enacting the action in a conversation. My account takes the form of a narrative about "what happened": I describe waking up early, taking a walk before breakfast, seeing the fishermen, watching as women arrived with empty pails, my fascination with the division of labor and women's economic self-sufficiency in India, where women are often depicted as subservient. I describe the setting, characters, unfolding plot, and stitch the story together in a way that makes my interpretation of the events clear. To capture the moment on that particular morning, I describe at great length the sunlight, the color of the men's lungis and the women's saris, bringing these objects from the real world of the beach to a narrative space in my friends' living room in Cambridge. My rendering draws on resources from my cultural context, notably the gender-based division of labor that all participants in the conversation value as a category of understanding. My friends listen, question, urge me to say more about particular aspects of the exchange between men and women; I, in turn, refashion the events in response to their cues and, to make the importance of the scene real for them, expand on what the moment means in the larger context of my life plans for living and working in India. By talking and listening, we produce a narrative together (level 2 in Figure 1).

In the telling, there is an inevitable gap between the experience as I lived it and any communication about it. Caught in the "prison house of language," in the words of Nietzsche (Jameson, 1972), there is no way to break through to the ideas to which my words refer, for language is "uncommunicative of anything other than itself" (Merleau-Ponty, 1962/1989). Yet without words, the sounds, movements and images of the beach experience cease to exist. Language makes them real, as it does the gendered practices of fishing, for as Merleau-Ponty suggests:

> [O]ur linguistic ability enables us to descend into the realm of our primary perceptual and emotional experience, to find there a reality susceptible to verbal understanding, and to bring forth a meaningful interpretation of this primary level of our existence. . . . By finding meaning in experience and then expressing this meaning in words, the speaker enables the community to think about experience and not just live it. (cited in Polkinghorne, 1988, pp. 29-30)

Meaning also shifts in other ways, because it is constructed at this second level of representation in a process of interaction. The story is being told to particular people; it might have taken a different form if someone else were the listener. In this case, I am not simply re-presenting the experience on the beach from some neutral place, but in a specific conversation with a mentor/friend and his partner, who mean something to me. In telling about an experience, I am also creating a self–how I want to be known by them. Beginning the new research project, my friends have raised questions that have forced me to confront difficult issues, including my position as a privileged, white, western woman studying South Asian women's health. My rendering of the narrative about the beach scene is colored by this context. Like all social actors, I seek to persuade myself and others that I am a "good" person. My narrative is inevitably a self re-presentation (Goffman, 1959).

Transcribing Experience

If either of my friends were acting in their roles as social science investigators, they would have taped the conversation. An audio recording would be more selective than a video, of course, but in neither case would the "entire" conversation be captured. Whatever form of taping used, they would ultimately have to represent it in some kind of text, a "fixation" of action, in the words of Ricoeur, into written speech (cited in Packer & Addison, 1989). Transcribing, the third level of representation in Figure 1, is, like the earlier ones, incomplete, partial, selective.

Kate Millett (1971), early in the contemporary feminist movement, commented on the tape recorder:

> [W]ithout this device to preserve the very sound of language, we should have no idea of how people really talk: their pauses, inflections, emphases, unfinished sentences, short periods. All attempts to mimic spoken language seem terribly mannered, and one comes to respect [Gertrude] Stein still more, and to admire how carefully she must have listened. (pp. 61-62)

Millett discusses the issues of making a written transcription from an audio tape of her interviews with women workers in the sex industry (prostitutes):

> What I have tried to capture here is the character of the English I heard spoken by four women and then recorded on tape. I was struck by the eloquence of what was said, and yet when I transcribed the words onto paper, the result was at first disappointing. Some of the wit of M's black and southern delivery had disappeared, gone with the tang of her voice. . . . J's difficulty in speaking of things so painful that she had repressed them for years required that I speak often on her tapes, hoping to give her support, then later, edit myself out. (p. 61)

Millett's solution, in addition to editing herself out, was to do "a good deal of work to transform spoken to linear-language" (p. 61) or to adopt a "loose oral narrative" and summarize what the women said. In an effort to display a polyphonic text that respected the different voices of the four women, she ultimately displayed the women's talk in her written text in four columns–a quartet where voices "were instruments expressing their diverse experiences" (p. 62).

Twenty years later, an investigator wanting to "capture" my beach experience faces similar problems, but in the interim a great deal has been written about transcription practices. Transforming spoken language into a written text is now taken quite seriously, as thoughtful investigators no longer assume the transparency of language.

Qualitative researchers now ask themselves how detailed transcriptions should be. How, for example, could they best capture the rhythm of my talk about the fisherman's chant? Should they include silences, false starts, emphasis, non-lexicals like "uhm," discourse markers like "y'know" or "so," overlapping speech and other signs of listener participation in the narrative? Should they give clauses separate lines, display rhythmic and poetic structures by grouping lines? Not simply technical questions, these seemingly mundane choices–what to include, how to arrange and display the text–have serious implications for how a reader will understand the narrative.

There is no one, "true" representation of spoken language. Mishler (1991) makes the analogy to photography, which supposedly "pictures reality." Yet the technology of lenses, films, printing papers, and darkroom practices, have made possible an extraordinary diversity of possible images of the same object. The form of representation reflects the artist's views and conceptions–values about what's important. Photographers, like investigators/transcribers, fix the essence of a figure. By denying viewers (readers) information, they paradoxically provide us room to supply our own. We can invent an entire world analyzing the figures (dialogue), though we know very little about them. But I am getting a little ahead of my story . . .

Transcribing discourse, like photographing reality, is an interpretive practice. Decisions about how to transcribe, like decisions about telling and listening, are theory-driven (Ochs, 1979) and rhetorical; by displaying text in particular ways we provide grounds for our arguments, just like a photographer guides the viewer's eye with lenses and by chopping images. Different transcription conventions lead to and support different interpretations and ideological positions, and they ultimately create different worlds. Meaning is constituted in very different ways with alternative transcriptions of the same stretch of talk (Mishler, 1991).

Analyzing Experience

A fourth level of representation in Figure 1 enters as the investigator explicitly analyzes the transcript, typically a number of them. Perhaps the research issue is defining critical moments in the awakening of work identity. Other social scientists narrativize turning points or epiphanies, like my moment along the beach (Denzin, 1988) in their work lives. The challenge is to identify similarities across the moments–an aggregate, a summation.

An investigator sits with pages of tape-recorded stories and snips away at the flow of talk to make it fit between the covers of a book, tries to create sense and dramatic tension. There are decisions about form, ordering, style of presentation, how the fragments of lives that have been given in interviews will be housed. The anticipated response to the work inevitably shapes what gets included and excluded. In the end, the analyst creates a metastory about "what happened" by telling what the interview narratives signify, editing and reshaping what was told, turning it into a hybrid story, a "false document" (Behar, 1993). Values, politics, and theoretical commitments enter, once again. While a kind of betrayal–the beach story and others like it are born again in an alien tongue–it is also necessary and productive; no matter how talented the original storyteller was, a life story told in conversation does not come readymade as a book (Behar, 1993), an article, or a dissertation, certainly. The stop-and-start style of oral stories of personal experience gets pasted together into something different.

Reading Experience

The fifth and final level of representation in Figure 1 comes as the reader encounters the written report. Perhaps an early draft was circulated to colleagues and their comments incorporated into the "final" product, or perhaps published work is returned to the people it is about, who may or may not recognize their experience in it, or like how they are portrayed. In any case, translations of my "original" narrative about India and analytic work on what it means by my social scientist friends in Cambridge inevitably gets into the hands of others, who bring their own meanings to bear. An extract about a beach walk might give some readers a shiver of recognition, while others might wonder about my relationship with my "subjects"–men and women of the fishing village in Kerala. What does my presence as a white English speaking woman signify, given that Malayalam is the native tongue? How are race and class inscribed in the text? It might be difficult if not impossible to get answers to these and similar questions. All a reader has is the analyst's representation.

Every text is "plurivocal, open to several readings and to several constructions" (Rabinow & Sullivan, 1979, p. 12). Even for the same reader, a work can provoke quite different readings in different historical contexts (imagine *Madame Bovary*, for example, before and after the recent feminist movement). Collaboration is inevitable for the reader is an agent of the text (Bruner, 1986). Critical readers include their understandings of the "makings" of a work in their interpretations of it. Because a writer cannot tell all (seemingly irrelevant personal and historical circumstances have been excluded), interpretation may focus on how power and history work through a supposedly objective text. Readers raise historical contingencies and excluded standpoints–of women, people of color, non-Western views–as they dislodge the seemingly secure ground under our representations. Written texts are created within, and against, particular traditions and audiences, and these contexts can be brought to bear by readers. The point is that all texts stand on moving ground; there is no master narrative (Clifford, 1986; Clifford & Marcus, 1986; Sosnoski, 1991).

Ultimately, it is unclear who really authors a text, although Western texts come with individual authors names penned to them, of course. The meaning of a text is always meaning *to someone*. The truths we have constructed "are meaningful to specific interpretive communities in limiting historical circumstances" (Clifford, 1988, p. 112). Any "finding"–a depiction of a culture, psychological process, or social structure–exists in historical time, between subjects in relations of power. While traditional social science has claimed to represent the experiences of populations and cultures, the new criticism states that we cannot speak, finally and with ultimate authority, for others. Our subjects "do not hold still for their portraits" (Clifford, 1986, p. 10).

The Limits of Representation and Student Response

I conclude the lecture by generalizing from my beach walk and its repeated transformations, and draw the implications for research practices. All forms of representation of experience are limited portraits. Researchers of all kinds face the problem, though it is typically hidden by the language of objectivity and quantification. Simply stated, we are interpreting and creating texts at every juncture, letting symbols "stand for" or take the place of the primary experience, to which we have no direct access. Meaning is ambiguous because it arises out of a process of interaction between people: self, teller, listener and recorder, analyst, reader. While the goal may be to tell the whole truth, our narratives about others' narratives are our worldly creations. There is no "view from no where" (Nagel, 1986), and what might have seemed "no where" in the past is likely to be somewhere in the present or future. Meaning is fluid and contextual, not fixed and universal. All we have is talk, and texts that represent reality partially, selectively, imperfectly.

Each level in Figure 1 involves an expansion, but also a reduction: Tellers select features from the "whole" experience to narrate, but add other interpretative elements. A similar process occurs with transcribing, analyzing, reading. Framing discussion of the research process in the language of "representation," rather than as "stages" or "perspectives," emphasizes that we actively make choices that can be accomplished in different ways. Obviously the agency of the teller is central to composing narratives from personal experience, but so are the actions of others–listener, transcriber, analyst, and reader.

The idea of representation brings into view the constructed nature of social scientific work. Edward Said (1979) goes even further, and his views have bearing for all researchers:

[The] real issue is whether indeed there can be a true representation of anything, or whether any and all representations, because they are representations, are embedded first in the language and then in the culture, institutions, and political ambience of the representor. If the latter alternative is the correct one (as I believe it is), then we must be prepared to accept the fact that a representation is *eo ipso* implicated, intertwined, embedded, interwoven with a great many other things besides the "truth," which is itself a representation. (pp. 272-273)

Whether we accept ultimate relativism, awareness of levels of representation presses us to be more conscious, reflective, cautious about the claims we make.

Returning to the issue of "giving voice" to women's experience, I prefer to think of research as a chorus of voices, with an embedded contrapuntal duet (Gorelick, 1991). There are strains because most researchers are privileged and white and many women we want to include are not. Some voices will have to be restrained to hear voices from below (Rollins, 1985), to create a particular harmony, but a different interpreter might well allow other voices to dominate.

Representing women's experience is limited further because language is often inadequate (DeVault, 1990) and the world as perceived by subjects may be confined, organized by structures of oppression not apparent to participants themselves (Gorelick, 1991; Smith, 1987). Just as gender is not enough in feminist research (Riessman, 1987), "giving voice" to experience isn't either, even as we commit to women's standpoint. Interpreting experience–and this happens at all five levels in Figure 1–involves representing reality; we create and recreate voices over and over again during the research process.

Not surprisingly, students find the lecture a bit overwhelming, and I am not recommending the ideas be conveyed in the form outlined here. I continue to experiment with how best to teach the material. But the concepts belong in the social work curriculum, probably the master's one also.

Students return to the idea of representation, and its levels, throughout my doctoral course, albeit with considerable individual variation–they "get it" at different points during the semester. Figure 1 is concrete and serves as a point of reference as students conduct, transcribe, and analyze interviews, and when the class responds to the students' research reports. The re-presentation of experience–subjects' and investigators'–becomes a refrain in the course. Feedback from students suggests the framework helps them integrate research and practice concerns.

Ultimately, the figure becomes limiting. One student made a forceful argument for depicting the research process as a spiral, rather than a series of steps. Her point is consistent with my general perspective–all representations are limited. They are constructed and can be constructed differently.

CONCLUSION

The following quotation, from John Steinbeck's *Log From the Sea of Cortez*, is relevant to social work research today:

> The Mexican Sierra [a fish] has 17 plus 15 plus 9 spines in the dorsal fin. These can easily be counted. But if the Sierra strikes hard on the line so that our hands are burned, if the fish sounds and nearly escapes and finally comes in over the rail, his colors pulsing and his tail beating the air, a whole new relational externality has come into being–an entity which is more than the sum of the fish plus the fisherman. The only way to count the spines of the Sierra unaffected by this second relational reality is to sit in a laboratory, open an evil-smelling jar, remove a still colorless fish from the formalin solution, count the spines and write the truth. . . . There you have recorded a reality which cannot be assailed–probably the least important reality concerning either the fish or yourself.
>
> It is good to know what you are doing. The man with his pickled fish has set down one truth and has recorded in this experience many lies. The fish is not that color, that texture, that dead, nor does he smell that way.

Social workers study human problems, of course, not smelly fish, but our field has adopted the positivist/natural science model of research, in an effort to be a scientific profession (Austin, 1983). "Empirical" has come to mean numerical counts, representative samples, objective measurement, the statistical aggregate. I have argued here for another approach, which brings into view the socially constructed nature of knowledge–including the "relational reality" Steinbeck writes of.

Teachers might wish to leave metaphors to the novelist, and philosophy to philosophers. But research methods depend on assumptions about reality and knowing, just as clinical methods do (Dean & Fenby, 1989; Hartman, 1990). As educators, we cannot avoid the problem.

On a practical level, teaching alternatives to positivist research is difficult because textbooks typically available for master's students do not support a phenomenological/ interpretivist perspective, or even the idea that different maps exist for inquiry (but in sociology see Goldenberg, 1992). Instructors who want to include alternative views locate readings from the social sciences, which are not always relevant to practice. It is a challenge to tack back and forth between texts that describe the research process in such opposite ways. We desperately need research volumes in social work that respect diversity in approach, and incorporate developments in social and clinical theory of the last decade.

The Council on Social Work Education, viewed by many educators as part of the problem, may offer an emergent solution. The most recent Curriculum Policy Statement (CSWE, 1992) mandates the teaching of qualitative *and* quantitative methods. (It provides no specifics about the former, in contrast to repeated mention of statistical procedures, however). Numeric compared to nonnumeric methods is a limited way to frame the problem (in my view), but the policy statement does provide an opening for the philosophies of social science that undergird *both* qualitative and quantitative approaches to enter the curriculum. As I argue elsewhere (Riessman, forthcoming), there is considerable diversity *within* the qualitative tradition regarding assumptions about reality and knowing. Some qualitative work is just as positivist in assumptions as quantitative research (see, for example, Strauss & Corbin, 1990). But comparisons between methods could open up philosophical underpinnings of different approaches for students. Organizing practice and research courses in terms of their basic epistemological premises offers another solution (Dean & Fenby, 1989), which could also heal the split between practice and research.

Returning to Steinbeck's metaphor, we can teach students that research means counting spines (e.g., a client's symptoms before and after an intervention). Or we can teach about the limits of the experimental/laboratory model for human studies, offering alternative ways of knowing and representing human experience. In Steinbeck's words, the natural science approach "records a reality which cannot be assailed," but is it the most "important reality" concerning the process between clients and social workers?

REFERENCES

Agger, B. (1991). Critical theory, poststructuralism, postmodernism: Their sociological relevance. *Annual Review of Sociology, 17,* 105-131.

Austin, D. M. (1983). The Flexner myth and the history of social work. *Social Service Review, 57*(3), 357-377.

Behar, R. (1993). *Translated woman: Crossing the border with Esperanza's story.* Boston: Beacon.

Bruner, J. (1986). *Actual minds, possible words.* Cambridge: Harvard University Press.

Charmaz, K. (1983). The grounded theory method: An explication and interpretation. In R. M. Emerson (Ed.), *Contemporary field research: A collection of readings* (pp. 109-126). Boston: Little, Brown and Company.

Charmaz, K. (1990). 'Discovering' chronic illness: Using grounded theory. *Social Science and Medicine, 30*(11), 1161-1172.

Clifford, J. (1986). Partial truths. In J. Clifford & G. E. Marcus (Eds.), *Writing culture: The poetics and politics of ethnography* (pp. 1-26). Berkeley: University of California Press.

Clifford, J. (1988). *The predicament of culture: Twentieth-century ethnography, literature, and art.* Cambridge: Harvard University Press.

Clifford, J., & Marcus, G.E. (Eds.) (1986). *Writing culture: The poetics and politics of ethnography.* Berkeley: University of California Press.

Council on Social Work Education (1992). Curriculum policy statement for master's degree programs in social work education.

Dean, R.G. (1993). Constructivism: An approach to clinical practice. *Smith College Studies in Social Work, 63*(2), 127-146.

Dean, R.G., & Fenby, B.L. (1989). Exploring epistemologies: Social work action as a reflection of philosophical assumptions. *Journal of Social Work Education, 25*(1), 46-54.

Denzin, N. (1988). *Interpretive interactionism.* Newbury Park, CA: Sage.

DeVault, M. L. (1990). Talking and listening from women's standpoint: Feminist strategies for interviewing and analysis. *Social Problems, 37*(1), 96-116.

Fonow, M. M., & Cook, J. A. (Eds.) (1991). *Beyond methodology: Feminist scholarship as lived research.* Bloomington: Indiana University Press.

Ford, J. (1975). *Paradigms and fairytales: An introduction to the science of meanings.* Boston: Routledge and Kegan Paul.

Geertz, C. (1983). Thick description: Toward an interpretive theory of culture. In R. Emerson (Ed.), *Contemporary field research* (pp. 37-59). Prospect Heights, IL: Waveland Press.

Gergen, K. J. (1985). The social constructionist movement in modern psychology. *American Psychologist, 40*(3), 266-275.

Gilligan, C. (1982). *In a different voice: Psychological theory and women's development.* Cambridge: Harvard University Press.

Glaser, B. G., & Strauss, A. L. (1967). *The discovery of grounded theory.* Chicago: Aldine.

Gluck, S. B., & Patai, D. (Eds.) (1991). *Women's words: The feminist practice of oral history.* New York: Routledge.

Goffman, E. (1959). *The presentation of self in everyday life.* New York: Doubleday.

Goldenberg, S. (1992). *Thinking methodologically.* New York: Harper Collins.

Gorelick, S. (1991). Contradictions of feminist methodology. *Gender and Society, 5*(4), 459-477.

Gregg, R. (forthcoming). Explorations of pregnancy and choice in a high-tech age. In C. K. Riessman (Ed.), *Qualitative studies in social work research.* Newbury Park, CA: Sage Publications.

Hartman, A. (1990). Many ways of knowing. *Social Work, 35,* 3-4.

Heineman, M. B. (1981). The obsolete scientific imperative in social work research. *Social Science Review, 55,* 371-397.

Husserl, E. (1939/1973). *Experience and judgement: Investigation in a genealogy of logic* (J. S. Churchill & K. Ameriks, Trans.). Evanston, IL: Northwestern University Press.

Hyde, C. (forthcoming). Reflections on a journey: A research story. In C. K. Riessman (Ed.), *Qualitative studies in social work research.* Newbury Park, CA: Sage Publications.

Jameson, F. (1972). *The prison-house of language.* Princeton: Princeton University Press.

Kolakowski, L. (1993). An overall view of positivism. In M. Hammersley (Ed.), *Social research: Philosophy, politics, and practice* (pp. 1-8). Newbury Park, CA: Sage Publications.

Lynch, M., & Woolgar, S. (Eds.) (1990). *Representation in scientific practice.* Cambridge: The MIT Press.

Merleau-Ponty, M. (1962/1989). *Phenomenology of perception* (C. Smith, Trans.). London: Routledge.

Millett, K. (1971). *The prostitution papers: A candid dialogue.* New York: Avon.

Mishler, E. G. (1991). Representing discourse: The rhetoric of transcription. *Journal of Narrative and Life History, 1*(4), 255-280.

Nagel, T. (1986). *The view from nowhere.* New York: Oxford University Press.

Ochs, E. (1979). Transcription as theory. In E. Ochs & B. B. Schieffelin (Eds.), *Developmental pragmatics* (pp. 43-72). New York: Academic Press.

Packer, M. J., & Addison, R. B. (Eds.) (1989). *Entering the circle: Hermeneutic investigation in psychology.* Albany: State University of New York.

Peller, G. (1987). Reason and the mob: The politics of representation. *Tikkun, 2*(3), 28-95.

Phillips, D. C. (1987). *Philosophy, science, and social inquiry: Contemporary methodological controversies in social science and related applied fields of research.* New York: Pergamon Press.

Pieper, M. H. (1985). The future of social work research. *Social work research and abstracts* (pp. 3-11). Silver Spring, MD: National Association of Social Workers, Inc.

Polkinghorne, D. E. (1988). *Narrative knowing and the human sciences.* Albany: State University of New York Press.

Polkinghorne, D. E. (1989). Phenomenological research methods. In R. Valle & S. Halling (Ed.), *Existential-phenomenological perspectives in psychology* (pp. 41-60). Plenum Press.

Rabinow, P., & Sullivan, W. M. (1979/1987). *Interpretive social science: A second look.* Berkeley: University of California Press.

Reinharz, S. (1992). *Feminist methods in social research.* New York: Oxford University Press.

Riessman, C. K. (1987). When gender is not enough: Women interviewing women. *Gender & Society, 1*(2), 172-207.

Riessman, C. K. (1993). *Narrative Analysis.* Newbury Park, CA: Sage Publications.

Riessman, C. K. (Ed.)(forthcoming). *Qualitative studies in social work research.* Newbury Park, CA: Sage Publications.

Rollins, J. (1985). Introduction. *Between women: Domestics and their employers* (pp. 5-17). Philadelphia: Temple University Press.

Said, E. W. (1979). *Orientalism.* New York: Vintage.

Schutz, A. (1932/1967). *The phenomenology of the social world* (G. Walsh & F. Lehnert, Trans.). New York: Northwestern University Press.

Smith, D. E. (1987). *The everyday world as problematic: A feminist sociology.* Boston: Northeastern University Press.

Sosnoski, J. S. (1991). A mindless man-driven theory machine: Intellectualists, sexualists, and the institution of criticism. In R. R. Warhol & D. P. Herndl (Eds.), *Feminisms: An anthology of literary theory and criticism.* New Brunswick, NJ: Rutgers University Press.

Strauss, A., & Corbin, J. (1990). *Basics of qualitative research: Grounded theory procedures and techniques.* Newbury Park, CA: Sage Publications.

Van Maanen, J. (1988). *Tales of the field: On writing ethnography.* Chicago: University of Chicago Press.

Author Index

Abbott, E., 167,171
Abbott, G., 167
Abramovitz, M., 153,162n
Addams, J., 167,171,172
Addison, R., 293,302n
Agger, B., 282,301n
Albee, G., 242,251n
Alcoff, L., 149,162n
Allen, J., 5,31,89,106n
Allen, J., 153,162n
Altany, C., 171,181n
Alter, C., 256,257,266,269,276n
Andersen, T., 49,53n,85,102,
    106n,188, 191,196n
Anderson, C.,83,108n
Anderson, H., 36,37,38,40,46, 52,
    53n,57,61,63,64,65,70,73n,
    86,88,102,106n,131,144n
Aponte, H., 92,106n
Aptheker, B., 149,162n
Argyris, C., 244,246,251n
Aries, P., 213,215n
Atwood, G., 115,127n
Auerswald, E., 92,106n
Ault-Riche, M., 83,106n
Austin, D., 299,301n

Baltes, P., 213,215n
Barth, R., 269,277n
Bateson, G., 79,84,106n,228,236n
Becker, C., 55
Becker, E., 201,202,216n
Behar, R., 278,295,301n
Belenky, M., 68,70,73n,148,
    162n,233,234,236n,261,276n
Bellah, R., 121-122,127n,173,
    182n,242,251n

Ben-David, J., 167,182n
Benjamin, J., 125,127n
Berger, P., 131,143n, 221,236n,
    241,251n
Berkowitz, B., 213,215,216n
Berlin, I., 198,216n
Berlin, S., 256,278n
Berman-Rossi, T., 60,73n
Bernstein, R., 18,29n,172,182n
Bledstein, B., 14,15,29n
Blumer, H. 276n
Blythe, B., 256,277n,278n
Bohm, D., 37,53n
Bordo, S., 150,162n
Boszormenyi-Nagy, 92,106n
Boscolo, L., 92,109n
Bowen, M., 92,106n
Bowlby, J., 225,237n
Braverman, L., 83,106n
Breckinridge, S., 171
Briar, S., 256,277n
Bricker-Jenkins, M., 147,162n
Brim, O., 213,216n
Brown, R., 131,143n
Brown, W., 209,217n
Bruner, E., 73n,86
Bruner, J., 68,69,73n,107n,131,143n,
    180,182n,200,201,202,203,
    205,206,213,216n,228,
    237n,296,301n
Bruno, F., 170,171,182n
Bunch, C., 153,162n
Burgess, H., 175,182n

Calame, C., 272,276n
Carter, B., 83,92,107n,109n,228,230,
    237n

Subject Index

Adolescence, 228
Adult development, and
  developmental irregularity,
    228
  family development models, 222
  normative models, 228
  structural models, 222
  systemic theories, 222
Adulthood, 228
Aggression, against the self, 125
American culture, as source of
    meaning, 204
Anthropological perspective, 86,221
  and families, 80
Art, and social work, 27-28
Assessment, criteria for, 63
  derived from medical model, 60
  revisioning, 101
Attachment theory, as transactional,
    230
Autonomy, 210
  individual, 209
  and health, 125

Battering, 149
Behavioral theory, 32
Beliefs, patterns of, 22
Borderline personality disorder, 120,
    123,124
  in cultural context, 124
  and sexual abuse, 124
  and women, 124
  social construction of, 123-126
Brief treatment, and managed health
    care, 113

Cases, intensive study of, 8,255
Casework, 167
"Challenge" model, 212
Change, and co-construction, 114
  as a co-evolutionary process, 87
  in family therapy, 85
Chaos, and constructivism, 24
Chicago School, 172
Child development, and culture, 227
  and stage theories, 226
Childhood, constructions of, 213
Children, with disabilities, 247
Circular causality, 229
Circular questions, 49, 65
Civic interests, 122
Class and field, as balanced partnership,
    171
  hierarchical relationship, 172
  integration of, 168, 180
  partnerships, form and structure
    of, 180
Classroom, assignments, 286
  and authority, 158
  coherence in, 222
  as co-constructed, 232
  and creativity, 188
  exercises, 285
  and knowing, 168
  as model of therapeutic
    environment, 190
  role play, 95-98
  and reflexivity, 191,194
  use of video in, 92,94
Classroom exercises, 59-60,64
  co-creation of meaning, 65-66
  and cultural awareness, 232
  ecomaps, 99-100
  family sculpting, 99-100

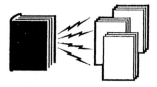

Haworth
DOCUMENT DELIVERY
SERVICE
and Local Photocopying Royalty Payment Form

This new service provides (a) a single-article order form for any article from a Haworth journal and (b) a convenient royalty payment form for local photocopying (not applicable to photocopies intended for resale).

- *Time Saving:* No running around from library to library to find a specific article.
- *Cost Effective:* All costs are kept down to a minimum.
- *Fast Delivery:* Choose from several options, including same-day FAX.
- *No Copyright Hassles:* You will be supplied by the original publisher.
- *Easy Payment:* Choose from several easy payment methods.

Open Accounts Welcome for . . .
- Library Interlibrary Loan Departments
- Library Network/Consortia Wishing to Provide Single-Article Services
- Indexing/Abstracting Services with Single Article Provision Services
- Document Provision Brokers and Freelance Information Service Providers

MAIL or *FAX* THIS ENTIRE ORDER FORM TO:

Attn: Marianne Arnold
Haworth Document Delivery Service
The Haworth Press, Inc.
10 Alice Street
Binghamton, NY 13904-1580

or FAX: (607) 722-1424
or CALL: 1-800-3-HAWORTH
(1-800-342-9678; 9am-5pm EST)

PLEASE SEND ME PHOTOCOPIES OF THE FOLLOWING SINGLE ARTICLES:
1) Journal Title: _____
   Vol/Issue/Year: _____ Starting & Ending Pages: _____
   Article Title: _____

2) Journal Title: _____
   Vol/Issue/Year: _____ Starting & Ending Pages: _____
   Article Title: _____

3) Journal Title: _____
   Vol/Issue/Year: _____ Starting & Ending Pages: _____
   Article Title: _____

4) Journal Title: _____
   Vol/Issue/Year: _____ Starting & Ending Pages: _____
   Article Title: _____

(See other side for Costs and Payment Information)

COSTS: Please figure your cost to order quality copies of an article.

1. Set-up charge per article: $8.00
   ($8.00 × number of separate articles)   _____

2. Photocopying charge for each article:
   1-10 pages: $1.00   _____

   11-19 pages: $3.00   _____

   20-29 pages: $5.00   _____

   30+ pages: $2.00/10 pages   _____

3. Flexicover (optional): $2.00/article   _____

4. Postage & Handling: US: $1.00 for the first article/
   $.50 each additional article   _____

   Federal Express: $25.00   _____

   Outside US: $2.00 for first article/
   $.50 each additional article   _____

5. Same-day FAX service: $.35 per page   _____

6. Local Photocopying Royalty Payment: should you wish to copy the article yourself. Not intended for photocopies made for resale. $1.50 per article per copy
   (i.e. 10 articles x $1.50 each = $15.00)   _____

GRAND TOTAL: _____

METHOD OF PAYMENT: (please check one)

❑ Check enclosed   ❑ Please ship and bill. PO # _____
   (sorry we can ship and bill to bookstores only! All others must pre-pay)

❑ Charge to my credit card: ❑ Visa;   ❑ MasterCard; ❑ American Express;

Account Number:_____ Expiration date:_____

Signature: X_____ Name: _____

Institution: _____ Address: _____

City: _____ State:_____ Zip:_____

Phone Number: _____ FAX Number: _____

MAIL or *FAX* THIS ENTIRE ORDER FORM TO:

Attn: **Marianne Arnold**
Haworth Document Delivery Service
The Haworth Press, Inc.
10 Alice Street
Binghamton, NY 13904-1580

or FAX: (607) 722-1424
or CALL: 1-800-3-HAWORTH
(1-800-342-9678; 9am-5pm EST)